Breakthrough insights from
52 extraordinary executive women...

Helayne Angelus
Brenda Barnes
Cristina Benitez
Kimberly Betts
Trudy Bourgeois
Shelley Broader
Michele Buck
Carolyn Carl
Betsy Cohen
Nancy Croitoru
Pat Curran
Linda Dillman
Jeri Dunn
Maria Edelson
Vicki Escarra
Kim Feil
Mary Gendron
Michelle Gloeckler
Beverly Grant
Cathy Green
Sandy Grimes
Kathy Hannan
Michele Hanson
Barbara Hartman
Janel Haugarth
Betsy Hosick

Sonja Hubbard
Dawn Hudson
Susan Ivey
Jennie Jones
Melody C. Justice
Jane Knaack-Esbeck
Lynn Marmer
Maureen McGurl
Rose Kleyweg Mitchell
Denise Morrison
Caroline Cotten Nakken
Kim Nelson
Bobbie O'Hare
Susan Parker
Marie Quintana
Irene Rosenfeld
Eileen Scott
Luci Sheehan
Judy Spires
Regenia Stein
Rosa Stroh
Joan Toth
Julie Washington
Tara Weiner
Mary Beth West
Meg Whitman

D0071734

The NEW Woman Rules

**More than
50 trailblazers
share their wisdom**

Fawn Germer

Also by Fawn Germer

Hard Won Wisdom

Mustang Sallies

To you. Lean on your sisters and let us lean on you. The world will change.

Contents

Acknowledgments

I'd just finished the closing keynote for the Network of Executive Women's Annual Summit when I was swept up by a whirlwind named Helayne Angelus. The summit had been a huge success, and Helayne was a Category 4 of energy.

"We need to get the stories from these women," she told me. "Somebody needs to write a book."

A year has passed, and now you are holding a book that never would have been written without Helayne seeing the possibility and daring to push hard for something that would have taken others years to accomplish. She is my hero.

As is Joan Toth, NEW's executive director, who worked this project on a daily basis, offering her guidance and support. She is now one of my life sisters. She's taught me so much, and we sure have laughed.

Thanks also to Luci Sheehan, the quiet guardian angel who led me to NEW and changed my life in so many ways without asking for anything in return. She is the essence of the mentor and friend I wish for all of you.

To my father, Fred Germer, who gave me the ability to interact with anybody, and my mother, Betty Germer, who taught me to think around corners and be a journalist who could change a few things in this world.

Thanks to Julie Hipp, my sounding board and best friend, who encouraged me from the first sentence—to the last.

To all of my friends. I love you.

To our great designers, Rob Wray and Bill Reuter. And copy editors Barb Jiannetti and Jennifer Bulat. And, in the galley stages, Elizabeth Roberts and Nathalia Granger.

Thanks to Evelyn Smith, who did a phenomenal job of putting together the contact lists. To Kim Feil and Kelli Lester-Brown at Sara Lee, Stephanie McFee at Wal-Mart and Anne Fink at PepsiCo for twisting a few arms to make some of the interviews happen. To all of the assistants who managed to schedule, reschedule and reschedule again all of these hard-to-schedule interviews. To Sandra Bushby for a dose of inspiration near the finish.

Finally, my thanks go to every woman in this book who so unselfishly shared her story and experiences in hopes of making it easier for the next generation of leaders to move forward. The only thing they will get in return for their time and honesty is the success that will come to you. ∎

Foreword

By **Helayne Angelus**, President
Network of Executive Women
Vice President, Global Customer Business Development Diversity
The Procter & Gamble Co.

A few brave women got together almost seven years ago to think about the possibilities and what could be different in one of the largest industries in the world: consumer packaged goods and retail. They each were brave pioneers, willing to invest in a vision to help attract, retain and develop women in this important industry. They asked, "Why aren't women at the table?"

We knew that 85 percent of all shoppers and spending decisions were made by women, but it was—and is—almost exclusively men who design the stores, determine what products should be on the shelves and market those products.

The Network of Executive Women incorporated a year later to help all companies in the quest to attract, retain and develop women and minorities in this important industry. The organization has grown from those few women to more than three thousand members in less than six years. We are creating a new model to help, enable, empower and inspire women in their organizations and to achieve a diverse and inclusive workforce.

Procter & Gamble was approached and the president of P&G North America asked if I would join NEW. Soon, I was heading up the education committee and, the next thing I knew, I was the president. I am a passionate believer that we have to turn, reach, pull and create—not just one seat at the table but half the seats at the table. Every single one of us has a responsibility and a duty to make that happen.

NEW is not like any other group because we are all committed to something bigger than each of us individually and each of our companies, respectively. We seek to complement each other's strengths, provide both formal and informal coaching, be a safe sounding board for both personal and career decisions, and provide inspiration and advice. Our mission is to "attract, retain and develop women in the consumer packaged goods and retail industry through education, leadership and business development." That is not just for top executives. We seek out young, recent graduates who can really add to our industry as emerging leaders. We are able to help build this leadership via a remarkable network across the United States and through the leadership and development opportunities within all the different committees and regional efforts of NEW.

NEW is a great place to try new things, get support and stub your toe and not have it ruin your career. This is a place where you can go to be who you are and not have to fit into a mold or wear a mask. You will have senior executives mingling with women who will find their way in the next ten or twenty years—all of whom are interested in individual and collective advancement and support.

We have so many wonderful male champions and supporters who also have been touched by NEW's mission. They have contributed so much to our growth and success. NEW aspires to truly be inclusive so we can be role models for the change that we really want to be, and help our companies leapfrog in this area. This is a place where companies share best practices, even though they compete fiercely with each other day in and day out. The mission of NEW is so much higher than our respective agendas.

The idea for this book came from my fear that we will lose the stories of the trailblazers. Those of us with twenty-five or more years in the industry can remember when we all were the "one and only." Today, 60 percent of the graduates are female, yet a lot of the lessons of how the initial pioneer group of women gained their success could be lost. We wanted to find a way to share those stories so we could accelerate the development of the next few generations, through inspiration, insight and wisdom.

This project had to come together so quickly that we had unthinkably tight deadlines. But these top executives made them work. Without them, this book would not be. These icons were as committed to mentoring the next generation as the Network itself.

Individually, we might be interesting. Together, we are a force for change.

Individually, we have insights. But put those insights together, and you have a movement.

We could not tell these stories without the wit, wisdom and chutzpah of our fabulous author, Fawn Germer. Fawn made the impossible possible. Fawn asked the difficult questions to get to the insights that revealed the NEW rules. Without her amazing gifts and talents, you would not be reading this.

My challenge to you is to read this book and let the power of the stories inspire you.

By **Joan Toth**, Executive Director
Network of Executive Women

I started hearing some buzz about a women's group forming in our industry late in the year 2000. As a more than eighteen-year veteran of retail and consumer packaged goods, I had never really given any thought to the specifics of women in the industry. Were they well represented? Were they in key decision-making roles? Did they advance? How did we fare versus other industries?

Some people were asking these questions, however. One of them was Michele Hanson, who was a sales director at the Minute Maid Co. Michele involved Don

Knauss, the company's CEO, in those discussions, and he provided the very first seed money to begin the network.

I went to my first Network of Executive Women planning meeting on March 30, 2001, in a conference room in New York City. There were about twenty women there. None of us really knew what the organization was going to look like, but we all knew we were at the start of something big.

With our seed money, we commissioned Catalyst to prepare a business case on our industry. Catalyst is the nation's premier research organization focused on advancing women in business. Its data showed that the retail and consumer packaged goods industries lagged behind the rest of the Fortune 500 in numbers of women in officer roles. Why? A lack of role models, mentors, networking, and critical assignments. Catalyst data showed that industries with women's networks had more representation of women in officer roles than the average.

We definitely needed a women's network.

What made the argument even more compelling were the consumer demographics. Women are the customers, but we aren't the corporate decision makers.

We spent the rest of that meeting crafting a mission statement that still stands today.

We have reached an important milestone in 2007—corporate sponsorship contributions have passed the $1 million mark. We have a healthy balance sheet and ensure that all projects and events are self-sustaining. We have eleven regional committees with more than two hundred committee members who will plan and execute more than twenty events this year. Our forty-three corporate sponsors, thirty champions and twenty-seven board members are a "who's who" of top companies and "C" level executives in the industry. This year we launched an extremely successful new program—the Executive Leaders Forum—geared to women at the VP level and above. The industry's most senior male executives participate in NEW and support their companies' journey to become a diverse mirror image of the customers that we serve.

We can't begin to name all the men and women who helped craft our first programs and spent countless hours volunteering for NEW.

In the past six years, I have heard so many stories and seen so many people take different paths in their careers. Our members tell us that the most powerful tool we can offer them is the opportunity to hear other women's stories. Our goal was to bring you those stories of inspiration and wisdom.

I know NEW has made an impact. While the Catalyst numbers have shown only very small gains in the number of female officers in our industry, the awareness is there. CEOs have embraced the issue of diversity and are adamant that the teams they build will listen to the many diverse voices they bring on board.

We still have a very long way to go. But we are so much closer now. I think this book will help take us there.

Introduction

Midway into this book, I realized what the women leaders I'd interviewed had done. They'd handed me the secret code.

I knew I'd been shown something that no one else had seen, and I was overwhelmed by it, partly because of the power of the content, mostly because of the sincerity of the women. They climbed over so many obstacles to get to the top, and now they are reaching down to you—through me. There are more than fifty women in this book, all of whom have no spare time—none—but they cleared time for you because they don't like being alone at the top.

Success is not a finite commodity. There is enough for all of us. If they help you to succeed and you help the next women, our place in this world will grow. And grow. They know that. They know we can only embrace our possibility if we embrace each other.

Sometimes it seems like we are just crawling along. This year, women run thirteen of America's Fortune 500 companies. Last year, it was ten.

Wow, thirteen women at the very top, and there are only 140 million American women in the running.

It is easy to be cynical—or jubilant. Your choice.

Not that long ago, women were banned from the Harvard Law School Library because we might distract men from their studies. We couldn't get credit in our own names. Employers fired us if we got pregnant, or didn't hire us because we might conceive. We were excluded from jury duty because, apparently, our opinion didn't count. There were male bosses who freely demanded sex from the women who worked for them—without consequence.

It wasn't so long ago that classified ads used to be split in half, with one set of jobs—the good ones—for men, and the rest for women. It was legal to pay men more because, well, just because.

Our history inspires me because our gains were the result of a brilliant, deliberate campaign for equality that began with the most crucial battle—the fight for the right to vote. Ninety years ago, we couldn't even vote! But our foremothers knew that, if we could vote, we could make change. In the 1960s and 1970s, the Women's Liberation Movement and the National Organization for Women executed a strategy that made discriminatory laws fall like dominoes. Reading that history is so exciting and inspiring. The women who are now in their fifties, sixties and seventies fought those battles—for us. We have a legacy to protect—and create.

There are times when I get so discouraged, like when I see a Catalyst report that says only 6.7 percent of the top-paying positions in the Fortune 500 belong to women.

But then again, there are times like this moment when I see the potential that exists because of who we are as women. We are growing into our power—together. We are learning from our mistakes and triumphs—together.

The first time I tried to get an interview with eBay CEO Meg Whitman, I got the same answer that I'd gotten from the other women CEOs on the Fortune 500—a polite-but-firm no. The reason was the same, every time. The CEOs wanted to be viewed as CEOS—not as "women CEOs." It was as if the qualifier suggested "less than." But I asked Whitman's spokesman if he would pass on a memo that I would write. He agreed, and I spent quite a bit of time composing my argument.

It came down to this:

Some women know innately what it takes to break through in difficult environments. They know how to use their strength without being punished for it. They know how to fly above the politics and build teams that perform.

It doesn't come so naturally to all of us. That doesn't mean the rest of us are less able or less deserving—it means we need a little guidance so we can get our chance to prove our mettle.

If the intuitive leaders don't share what they know instinctively, they always will be viewed as "women CEOs" because they will be the only ones up there. If they share their wisdom and enlighten the rest of us, they won't be so rare.

Whitman wound up giving me an incredible interview. I loved her. The other "women CEOs" didn't come around in that book, and I couldn't figure out why they wouldn't share their mentoring wisdom. Fortunately, a new lineup of great women is in power, and they not only agreed to participate this time—many said it was their duty. Whitman came through again in this book.

You are their legacy. What you do with what they teach you here will play out over years and even decades. Just don't do it alone. Remember the women coming up behind you, and help them along. The more success you create for others, the more you will succeed for yourself.

When I went through the interviews in this book and distilled "the rules," I realized that, collectively, their words created a legacy that could have a life-altering impact on the careers of thousands of women leaders. Will this book create one more Fortune 500 CEO? A book won't do that. But a movement to continue to share and reveal and help and mentor will create one, then two, then a dozen, then a hundred.

It's our moment. Our turn. Our rules.

If one woman gets over the wall, then brings two more, who each bring two more... You get the point. The world is ours. ■

Performance Matters

First off, you've got to want "it."

"It" being the operative "it" in "Go for **it**" or "Just do **it**," "Do what **it** takes" and "Give **it** all you've got."

"It" is significant because it isn't always definable, but it is ever-present in the mind-set of the people who actually combine talent + drive + brains + ability to come up with a level of success that eludes 99.9 percent of the rest of the world. They might sense they can do great things and they might know full well they have superior skills, but a lot of super achievers admit they did not lay out a plan that would get them as far as they went. Essentially, they went for "it" without knowing what "it" was.

So there is a lesson there.

It's about making a decision about achieving a level of performance that will accomplish what others can't or won't dare try, then following through with such forceful, determined effort that you rightfully deserve the exceptional success you will ultimately and inevitably build.

Every person in this book stressed that you can't win if you don't perform. But, there is that critical caveat, which is that you must perform and build the proper relationships that will advertise and advance your performance. Networking and self-marketing are so key that we'll talk about them in depth in other parts of this book. But you have nothing to market if you don't perform.

So perform.

The first step is to decide to go beyond average, above average, excellent and extraordinary. I have interviewed so many women who have achieved unthinkable things. They did it because they didn't talk themselves down. I remember how my life changed when I interviewed Jody Williams, who won the Nobel Peace Prize for leading the International Campaign to Ban Landmines. Williams received the award because she got foreign ministers from 135 countries to sign off on the treaty banning landmines, and eighty-one of their countries to subsequently ratify it into international law.

She did it by herself, without even having a secretary.

I asked her, "What separates an ordinary woman from an extraordinary woman?"

She didn't hesitate with her response. "The belief that she is ordinary."

I have seen that play out in the hundreds of interviews I have done for my books. It is the choice to go beyond—and the belief that you can—that lets you do what others can't or won't.

So the first step in moving on this fast track is deciding to get on it.

The second step is realizing you belong there.

The third step is making your engine perform harder, faster and stronger than you ever imagined any engine could perform.

It is so easy to slow yourself down by comparing yourself to everybody else. If everybody performs at one level, and you perform above that level, aren't you doing extraordinary work? Well, maybe.

To be honest, that is the zone where I operated for most of my career as a journalist. I delivered more front-page investigative stories than anybody else at the paper, my work was excellent, and I was treated like a star. But the truth is, I could have done much, much more. I just didn't feel like it. I had other priorities and distractions. That is perfectly okay, too. I set my priorities and honored them.

But when you hear that I was nominated for the Pulitzer Prize four times, you should also note that it also means that I did not win the Pulitzer Prize four times. Granted, some of that comes down to newspaper politics, but let's get real. If I had pushed as hard on my work as the women in this book pushed on theirs, I'd have won it. I had the ability. I didn't have the drive. I will never minimize what I accomplished as a journalist because I know it was extraordinary. But I always will know that I gave it 96 percent of my energy. That last 4 percent is what makes the difference.

And that is the 4 percent you need to commit to give if you wish to attain and sustain yourself at the highest levels of business. If you want to go where these women have gone, you have to commit to an exhausting level of performance that pushes you every day. The only thing stopping you from getting there is your own mind-set.

Make conscious decisions to advance yourself without waiting to be advanced. Numerous leaders told me they get a bad taste in their mouth when they hear someone coming right out and asking for a promotion or a raise. Promote yourself, and the raise will come. You do that by raising your hand and taking on challenges that expand your value to the company and showcase the breadth of your experience and abilities. If you are constantly taking on more responsibility, the promotion or raise should come. If it doesn't, you should talk to your boss and say, "What else can I be doing in order to advance to the next level?" Then do it.

Oh, and don't forget the most important thing. Make sure you advertise your performance. There are all these different terms for it. Market yourself. Self-promote. Toot your own horn. Whatever. What good is stellar performance if you are the only one who knows about it?

Okay, let me repeat that again. Don't assume your excellent work will be noticed. Bosses are busy. They have a lot of things to worry about. Their attention generally goes to what they are worrying about, instead of the things that are going well. They might notice what you are doing, but they might also forget it as soon as something bad distracts their attention. They aren't keeping running lists of all your accomplishments that they can review before they sleep at night just so they can feel good about the world.

In her interview, Procter & Gamble's Maria Edelson gives some especially insightful advice about how to put the word out there, and numerous women in this book will tell you why it is so critical that you do it. Accept it. As uncomfortable as it may feel to show how great you are, you must develop the talent. I liked Kathy Hannan's story, which showed how her failure to self-promote left a window wide open for a less diligent, less able, less deserving co-worker to claim credit for what she was doing.

Performance alone will not make you the CEO. But you will not become the CEO without CEO-worthy performance. And you do belong at the highest level if you think you do. I love what is in Sweetbay CEO Shelley Broader's interview because she so perfectly hits us with our misperceptions about what it takes to belong and operate at the top level of the business hierarchy. We assume that people at the top are more naturally brilliant and possess far greater brainpower than the rest of us folks, but Broader says that assumption is just plain wrong. Granted, it may be easier for some people to operate in that realm than others, but we do have far more control over our own destiny than we acknowledge. And we can exercise that control by making the decision to perform, learn, and deliver results.

The NEW Woman Rules of performance:

- Do your absolute best work on everything you are asked to do, from the simplest assignment to the most complicated.
- Be willing to take on tough assignments.
- Overdeliver. Overdeliver. Overdeliver.
- It is a mistake to wait for the "big project." The way to get the big project is by doing a lot of small ones very well.
- Evaluate your progress and be flexible. It is dangerous to get so committed to what you are doing that you stop evaluating whether you are moving in the right direction.
- Don't hesitate to raise your hand. There are opportunities to broaden your skills base and be seen as a real contributor because you are willing to say yes.
- Any leader is glad to have somebody willing to take on more so they don't have to hire more people.
- Understand the expectations and what success looks like for every assignment, and make sure everybody who evaluates you understands what you are going to deliver.
- Don't compete against your peers—compete against a standard. Do what differentiates you against the standard for excellence. Judge yourself against the very best you can be.
- Perform. Perform better than anybody else.

- Ask others for help.
- When others try to help you, don't be stubborn. Listen to them. Take the help if it will move you toward your goal.
- Keep your end goal in mind at all times.
- Know that there are always multiple ways to solve a single problem.
- When you are struggling, change your game. Win by playing a different strategy.
- Learn the business model: Build trust, communicate, create alignment with goals, find the sweet spot, know how you will grow the other person's career or business, execute and follow up.

Eileen Scott started as a part-time cashier and ascended to become CEO of Pathmark Stores—one of only seven female CEOs of a Fortune 500 company at the time. Her position gave her visibility on the way up—and out. Today, she is Eileen Scott the woman, not the title.

Scott left Pathmark in 2005, the same year Carly Fiorina left Hewlett-Packard and Marce Fuller left Mirant. The media jumped all over women leaders that year, saying things had soured for women at the top and linking stock performance to gender. Scott had taken over a company that already had filed for bankruptcy, and her story is one of leading through self-sacrifice.

It's lonely, lonely, lonely at the top. But Scott inspires and challenges a new generation of leaders to succeed by making others succeed.

1 Strive for Leadership, Not Power
Eileen Scott
Former CEO
Pathmark Stores

I come from a family of ten children. My dad worked three jobs, and when you talk about a team, for us, survival was that team. We took care of each other, so teamwork began at home for me.

My mom collected food stamps. I can remember going to the supermarket with my mother and dreading going in because she would take out those food stamps. You could hear the people in line, whispering.

My dad said I could do whatever I wanted to do. My mom reinforced it. We didn't have a lot of money to send the kids off to college and my father said, "Let's send the boys." My mother said, "My girls will be afforded the same opportunity." One of my greatest memories is of her sitting at the table, filling out the college financial aid forms. Every one of us was afforded that opportunity because she helped us to fulfill it.

I'd started working for Pathmark Stores when I was a sophomore in high school and, while working my way through college, I never gave staying in the supermarket industry a second thought. At least, not until my first business mentor—my district manager—asked if I'd thought about staying with the company.

I hadn't.

He asked if I would consider taking the assistant-store-manager assessment test, which measured leadership skills. I did really well, and he asked if I wanted to go in the training program to become a store manager. That was pivotal to me. I was a twenty-one-year old who really didn't have a clear direction, and this mentor took such an interest in me.

The industry is addictive. It's fast, it is exciting, and although I worked for the same company, I had as many different jobs as people who worked for a dozen companies. My experience goes from cashier to secretary to assistant store manager to buyer to merchandiser to director of procurement to sales director to vice president in numerous roles to EVP of merchandising and logistics, then EVP of store operations and, finally, chief executive officer. All within one company.

I was pinching myself when I found out I was going to be CEO. I'd worked so hard to get there and, finally, it happened.

The job was very hard. We were a company that had struggled since the 1980s after an unsuccessful takeover attempt. In order to stave off that attempt, the company entered into a management-led leveraged buyout in 1987. The company became so highly leveraged that it struggled from that moment on. Although there were some periods when things started to look a little bit better, we never recovered from it, and we wound up filing for bankruptcy in July 2000. We emerged as a publicly traded company in September of the same year, one year before I became CEO. Very soon after taking over, it became clear to me that we could not survive and be successful as a stand-alone, regional supermarket company. The competition was getting more intense, and the Northeast is probably the most competitive supermarket region in the country. So, the hard decisions came into play.

That was probably the hardest period of my life. In a situation like that, you have to trust yourself. You have to have the self-confidence to know that you are making the right decisions. It is the time when the rubber really meets the road.

It is where leadership versus power comes in. Power can only get you so far. Leadership is what will help you put your head on the pillow at night knowing you have made the right decisions. Maybe that is backwards. Maybe making the right decisions is what leadership is all about.

I had to go to the board of directors and recommend that we explore strategic alternatives that included the possible sale of the company. This was a company I loved. I grew up in this company and it was the only company I'd ever worked for, so this was a very hard reality for me. My responsibilities were to maximize shareholder value and take care of our twenty-five thousand associates. I felt like I knew most of them, so it was a very hard time for me.

We sold 40 percent of the company to a private equity firm and, although you never like to admit it, I knew my time was going to be coming to an end at Pathmark. Generally, a private equity company coming in needs a change agent, and a thirty-six-year veteran doesn't fit the bill.

I was the first and, sorry to say, only female CEO of a public supermarket company. To be honest with you, I was in the limelight because I was this token.

I read an article a few years ago that said women can't get ahead because power feels like a dirty word to us. But, when you think of running an organization in terms of leadership instead of power, women will step right up and say, "Yeah, that's what I am talking about." That's what I gravitate to. It is the leadership role. Leadership really means creating that team and being successful as a team, as opposed to power, which kind of gives the connotation of one person doing it all.

So, if you take it back to my situation, it took a strong leader to take the company where we had to take it. Although it was hard, it was something that I could say I have absolutely no regrets over, and something I am, quite frankly, pretty proud of.

After we went through the transition, they asked me to leave. There were so many mixed emotions there. I knew the time was right for me to leave. I'd been CEO for just under three years. But I knew in my heart that it was the right thing for the organization. We absolutely needed to do that, and I have no regrets at all.

Walking out the door was a lot of things. It was sad. There was some relief. But can you imagine waking up the next day and not going to the place you'd gone for the last thirty-six years? It was different! Initially, there were a lot of phone calls from well-wishers and then it became, "Here today, gone tomorrow."

But, if you need a title for a clear identity, then I don't want to be tied to a title. I want to be tied to who I am. Certainly, that is about what I have done, but I don't want to be known as, "She was the CEO of Pathmark." I would much rather be known as, "She was the generous, self-confident, team-building person who made a difference in lots of people's lives."

I'm on four boards now. One is a public board, one is a private board that operates with independent directors who are paid. I am on the board of the Food Bank For New York City, and am chair of the Food Policy Institute for Rutgers University. I am also fulfilling a lifelong dream to further my education, so I am enrolled in NYU-Stern's MBA program. I guess I'm doing things backwards, going to grad school after being a CEO! I have stayed very active the last two years.

I am still in the process of developing my plan for the rest of my life. There are many ways I could go. I may go further into the nonprofit world. I have been very fortunate. I have worked very hard for what I have gotten, but I have gotten it. It is time for me to give something back.

Each of us has a responsibility to mentor other women. Unfortunately, one thing we don't do well as women is help each other. Men do that really well, and that is what the old boys' network is all about. Women stand on the sidelines and don't get involved helping other women. It is like Gail Evans wrote: "Every time a woman succeeds in business, other women's chances of succeeding increases. Every time a woman fails, our chances of failing as women increases." So it is very important for us to take the time to mentor as many women as we possibly can.

I think that women have come a short way. I'm sorry to say it's not a long way, but we've come. We have a long way to go. ■

First, **Trudy Bourgeois** heads The Center for Workforce Excellence, a coaching, consulting and training firm.

Second, she built an eighteen-year corporate career that culminated with her managing a $3 billion business: Brown & Williamson Tobacco, then a subsidiary of British American Tobacco and now Reynolds American.

Third, this is one of those times when the author just needs to shut up and let the woman talk.

Look Within

2 Trudy Bourgeois

President and Chief Executive Officer
The Center for Workforce Excellence

I was fortunate to have many great opportunities afforded to me, but they did not come easy—I will say that.

I was raised in the Deep South and was born in Mobile, Alabama, at a time when the South was still segregated: 1959. My sisters and brothers and I were among the first African-Americans going to an all-white school. My first two years of grade school were in public school. After the Brown decision, the priest and nuns at the Catholic school came to my parents and said, "We want your kids to come to our school." My parents couldn't afford it, but they worked out some kind of scholarship.

The kids in that school were not ready for us to be there. My sister and I were the only African-American students there. I loved to learn. I didn't understand that I would not be welcomed.

We were on the playground and one little kid shouted to me that they didn't want any "doo-doo babies" at the school. Another boy said, "They don't call those people 'doo-doo babies.' They call them niggers!" Another kid said, "Yeah, you are a nigger and you need to go home." He spat in my face. There was a frenzy of activity.

The nuns had no idea what to do. I was wailing—beyond the murmur of tears, but the kind of tears that come from the bottom of your toes. My mother came to get me and take me back down the hill. Rich people lived at the top of the hill; poor people lived at the bottom. My grandmother was waiting for us. I was saying that we were going to get my brothers and go back and somebody was going to feel the pain I felt. I felt anger and hate.

My grandmother took me in her arms and said, "You will do no such thing. You will pray for those people and you will clean your face off and you will go back to school tomorrow. You must remember that God has put you on this earth for a time, a season and for a reason. It is not what you are called, but what you answer to."

Oh, it was profound. It changed my life. I could have been the angry black woman. I could have grown up hating people because we all come to where we are, based upon our life experiences. Those experiences shape us, and they can either go for the positive or carry you to the negative. However, because of her words, it became positive.

That values foundation carried me many days when I was the only person of color, the only woman. I was not spat upon in the corporate environment, but I was made to feel "less than" because I was a woman and an African-American woman. We all have to own our life's experiences and find the lessons in those experiences and be willing to serve in the season that we were placed in. That is why I believe women are going to be the ones to transform corporate America. I don't believe we have stepped up to the plate yet. I don't believe we have found our voice. Collectively, women are so powerful.

Look within.

Another defining moment came when I was a sales rep. I said to my boss, "I really want your support. Here is my personal career vision. I want to be ready for the next position. I need for you to give me candid feedback and help me understand what it will take to get to that position." Here was his response: "I have been grooming two men, and once I get them promoted, I will turn my attention to you." I said, "Thank you."

Thank you, because that was the day I said to myself, "If it is going to happen, I have to make it happen. If I want it, I have to go get it." There is no they, them, this. There isn't. It is you. The personal ownership was solidified when someone rejected me yet again. And it is funny. As I look back on my life, it is in those low moments that I have discovered my strength and resolve. It is about claiming your life experiences and using them to your own benefit.

I went about the business of working hard and doing more than anyone else had done to get promoted. I got a promotion—to be manager of eight men. I would be managing Watts, Compton, South Central Los Angeles and Skid Row. It was the highest gang-infested area on the planet, and I was this little country girl from Alabama thinking, "Lord, I said I wanted this, and now it is being presented. I am scared. I am frightened beyond words. But I am going to do it." I could have fallen flat on my face, and to this day I think that is what my managers thought would happen. And, literally, I was so afraid that I would cry myself to work.

On the first day, I assembled my team together and told my people I expected excellence. I was pontificating as a leader. One of my direct reports said, "Listen. Ain't no bitch gonna tell me what to do." And that humbled me to my knees. So I was scared, and somebody called me a bitch. I had grown up in an era where leadership was supposed to be about a title and power and authority. I was reminded that it is none of those things. It is service. It is transformation.

That morning when Marco called me a bitch, I didn't process it well. First of all, how dare he call me a b-word! I was going to work with one of my direct reports and he took me down to Skid Row. He said, "I am going to give you an orientation of what you are going to manage." The scene was crazy. As we were driving, police were chalking the outline of dead bodies on the cement. There was Skid Row, Heroin Alley—it was all an over-the-top experience. I was mesmerized. It was as if I had gone into a war zone.

Vincent pulled in front of the store and I didn't realize he had left me in the van by myself. We were making a call to a mom-and-pop convenience store, but there were people right in front of the store—that's right where they lived, sleeping right in front of the store. There was a dog with the teeth of a freakin' lion; it growled at me and I almost peed in my pants. I was so nervous. Inside the store, behind the counter, there was a sawed-off shotgun. I thought, "Oh my God, what have I done?" Vincent was the one who told me where not to go, what time to go into certain neighborhoods, what colors I could wear because of the gangs. He also told me, "We know you are smart and have a lot of skills, but if you don't teach us how to do things differently instead of telling us, we will never grow."

I said, "Say that again."

He said, "You need to teach us."

I decided that day that my whole leadership platform was going to be about teaching others. I told him I was so sorry I'd come off sounding as if it was all about the power.

I managed that team for five years. I learned to meet people where they are instead of thinking they should be where I think they should be. I learned that people learn differently—not with a cookie-cutter approach. I learned that people will go to the wall for you when they know you care. I learned that humility is a great leadership trait. I learned that there is more power in asking a question than making a statement. I learned that simple acts like saying "Thank you" are worth their weight in gold. I learned that people are the company's greatest asset. And I learned a lot of business stuff. I got promoted because I did first-time things that made the company millions of dollars, but it was like a class that wouldn't end. ■

Kathy Hannan is all about supporting, mentoring and promoting women. She doesn't like being one of the few at the top.

Her bio shows the breadth of her professional knowledge and commitment to community. It is filled with the kinds of awards and achievements we'd all love to boast (Athena Award, Woman to Watch, Woman of Achievement...). But what the bio leaves off is Hannan's exuberant personality, quick wit and bright aura. She's a lot of fun—and not what you'd expect from a super CPA.

Hannan was appointed as Managing Partner of Tax Services for KPMG's Midwest Area in 2004 and was the first woman to be named to the rank at the firm.

"I don't like being the only woman," she said. "I hate when women say, 'I'm the first woman to do this; aren't I awesome?' I say, 'I'm the first to do this and I think it's pathetic that in this day and age I am the first to do this.' "

The woman rocks.

3 Don't Be Humble
Kathy Hopinkah Hannan

Midwest Area Managing Partner, Tax
KPMG

Women really don't ask for things. We assume that, if we work really hard, others will recognize it because we are killing ourselves.

It doesn't work like that.

Years ago, I was in a senior staff position working next to a guy who was my age. I worked so much harder than he did—soooo much harder. But, I was going over my evaluation with the firm partner and he said to me, "So you think you do a pretty good job." My first reaction was that he'd read my self-evaluation and thought I was boasting. I said, "Yeah, I do." He asked, "Do you think you work harder than your co-worker? Do you think you are better than he?" I thought, "Oh my God, he is going down that path." His question was, "Are you better?" But I was not going to brag. I knew I worked harder than my male co-worker, that I had a much stronger work ethic, and I thought I was smarter than he. But I didn't want to appear to be an egomaniac. I said, "I think I work as well as my male co-worker, yes." The partner said, "Well, I have his self-evaluation." He started giving me pieces of what the male co-worker said. That he was better than his colleague, that he worked harder than I. He took credit for what I was doing.

I was furious.

That's when the light bulb went off. You have to toot your own horn, or at least be very honest in your self-assessment. Don't be humble to a fault. Other people will be taking credit for things they don't do. You have to take credit for what you are accomplishing.

That partner knew what he was doing when he told me what my male co-worker had written. He got my blood boiling. He told me, "If you are going to do a good job, you have to say you are doing a good job. If you are doing a great job, say you are doing a great job. And don't let other people take credit for what you do!"

I took on another leadership role when the company was merging two geographies. We had two senior men who were in leadership roles for each of those geographies. When the areas merged, each of these men thought he would get the role. They didn't. I got it. I came out of left field. They were senior partners and I was a young partner at the time.

One of the men worked in my office, and if I would say black, he'd say white. It was constant. Finally, I sat him down and said, "Listen, I didn't ask for this job. We are all going to look like idiots if we fight on everything." He agreed, and I felt good about it. But, it wasn't long before I happened to be on another floor and another person had this guy on speakerphone, and he was ripping me to shreds. It was, "Who is she? She is a kid, she doesn't know anything …" I was mortified because I could hear this and I was right there with one of my managers.

I talked to another partner who was one of my mentors and asked, "What should I do? He just annihilated me." His advice was not to do anything. Just let it roll off my back.

That night, I went to bed and I was so angry. I couldn't live with myself if I'd let it roll off my back. So I went to see the guy and said, "Listen. I heard what you said about me the other day." He said, "What? I don't know what you are talking about." I said, "Oh my God, yes you do. You were on speakerphone and I heard everything you said." Then, I looked right at him and said, "If you want to stab me in the back, do it right here in front of me—in the chest." He apologized. "He said, I'm really sorry. This has been very difficult."

I got so much satisfaction from him saying that, and we've worked together beautifully ever since. In fact, we are really good friends. You have to stand up for yourself. You can't just turn the other cheek because it shows weakness.

Another lesson is, it is okay to say no. Remember that. I was told the company wanted me to move to California for a promotion. I had to decide within twenty-four hours whether I would relocate my family to the West Coast. But my husband was at the FBI Academy. My girls were seven and five. And I had to decide in twenty-four hours? People told me I couldn't say no to the opportunity, but I wasn't comfortable with it. I came in the next morning and said, "I'm not going to take it." Other people told me I was making a career-limiting decision, but I couldn't do it that fast. That was that. If it limited me, it limited me.

Within two months, I was asked to be the vice chair of human resources and development. So I learned something. It really is okay to say no. It doesn't mean you never will have another opportunity.

I love that phrase by Ralph Waldo Emerson, "The years teach much which the days never knew." I try not to look back and say, "I wish I would have done this differently," or "I failed at that." I really believe you learn more from your failures than you do from your successes. You can't ever really succeed unless you fail. I tell my kids, "I hope you fail at things because then you will learn what it takes."

I've made my mistakes. Mistakes on projects, mistakes in hiring people, mistakes in relying on certain people too much.

I learned one lesson early on—about preparing. Actually, that one was in college. I was in a class and I figured I was smarter than all the other kids in the class, and we had to get up and read something and then do a critical review. Well, I read the book but didn't put any thoughts down, and went in to give my presentation without any notes. It was to last a half hour. Well, I had two minutes of material. I think that, for twenty-eight minutes, I said again and again, "Any questions?" I was totally mortified, but it taught me how you really have to prepare. You have to think about what you are going to say.

Years later, I was getting ready for a presentation and my mentor asked if I needed any help because there were some questions the chairman was going to ask. I was vice chair of HR and didn't want him to think I needed to run it past him, so I didn't ask for help. I should have been smart enough to realize that he was giving me a sign that it was a sensitive issue and I should have gotten help and built some support around the table. Instead, I went up by myself and the chairman came out and said, "I don't like this because…" He asked a question that I couldn't answer because I hadn't asked for help and I didn't know what he might ask. I saw my mentor put his head in his hands. Gong! I heard the gong go off.

Well, what I learned from that is, you are never too high up to ask for help. Actually, you are an idiot if you don't. If people want to offer advice, listen to it. You don't have to take it.

I have learned you have to make fun of yourself and take some risks. It's like golf. Guys lie about how well they play golf. Most people are pathetic. I remember when I told a friend that I was going to go out and play golf, and she thought I was crazy because I'd never played it.

I went with this guy who said, "I'm not really great at it—just okay." Well, he was terrible! He got up to the tee, missed the ball on the first swing. He just swung hard and missed it. Then I learned what a mulligan is. He hit the ball, it went straight in the air, and it landed right behind him! I thought, "This is great. I can do that!"

Another thing: These guys cheat. I was golfing with this guy in Baltimore and he was swinging in the weeds. I mean, *swinging*. It was like he was going to cut the grass with a machete. Swinging, swinging, swinging. And when he came back and was asked what he'd hit, he said, "I got a four." Four? It was twelve. At least eight.

That's how guys are. If something goes wrong or they get embarrassed, they can brush it off. A woman will worry that she can never be seen after that, that everyone will remember how awful she golfed. ■

The night she grew up, **Betsy Hosick** was nine. Her father was in the U.S. Army in Vietnam and her mother was upset and drinking wine before bedtime. Hosick heard her mother vomiting, so she went to her to clean the mess. Her mother went to bed. When Hosick awoke the next morning she couldn't rouse her mother.

Her mother's stroke and recovery changed her—forever.

Hosick was the youngest of four children. Her twin sisters were fourteen, her older brother was sixteen, but they didn't know how to cope with the situation. It all fell to Hosick, who now says, "Leadership doesn't necessarily come with age. When life is in chaos, somebody has to be the person who is not in chaos. That was me."

Her mother lost her independence and had extreme difficulty communicating. Hosick took care of her for many years, cooking and caring for the entire family. "Somewhere inside I knew that, when something goes terribly wrong, you can choose to be a victim or you can choose to take responsibility. Events happen every single day. Some of them are in our control, some are not. The only thing you can control is your response."

Her father returned home after the stroke, but Hosick was the point person for her mother's care. Her father didn't want her sharing her feelings about what had happened, or how she was dealing with it—with anyone. It was her first experience in holding in the deepest truths and covering it all up.

4 Step Up
E. A. "Betsy" Hosick
General Manager Midstream Procurement
Chevron

I used to work for 7-Eleven. I was responsible for thirty-three stores in the inner city of Dallas. There was a lot of crime—so many store robberies that we had a robbery every night for forty-two days straight. We had employees who were shot.

One of the things that I always did was meet everybody who works for me because I just think business is about relationships. The better you build relationships, the better things happen. Then people want to do the things they need to do. They don't want to feel they are made to do them. They want to feel that they are important enough to be a part of the process.

I was doing night rides in a really tough neighborhood, and I went by one of my stores and the employees who had gotten off at 11 p.m. were still standing outside. I wanted to know why they were there. One employee told me his ride home forgot to pick him up, and he was afraid to walk. He lived in the South Dallas projects. I said, "You know what? I'll take you home. I don't want you to stand out here all night. I don't know if it is any safer for you to stand outside this building all night than it is to walk home."

We got to his home and, I admit, my palms were sweating. I wasn't comfortable and I didn't feel completely safe. He said, "I really want you to see my house." So I did. It was two o'clock in the morning. But, we went in there and everything of value was locked up somewhere. There was no television set out. There was nothing of value sitting out, other than his couch and chairs. I didn't ask about it, but he explained that he had a TV, but it was locked in a special place because, if he didn't do that, it wouldn't be there when he got home. Then he showed me the laundry room in his apartment. There was a hookup for a washer and dryer. He didn't have a washer or dryer, but the point was, he was proud to live in a place where, if he did have them, he could hook them up right there.

Seeing his home with him changed the whole way I managed people. This guy could have lived like a victim. A victim of society, a victim of the system, saying it was somebody else's fault. But he didn't live like that. He had hopes. He had courage. He had pride. And, I suspect, more than I did at that particular point in my life.

Our job as leaders is to help people be the best they can be. You have to understand them and know what makes them tick. I do think motivation comes from within, but a good leader creates environments that help people tap into their motivation.

You can't make judgments about the people who work for you because you don't know everything there is to know about them. It is our job as managers to help them work in the circumstances they are in and be available to help build their own confidence in themselves. That was the turning point for us in that market. We went from the worst district in the company for 7-Eleven to the top ten in just that one year. It was just because I changed the way I thought about the people who worked for me.

I started doing fun things. We would have regular meetings. I started a contest where we'd award the best audit control or the highest sales—the things that were important to the company. The reward for the store that won was that everyone in the store would get the day off—on us. We would work in their place. It was important to them. They needed the money. This was a way to show them that we appreciated all the hard work they did under those difficult circumstances. Those were such difficult stores.

We stopped having shortage problems. Turnover dropped. People say you have to drive for results and, yeah, you do. But you can do it in a lot of ways. Finding those motivational keys is a good way to drive for results.

And, the employee who showed me his home and taught me so much about the people who work with me continued to work for 7-Eleven. He became a store manager.

The other piece of leadership is about being honest. Honesty and integrity. Those are big leadership qualities, which also, I think, drive success.

I learned something about that when I was trying to get my son to go to college. He didn't really want to go. He is very artistic, very good with his hands, likes music and those kinds of things. He didn't want the discipline of going to college, but he complied because I am his mom. He went and dropped out twice. It was very tumultuous for the two of us. I said all the wrong things like, "You are spending all of my money..." He said to me, "Mom, if I am happy flipping burgers for the rest of my life, why is that a problem for you?" That comment helped me to understand that I wanted him to succeed—not just for himself, but for me. It was my pride and my ego that was wrapped up in the child or adult he was to be.

That taught me that I wasn't honest with myself about what I wanted for him. Parents say these things all the time: I want you to be happy. I love you and I want you to be the best you can be. I want you to fulfill your dreams. But, I realized that, at least for me, I wanted him to be the best he could be so I would be proud of him. I obviously didn't want him to be happy because I was certainly forcing him to do things that weren't the things he really was interested in doing. So I learned that lesson.

And now, my son is a very successful business person. He works as a construction superintendent and he plays in a band in his spare time.

That lesson translated into my work. Be honest with your people. Allow them to face their natural consequences—no matter what those consequences turn out to be. If you are setting an expectation, or any kind of standard for your folks, be honest enough with them to let them know how you feel about what they are doing. The rest is in their court. I've even had people whom I have terminated who actually ended up thanking me because the job wasn't the right fit for them. If I act with integrity, I never have to worry if I am doing the ethical thing.

People who work for you know whether or not you are honest. If they think that what you are saying to them only makes it good for you, they will know it right away. If you are having them work on a project because it is going to get you something, rather than how it will develop them or be for the overall good, they will know it right away, and you will lose your integrity. With my son, I lost my integrity. He knew I wasn't in it for him.

Again, be honest.

Being a lesbian is just an honest part of who I am. If you are afraid that people will reject you, you are really saying more about you than you are about them. I have to be true to myself. If I really accept myself, I can't be shy about who I am.

Of course, it is not as simple as I just put it. I was married for nineteen years. I grew up as a Catholic, and I had all of that stuff in my head about not doing anything wrong or my mom would be sick again. So I stayed married to a man who was an alcoholic. My kids grew up telling stories because we couldn't let that secret of my husband's alcoholism out. And there was so much codependence with me trying to fix it, thinking it was my fault. I really thought that, if I were a better wife or mother, the problem wouldn't exist.

My son caused this change to happen because he started using drugs as a teenager. He recognized it wasn't a good thing and actually admitted himself to a treatment center when he was sixteen. During a facilitated family meeting, he was very honest about what he needed from us. He told my husband, "I need you to be my father. I need you to stop drinking. I need to be able to have a real conversation with you." My husband denied he had any problem at all, and that was the straw that broke the camel's back.

It wasn't like there was this light bulb that went off and I thought, "Oh, I'm gay." It was a slow process that started with this friendship. I literally fell in love. It felt like the most natural thing in the world to me—more natural than anything I have ever felt in my entire life. It was a journey for me to realize I had found my soul mate. In the midst of my counseling and trying to get divorced, I told the counselor about Barb and what I was feeling.

He asked me the question of a lifetime, which was, "Are you going to let people know?"

My first response was, "I just can't." I was scared. I didn't think my kids would love me, and all those other lies we tell ourselves.

He said to me the most profound words of wisdom I have ever heard. He said, "So, Betsy, are you going to trade one lie for another?"

Right then and there, I knew I couldn't be true to myself or my partner or anybody else if I were going to lie. In that moment, I decided I was going to be honest about it. I would share my happiness about finding my soul mate. That was when I was thirty-seven. I am fifty-three now.

I started sharing with people. I told my dad what I was doing. My dad said, "It's about time. I can't believe you waited so long." Now he introduces us as his daughters.

I was working in a pretty high position. Barb actually worked for me, so I went to my boss and said I really need to change this. I had to tell him right away why I wanted to change it. She ended up leaving her job there. I can't help but think that, ultimately, prejudice and homophobia led to her quitting because her job got to be so stressful, she had no other choice.

A friend of mine joined Chevron and persuaded me to work there.

I was very upfront about my lifestyle in the interview. Every interviewer asks you to tell about yourself, and I talked about my kids, my grandkids and my partner—Barb. It is a regular part of the conversation. Chevron may be the only oil company with domestic-partner benefits. Barb attends all of our functions.

I can't tell you that everything has been easy. My sister, a Southern Baptist, used to send my Christmas presents back. But we've worked through it.

Barb and I had a wedding in 1998, and we've been together for more than fifteen years. People from Chevron came.

You have got to be okay with yourself. If you aren't true to yourself, you can't be true to anybody else. It's really been nice. I wish I'd gotten here sooner. ∎

Susan Ivey is always ready for the questions of how she defends her industry—and why. Such questions are cliché when you become the face of one of the world's largest tobacco companies. "You have your moments in a job like this," she said. "The difficulties about the controversies are that you are trying to solve a dilemma with facts when, actually, it is an emotional debate. Nobody wants to hear facts. It's one side or the other."

Ivey described what it was like to endure an excruciating deposition in which she was asked to interpret a document written in the 1950s. "I always tackle the most difficult situations with a clear mind-set that I can do anything for four hours. Like, a deposition, or testifying at the Department of Justice, or even our annual meetings. I say, 'I can do anything for four hours. This too shall pass.' "

Being such a visible CEO requires conviction in her beliefs, she said. "This is an adult product for adults, and we have to market it responsibly," she said.

Ivey is chairman, president and chief executive officer of Reynolds American Inc., the parent company of R.J. Reynolds Tobacco Co., Conwood Co., Santa Fe Natural Tobacco Co., and R.J. Reynolds Global Products. She is also chairman of R.J. Reynolds, the second-largest U.S. cigarette company, which manufactures and markets about one-third of the cigarettes sold in the United States.

5 Visualize Success
Susan Ivey
Chairman, President and Chief Executive Officer
Reynolds American Inc.

Everybody wants to know how I wound up in this industry. Well, I moved to Louisville, graduated, went into sales and took a job for an office-equipment company. I did it for nine months, and I hated everything about it. It was a disaster. So this goes back to the philosophy that you have to do something you like. And there I was at the ripe old age of twenty-two and I asked myself, "What do I like?" Well, that would be alcohol, cigarettes or cosmetics. I called up the company and asked, "Do you need a sales rep?" I was hired within two weeks.

I was a sales rep, then a district manager. I got my MBA on nights and weekends and bought my dream house. I hadn't even been in that house for thirty days when the company came to me and said, "We would like you to move to London and you have forty-eight hours to decide." Living overseas had never even entered my consciousness. The parent company was in London and they thought it would be a good experience for me to go there for two years. I'd just moved into my house! But I thought, "I am going to go. I can always come back."

These are some of my words of wisdom: You can always go home. You can't always reconstruct an opportunity. You can always have a run at it and give up later if that is necessary, but it may never come again.

The worst situation would have been sitting around ten years later and wondering what would have happened if I'd done it. So I went there. I knew nobody.

Those two years lasted for nine. It was the most broadening thing I could have done. I traveled to sixty countries along that path and really learned about the world and about people and business. I went there in 1990, and at that time, we were not long on women in the tobacco industry—especially not in senior leadership. But what I didn't appreciate was that it was even worse in London. There, they had no women. When I got there, they wondered what a woman was even doing there, and what any-one was doing there who was that young. I was thirty-four and, by their standards, that was young. Plus, they didn't have the highest regard for Americans.

The women in middle management came forward and told me they were support-ing me, but I should remember, "If this goes wrong and you aren't successful here, you could set us back." I had not appreciated that burden until then. I never walked around thinking I was carrying the gender, but in their case, that was how they felt about it. It had been an old boys' club, like British public school. The cabal had been running the thing forever. After six months, the men figured out I had a reason for being there. Then, I was actually championed very well in that system, even though there weren't a lot of women. I had some very strong sponsors.

I was not expecting to come back to the States but, nine years later, the parent company decided it would be a good idea. Their subsidiary here was in pretty bad shape, and there was a coup among the leadership, so I came back to run the marketing and sales departments.

Until 1999 or 2000, I'd never thought about being the CEO. Sometimes you just grow up into these things. I didn't expect it to happen for three to five years, but then it happened. There was no turning it down. There was nobody else to do it. I didn't feel ready, but then again, there is another lesson. You are not always ready. You are not the No. 1 until you are the No. 1. You are the No. 2. You can't practice to be the No. 1. After the company sold its assets to Reynolds, it sold me as well and I was made CEO of the public company. Those have been the biggest career-changing, defining moments.

You don't always have to know what you want. I am a big believer in positive visioning. Young people ask if I knew I wanted to be a CEO when I was getting my MBA and the answer is, certainly not. I wanted to be a brand manager or a brand director. But, after I got back from London, I was watching the dynamics unfold in the top team and it occurred to me: "I could run this thing. I don't have all the expertise; nobody does. But I have enough end-to-end knowledge and the instincts to run this entity." I thought I'd get myself ready so that, in two to three years, when my boss retired, I'd be next in line. But, the next thing I knew, my boss was leaving and the Brits came to me.

I remember, it was in an Atlanta hotel. The managing director at the time said, "We are going to make some changes here and we would very much like for you to be the CEO of this company. We think you are ready. And, we know you." I was promised all the support I would need. I don't remember it being too optional. I don't think they had a Plan B. It was just shocking for me, in terms of the timing. I said, "Yes, I'll do it." I needed to step up and take it on.

You have to believe in yourself. You have to love what you do. You have to have that commitment and passion for what you are doing—whatever that is. You have a core level of aptitude. Beyond that, it is passion and commitment. It is being prepared to keep taking challenges and to keep pushing yourself. It is wanting to have new experiences and embracing change so you don't get comfortable in your own job and do the same thing for twenty years. You have to have a thirst for adventure and an attitude that makes you try new things.

If you don't love your work, you need to get out and get another job. If you are going to do something for ten to twelve hours a day, you really have to love it. If you don't, you aren't going to be any good. A lot of people get in ruts and keep doing what they are supposed to do. But, if they don't like it, it will dead-end them.

I really, really like what I do. There are aspects of any job that you won't like. There are days in my job that I don't like. But be passionate about the role you play and the issues you take on—you have to love it. In my case, it is shaping and defining a successful organization. I love that.

Prior to the merger (between Brown & Williamson Tobacco and R.J. Reynolds), Reynolds had a female president and chief financial officer. When the merger happened, their CEO retired. I was the CEO of the other company and was nominated to be CEO of the merged company. It ended up being the three females at the top. We are the only company in the Fortune 500 at which the top three officers are female. So it was rather lucky and it worked out exceptionally well.

We don't vent because we all come from the same team. If we get together, we're talking about the company. There are differences between men and women at this level. Women will tell each other if there is a run in their hose or if there is something in their teeth, whereas the guys will let it go all day. We'll ask, "Where did you get that?" and we'll talk about shopping.

Men do exceptionally well with us. We tease about it. They'll say, "Oh, here they come again," or, "We need a man in here." But, people react, in the end, to the vision and the direction, the communication. It doesn't matter if it is female or male. We are past the generation of men who didn't grow up working with women. The last bastion of guys who think we should all be secretaries are older than sixty. We are ending that. Men now have grown up with women alongside them in their careers.

Working in this industry is a constant challenge. I've been in it twenty-five years and the controversial nature of it is a given. We have so many different constituencies and stakeholders, and that is a challenge. There are people who would like to see us go out of business. Others think it is better to have a more responsible industry. This is a challenge I have grown up with, and I take it in stride.

The job I have today is the best job I have ever had. And I would probably have said that about every job I've had along the path. I now have an opportunity to build a company of more than 8,500 people, and that is enormously rewarding. ■

Jane Knaack-Esbeck's father used to tell her, "I'd rather be lucky than good." There's a lot to be said for that, she said. "Sometimes you are lucky. But you have to be good, too. And sometimes you have to make your own luck." She is a warm, honest, approachable storyteller with an "oh gosh" view of her extraordinary success.

She is also a giving mentor who truly wants to help. Proof was the e-mail that came soon after her interview:

"Fawn, I went to lunch and was thinking about the interview. One question I didn't answer with as much conviction as I really wanted was, 'What advice would you give your daughters?' I would like to add to my response, if you would allow.

"Don't take yourself too seriously. I have found that when the majority of my focus is on my job, I start to worry about the wrong things. When that happens, I take a class, and, in many cases, I would teach a class. I get my balance back as well as a quick reminder regarding good time management.

"When you feel under lots of pressure or stress, go immediately to the gym and exercise. It's amazing how quickly you put 'stuff' into perspective after a hard workout.

"If someone is creating problems for you, step back and, as objectively as possible, evaluate their motives. The problem could be you and not the other person.

"Try to find something to laugh about every day.

"If you make a mistake, admit it immediately. We are humans and we make mistakes, but learn from it and try not to make the same mistake twice.

"Don't ever forget who got you to this point in your career and, whenever possible, thank them for their help.

"Give back—help someone else move up.

"This is not a smooth road. There are dips and curves—go with them. Be patient, but find ways to learn new things and pretty soon you are back on track."

About sums it up, eh?

6 Work Well with Others
Jane Knaack-Esbeck
Senior Vice President of Human Resources and Administration
Hy-Vee Inc.

About twenty-five years ago, I was divorced with three small children—three, five and nine—and we were traveling to see my parents on the eastern edge of Iowa. It was Christmas Eve, and very quiet, because there weren't many people on the road. It was seven or eight o'clock at night, and I was tired and needed to stop for coffee.

The lady sitting at the next table struck up a conversation. She was also a single parent on the way to her parents' house. She had two boys; I had two boys and a girl. She heard me talking to my kids about going to Grandma's, and she started talking. It was one of those moments when you feel like you have been touched by someone.

My divorce was an ugly situation. My husband left me with support, but the situation was emotional and messy. We lived in a small community and I couldn't get away from it. I needed to shake myself off.

If it hadn't been for that one moment in time at that restaurant, I don't know where I would be today. I'd been thinking about moving and the woman encouraged me to take a risk and move to Des Moines. I'd never considered myself a risk-taker, but a week later, I drove to Des Moines with the kids and drove to the neighborhood where she lived. She helped me find a house. I started looking for a job. All of a sudden, it hit me: "I can do this. I can make this change."

It was exactly what I needed. I needed to get away from a very depressing situation. I needed to shed a lot of sadness and redefine who I was. I have, honest to God, never looked back.

All these years later, she and I are still friends.

It is not always easy to make change, but once you make the life-changing decisions, everything else sort of falls into place. We'd moved fifty miles away, but it was a whole new world,

I went to work as a headhunter. Then in banking. Then I worked in human resources for *The Des Moines Register*.

My first husband actually did me a favor when he left me. Because of that, I had the opportunity to meet the person who was my true soul mate. He worked at the bank where I was, and we dated a while and then married. He is my best friend, partly because he doesn't always say what I want to hear. I might be having a hard time and he will say, "Have you thought about how you came across?" instead of "You're right." I give him as much credit for my career as I do my best mentor, which is my boss.

When I was at *The Des Moines Register*, I got a call about a job at a place called Perishable Distributors of Iowa. My boss was Ric Jurgens, who is now CEO at Hy-Vee. He has the ability to sit down with you and work through problems. He shows that issues you have with other people may not be the fault of the other person. I once worked with a guy who was tough, tough, tough. He had a forceful personality, and he was pretty sure he was always right. There were times when I needed him to slow down and listen to me.

After one encounter, I went into Ric's office, grabbed a box of Kleenex and unloaded. By the time I left the room, I realized that I was the reason there was a problem. I learned a valuable lesson, and that is, when you have an issue with someone, you need to look at it from his or her perspective. In order to change how you deal with the issue, you have to figure out how to work with the other person from where he or she are. In this case, I learned I had to meet that man where he was. I didn't need to change him; I needed to change how I dealt with him.

That is a lesson I have tried very, very hard to use. Over the years, I have had to learn to say, "I have a tough time understanding. Share with me how we can work together. I am having a tough time communicating with you." So I learned that the most important thing is figuring out how we can work together.

You have to listen. You really have to listen to people, and you can't believe you are always right. If you do, you shut people off from thinking about how to do things differently—or better. The longer you do a job, the more you have to step back and listen and encourage other people to help you find a new path.

I tell my kids that honesty and integrity are the two things you never can let go of. If you are in a situation where you are uncomfortable, be forthright. Communication problems are ninety-nine percent of all issues in all companies. When you have one, back up and try to clarify the situation. Ask a lot of questions. Make sure you are clear. If you don't like what someone is saying, you can disagree and not put somebody in a tough position. You have a responsibility to express why you don't agree. People are afraid to share the truth, and that is how companies get into trouble. I want people to step up and be honest. That's what I tell my children. Just be honest.

I always knew there were things I could do. I never dreamed I would end up on the executive committee of a company of this size. I never dreamed I would get on a corporate plane and fly here or there. I wonder how this kid who grew up in the Midwest was fortunate enough to be in the right place at the right time and know the right people. I am not a genius. I am a nice person. I know my craft well. I love my children, I love my family.

And, guess what? You can do this. All of this.

There are moments when it is hard. You just have to back up, square your shoulders and go right back at it. Be resilient. Understand that not every day is a wonderful day.

You have to smile and work your way through it. Go out and run. Take care of yourself and come back at it tomorrow. ■

Dawn Hudson was running late because she was in the middle of something and it was big. Suddenly, she was on the phone, talking quickly with a move-it-move-it-move-it intensity that was completely focused and on task.

Asked if she has always been so intense, she said, "I wouldn't describe myself that way. I am intense and focused and hard-working, but I like to think I am fun-loving and approachable at the same time. That's my goal."

Hudson oversees all functions of Pepsi-Cola in North America: sales, marketing, and operations, strategic direction and financial performance. She is also CEO of the PepsiCo Foodservice Division, which integrates the relevant units of Pepsi-Cola North America, Frito-Lay North America, Quaker, Tropicana and Gatorade.

7 Use the Drop Shot
Dawn Hudson

President and Chief Executive Officer
Pepsi-Cola North America

My father raised me to be the son he didn't have. I was the oldest of three daughters, born to a father who was one of four boys in a very athletic, hard-driving, hard-working ethnic family. There was a huge emphasis on sports, and I often ascribe my focus and success to that sports background. I took lots and lots of tennis lessons, and I wanted to compete. I was a ranked tennis player throughout college.

When you compete at a tournament level, it is not about having fun. It is about being faced with competitors on the court and knowing how to bring out the best in yourself when you get down and upset, or when you are up. You have to know how to close it out. It is that fortitude of focus that brings you the win.

Our board chairman used to say that if he had to be in a foxhole, he would want me in there with him. When challenged, I get stronger. I get stronger under pressure. That doesn't mean I want pressure all the time, but the ability to get stronger under pressure comes from athletics.

You have to have the confidence that you can fix a problem. Reach out for help from the people you know, pick a path and be decisive. Nobody is perfect. Nobody has a crystal ball. You want to get the facts, gather the experts, assess the situation, make a decision and move.

I have learned that there never will be enough time in the day. Focus. Be very adaptive. Move. This is a tennis analogy because when you are down and they are killing you and making you run around to get to the ball, what can you do? Drop shot.

Change your game and get it done.

I didn't wake up at age twenty-five and say, "I want to be a general manager of a company." I'm somebody who takes opportunities. It takes a vision and an ability to communicate and articulate and motivate and lead others toward that vision. It takes confidence—that is critical. But it also takes common sense. You can do the analysis you need in business, but there is so much common sense involved and you have to trust it.

You chart your own path. Life is too frenetic, and as much as people want to coach and develop you, they don't have time. You are the one who has to use your opportunities and skills sets to get ahead, be your own advocate and know when the time is right to make moves.

The best learning in life happens when you are faced with a tough situation. I once took over leading a company that was very male-oriented, which was fine, but it was a company—an advertising agency—that was in a lot of pain. At least 50 percent of the people were actively looking for jobs. The creative director I'd partnered with had been asked off the business, and I was joining this agency with no leader of the creative department. I found myself walking in without a senior team and getting a company in crisis. That is an uncomfortable place to go for your first general management role.

I learned you have to reach to your top talent, put faith in them, pick one or two things you can do to create a win, and then create a win. I focused on bringing an esprit de corps, which had vanished there. We brought in a new piece of business, people felt good, and the lesson was invaluable.

Another situation that taught me a lot happened after I joined the Pepsi-Cola team from Frito-Lay. Five weeks into my tenure, we had a potential national recall on a product because of some packaging that wasn't working properly. In that kind of situation, you have to get in the trenches and figure out what to do, so we all got in the trenches and worked all weekend long. We pulled everything apart, rolled up our sleeves, strategized what we could do, made decisions—and made them quickly. I learned more in that two-day weekend about leadership and working with a team than in any other experience. Usually, a packaging problem takes months to fix, but we were able to pull it out of the trade and quickly fix and replace without having to do the recall.

I am not the first to break through the glass ceiling. I may be five years after that. My first boss in advertising in 1979 was a woman. The head of the advertising agency I worked for in Chicago was a woman. I never had to be that "first one." I had other firsts before me who took me along and helped me. A lot of those who were first viewed other women as competitors. I don't want to and I don't think I do view other women as competitors. My role is to give back. I always wish I had more time to mentor women.

I hate office politics. I think spending a lot of time worrying about office politics and talking about it with others doesn't get you anywhere. It takes time away from your job. I am a believer that good things happen to good people. Spend your time on the things you need to get done and you will be more successful than you will be by spending time on office politics and putting your energy into the one person in ten at work who is divisive or difficult for you. Spend your time on the other nine.

I do believe that, in the end, you will be rewarded by what you can contribute. I focus on what I can do and look for the opportunity to demonstrate what I can do by looking for the things that are significant to the business. One person rarely does anything by himself or herself. Give the team credit and you will be rewarded.

There is a saying that I'll take a 70 percent idea executed 100 percent any day over a perfect idea executed 70 percent. Power is getting people aligned around an excellent idea and getting movement.

I have high standards, but I don't let that keep me from moving. You've got to be willing to make your move. ■

You can't help but fall in love with **Shelley Broader** because the woman is unabashedly who she is: bold, inspiring and irreverent. There doesn't seem to be much pretense there.

"I don't put on my game face," she said. "I am a unified individual. My public and private persona are all the same deal." She is conscious that, as a CEO with eight thousand associates, she is being watched all day long. "They are watching what I am putting in my coffee, the dress I have on, if I have a crabby expression on my face. So, they see if I am sending signals, positive or negative, that I intend or don't intend to send. But I have integrated my public and private personas. It's all one person. You waste so much energy and effort and stress if you have to change your behavior when you are alone and in public."

Broader is a natural mentor who said she'd much rather develop leaders than followers. She runs the Tampa, Florida-based Sweetbay Supermarket, a chain of more than 100 retail stores with more than $1 billion in annual sales.

8 Know Who You Are
Shelley Broader
President and Chief Executive Officer
Sweetbay Supermarket

I had a wonderful childhood. I had a lot of friends, played sports and did the cheer-leading thing. I don't have those memories of adolescent angst.

Real tragedy hit our family in the late 1970s when my father died in a car accident. He was 43, leaving us four kids behind. I was in the eighth grade, my sister was a freshman in high school and my two brothers were in college. Mother hadn't worked since she'd married. This was a huge shock to the system, but she was amazing. She went back to college and got her teaching degree, and she made a life for us.

As sad as we were about my father passing away, we never were allowed to be scared by it. I am sure my mother was very scared, but she put on the front that she was in charge of the family and we were going to be fine. Talk about pivotal points in your life.

Because of that, I don't live a dramatic life. I never have. That is because, at an early age, I knew about real drama. It gives perspective to the scale of what is truly bad versus what is annoying and can be solved. If everyone is alive and well, it is not that bad. It isn't. The angst of first jobs or boyfriends or bad bosses—on a scale of one to ten—didn't rate near as high as what I'd gone through. It gave me excellent perspective on life.

Life is fragile, and you don't know what is coming. You don't know. You never know what the next day will bring.

But the real lesson is that you will recover. If my family recovered from that, people are really resilient. You can recover from personal and professional tragedy. Humor helped my family; it certainly helped me. Life and work are serious. But it can all be intertwined with a lot of good humor. I probably compartmentalize a bit, saying I might not think about this or that right now, saying I will focus on something else. I try to intertwine positive energy and positive outlook.

Surround yourself with people with positive energy, with people who are optimistic, but also realistic, so you aren't just hearing good news, but all of the news.

On the flip side, you don't want the spin of doom on every report. If it is a sunny day, some people will say it must be the thin ozone. Can't anything be good?

I work with a terrific team. There are always some people who are exhausting. Sometimes, people are exhausting in a positive way because their energy level and commitment and desire are so intense—all the time. But there are those who are always looking for the Achilles heel—why things won't work.

You have to make some decisions about who you are going to spend time with, who you are going to align with in the workplace, and I have to admit that there is more time in my life—and more joy—when I am not around the people who are exhaustive on the negative side. Those people never take anything for face value and look for ulterior motives for every single move. Not that you want to be Pollyanna, because there are occasionally dark sides. But you don't want that every single minute of the day.

I once had a conversation with my boss, (Hannaford Bros. CEO) Ron Hodge, which really stayed with me. I asked, "What can I do to move to the next level? Where can I improve?" He said, "You have to quit trying so hard." I remember thinking, "What? Quit trying so hard?" I thought it was all about trying so hard. He said, "You've made it. You could do nothing more developmentally and still have a very good career. Or, you could quit being the one always raising her hand, volunteering to do something. You can sit back in a discussion and watch and see if your answer comes up before you say it."

I was senior vice president of business strategy, marketing and communication, and was one of the most senior people at Hannaford, next to him. But I was still behaving like I was trying to move up the ladder and get points. I was already at the top. I didn't recognize it.

That was a very enlightening view on senior executive posture, about leaning back in your chair and hoping the answer comes out of someone else's mouth. It doesn't mean relax and don't work hard. It is about developing a more serious leadership voice. Letting answers come out somewhere else, and directing them.

Another thing Ron did for me was demystify management. People think that the people on the top floor have loftier minds, are craftier individuals and better strategic thinkers. What he taught me was, it is just the same on the top floor as downstairs. The people downstairs think we must have the answers, but the people on the top floor are doing the same thing they are: sitting in a group and coming up with ideas. The upstairs group is just a different group of people with a little more experience. You might think you don't belong "up there" because you assume there is a level of thinking far above what yours is, but you are wrong.

Leadership has to do with knowing what you want, and communicating a desired outcome to different levels in a way that is not intimidating, threatening or the only option. There are a lot of times when I know exactly what I want, and lay it out clearly and communicate it very well. And, in the process, people will come up to me or there is research that shows it is not the right outcome. I don't hold onto the original plan too tightly. You'd better change your mind. It has to do with being flexible in your outcome. There are a lot of people who can set direction and communicate a plan, but who are too autocratic or inflexible. If the plan goes awry or the facts say you should change direction, take action. It doesn't mean you are wrong; it means you are smart.

It is hard for me to quantify my mistakes because I don't make them in the way people traditionally make them. I have made tons of mistakes—hilarious, legendary ones. But the mistake would be staying the course. The real mistake is when you recognize something is a bad mistake and keep trying to force a bad decision into success. You are much better off saying, "Does everyone agree that this is a bad plan? I thought it was terrific, everyone thought it was terrific, but we are four months into it and it is not working. We can try one two-week generation to fix it, but if it doesn't work, we're outta here." The mistake is forcing something until it is dead.

There are very few decisions in life that can't be corrected if you make a wrong call. But there is a lot of misery if you stick with a bad decision forever.

A big theme in my life is using your right to complain. If you are not going to take any action on what is bothering you, you have no right to complain. I have raised my children that way and I run my business that way. If you don't like how someone is doing something, I don't want to hear about it until that person has heard about it. There are people who would rather complain than take one action to fix something. If you don't like how someone is treating you, try to change it. And, if you don't like something, either change it or get over it. There aren't many things worth being miserable over all the time.

Know who you are. You don't have to get an A-plus in every subject. It's nice to hang with friends who get the A-plus in the subjects that you don't. I see myself as a coordinator of experts. That has allowed me to be more strategic and grow the talent. They are the masters of their own domains. If you are the master of operations, I expect you to run them. I don't want to be making the advertising buy. If I need to, I don't have the right person in that role.

I will tell my people to imagine that today is their last day, and they need to give the next person the five things they need to do in order to hit the ground running. Is it a vendor who needs to go? Is there an issue with the age of your facilities? What five things would catapult the person forward? Then I say, "Why aren't you doing those things? Start!"

One of the most pivotal moments in my life happened in the fourth grade.

I had a teacher named Mr. Jared, who was the cool teacher everyone wanted to have. Every few months, we got to change seats in his classroom, and I remember Mr. Jared coming up to me at recess the day of the switch.

He said, "We're going to switch seatmates again," and I said, "I know. I'm going to sit next to Kim."

He said, "I'd like for you to do me a favor. I want you to pick Rick."

Rick was the boy in the class that no one would pick. Now that I look back on it, he was probably a child in the early mainstreaming. He had physical difficulties as well as emotional and developmental difficulties.

I said, "Mr. Jared, I don't want to sit with Rick. I don't want to pick him."

Mr. Jared said, "I want you to do that for me. No one ever picks him. If you pick him, you might make a difference for him his whole life because no one ever picks him."

Then he said something I will never forget: "There are certain people in the world who have powerful gifts that can either be used for good, or they can waste them. I think you have those gifts and you should use them for good."

That is what I have tried to do. ∎

Beverly Grant does not cower from criticism. She seeks it out. She uses it. She appreciates it. She knows the cost of a varnished truth.

During nearly twenty-two years at Procter & Gamble, Grant has proved her mettle by acknowledging that there is a "game" involved in working in the corporate world, and then learning the rules. That hasn't always been easy, but it has led her over and around obstacles that would have defeated a less-savvy—and less-hearty—individual.

"If you don't understand the game and how it is played, you don't know what game to play," she said. "I was in a situation where it was as if I were playing basketball and wondering if I should be playing golf, then finding out we were really playing soccer. Once I understood what the game was, I knew what the rules were and I could play it."

9 Master the Game
Beverly A. Grant
Chief Customer Officer, U.S. Grocery
Customer Business Development
Procter & Gamble

I remember everything. I remember what my boss had on. I remember every single word he said. It was 1993, and based on the feedback I'd been given about my performance, I should have been promoted from what we call "band two" to "band three." I'd always gotten such glowing reviews. But, instead, I was transferred. I couldn't figure it out.

Finally, my new boss told me what was holding me back.

He shared very candid and actionable feedback with me. He said, "This is how you are viewed: People believe you cannot sell."

I was shocked. I'd been a salesperson for seven years and had been told I was a superstar, and now I was being told people didn't think I could sell? But, I had been getting all of that positive feedback during a time when white male managers were afraid to share candid and actionable feedback with African-American female managers. They didn't want to be labeled as someone who was getting in our way. They weren't helping us by holding back.

What my new boss had told me was true. That perception is what was keeping me from getting to the next level. I had demonstrated capability in assignments that my other managers considered safe.

His frankness was exciting. It was like a barrier had been removed. I celebrated that.

He told me, "I think you have the capability. Let me put you in a place where you can demonstrate it." He put me with a tough manager in a tough part of the business: food and beverage sales. I was there for two years, introducing Fat-Free Pringles, which was really challenging because the launch was terrific, but the product did not meet expectations. The chips were made with Olestra and, well, the product was a failure because of the whole diarrhea thing.

But I did well with it. The experience taught me that you have to understand what the playing field is. You have to understand the game.

Sometimes we walk away from the chance to get that kind of clarity. We don't want the criticism. And sometimes I talk to some women who don't believe corporate America is a game. It is a game. Not from a manipulation standpoint, but there are rules you need to understand. You need to understand what is required, and all the moves and pieces that go with it.

That boss became a real mentor and career sponsor to me. He retired in 2002, and

I still have lunch with him once a quarter because he is such a great coach and advocate. When I have a tough business problem, he can help me think through ways to solve it. I always trusted what he told me. I didn't debate him. I asked some penetrating questions, but I trusted what he was asking me to do because he was the one who was willing to take the risk and give me the feedback I needed.

Six years later, I was still working for the same manager and I needed to do an assignment that required relocating. I had a son who was going to be a senior in high school, one who was beginning his sophomore year and one who was a first-grader. We were living in Cincinnati and were very happy because we'd just bought a new house.

My boss came to me and said, "I've got this great opportunity for you. You need to do it and do well in this type of role before you can get promoted. You would probably do it best if you relocated to where the customer is."

I talked to my husband and kids, and they didn't want to move. So I told my boss I would do it, but only on a commuting basis. He said, "You have one more year with a son who is going to be a senior and three more years with your son who is going to be a sophomore. Do you want to make a decision that will affect fifteen more years of your career based on what is going to happen to them during the next three years?"

I went home and talked to my husband. We ended up moving.

For my one son, his senior year was the best year of his life.

But for my son who was a sophomore, the move was traumatic. He didn't speak to us or eat a meal with us for six months. I had a lot of guilt about it. It was a family choice, but it was really more about me.

I went back to my boss and said I needed to move back to Cincinnati. He said, "If you do that, you will have lost control as parents." And he was right.

Over the Christmas holiday, my son snapped out of it and got in the game. Today, he will say that move is the thing that pushed him to excel and succeed at a higher level. But it was very difficult.

I want to tell you about a few of the things I've shared with other women. A lot of people don't realize that information is power. I don't think a lot of women quite understand that. Even if a discussion at work is "confidential," all information that is shared is really public. If you are sharing information about yourself and a project that has implications, it is public and can be used to influence an outcome. If you are sharing something and there is an obligation by the listener to do something with it, it will be public.

I remember an instance when someone shared with me something that one of my employees had told her about her plan not to relocate for career development. I learned that the employee was planning to wait it out until I changed my mind. But the person she told shared that with me. Just know that when you open your mouth, there is a possibility that it will come back to you.

Competition is very helpful and healthy if you have your eye on the right goals. I don't think I am competing against any of my peers. I am competing against a standard. I need to do the one or two things that differentiate me versus the standard. What is the standard for excellence? Deliver toward that, and execute. People need to know what you are known for. At P&G, I am known for delivering. If you give me something, I am going to get it done. Do that so people can think about the value-added work that you do.

I just got to the VP level two years ago. I spend a disproportionate amount of my time focusing on performance because, in my opinion, performance gets you exposure and frees up time to allow you to work on your image. I ask myself, what are the one or two things that need to be done that haven't been done? If I am replacing someone who is moving to another job, I ask what they didn't get to, and why. I ask myself, "What are the degrees of difficulty in order for me to do it?" People think about the barriers that keep them from doing something. I don't think about the barrier. I think about the degree of difficulty. That is what I focus on. If you get the right operational people in there, the barriers are going to go away.

Office politics do exist. Acknowledging that and understanding what the political game is so you have a game plan to work through is critical. I was at a meeting with 250 women who were challenging me on the notion that there is a game, as if it is a negative. It is not a negative. It just is. If you have people competing for opportunity, it sets up the rules for the game.

Acknowledging it is half the game. ■

If **Nancy Croitoru** thinks she can move a mountain, the mountain is going to move. Because she has had the confidence to take risks and happily plunge into the unknown, she has had enormous success in the corporate world and in her own consulting business.

Croitoru currently heads Canada's largest association of food, beverage and consumer-packaged-goods companies. Food and Consumer Products of Canada (FCPC) supplies legal, scientific, communications and political expertise to the industry, which annually represents more than $86 billion in sales and is the largest employer in the manufacturing sector in Canada.

She credits her mother with making her feel strong, secure and powerful in her own self.

"My mother gave me a lot of confidence," she said. "I thought I was this fat, ugly kid, but my mother told me I was beautiful. She said it all the time, and I always thought I was beautiful and terrific. Success is always about confidence and self-esteem. You walk confidently and people think you are the leader."

10 Be Authentic
Nancy Croitoru
President & CEO
Food and Consumer Products of Canada (FCPC)

had guts at a young age. I was twenty-six and was a dietitian working for the school board. They had thirty-five or forty cafeterias that they ran across the city, and my boss was in charge of them. He wasn't around much. Needless to say the cafeterias, which had a significant operating budget, were running a significant deficit. After a couple of years, the director general of the school board recommended bringing in a third party in to do the job. Contract out. They made recommendations to the board and brought in a consulting firm that interviewed me. I was told I'd have the option of working for them after they took over.

I thought, "This is insane. I should be running those cafeterias."

The contractors would break even, but the school board was missing out on the opportunity to actually make money. I went to my boss and said, "I don't agree with this. I want to make a presentation to the board that we do this ourselves." He disagreed. But, I went home, thought about it over the weekend and I called all the board members at home and said, "I've been working in this department, I know we can turn this around and I'd like to come to the board to make a presentation."

The chairman of the board told me to come on in.

I worked hard on that presentation. I crunched all the numbers, analyzed everything, and identified opportunities to cut and areas where we could make money. I strategized what needed to be done, then went up to the executive boardroom in a very prestigious building. All these people were sitting around a very long, mahogany table, and I was scared out of my wits.

They hadn't told the director general, who is like the president of the school board—the top employee of the board. And, when I spoke, he looked like he was going to leap across the table and throttle me. The contracting firm walked in as I walked out, and they were shocked to see me. But I waited outside as they deliberated, and then I was called in.

I was told they were accepting my proposal. They demoted my boss and then gave me the job.

What I learned was that you have to stand up for what you believe in. You've got to do your homework, get your facts and figures and make your case. Granted, I was young and probably didn't realize all the political implications of what I was doing, but for me it was very much a defining moment for my future.

I did very well there, and stayed on for a few more years before being recruited to work somewhere else. I only stayed in that job for five months. That was another defining moment.

The person who recruited me to the new job was retiring and told me I would take over his job as vice president. Within a week of my joining, he was fired. I ended up having a different boss who was a very paranoid and insecure individual. He would search my desk at night to see what I was doing. Also, it was a communications job and I wasn't comfortable with some of the statements he was making publicly. They weren't based on fact.

I went to the CEO and explained my challenges. I said, "It is going to be him or me? I can't work like this." He said, "You've been here five months and he's been here six years. It's gonna be you." So I left. See? I had guts at a young age.

People stay in situations when they shouldn't. It's the security issue. The old story that you know what you've got, and you don't know what you don't have. So many people have that fear of what they don't know. You have to know that you are good at what you do, and believe you are good at what you do, and know you will always have something to do and you will always do a good job. You will always have opportunities. It's the mediocrity that is the issue. If you allow yourself to be in a situation that is demeaning to you and hinders your ability to succeed or impedes your self-confidence, you are going to become mediocre.

Security is comfort. It is familiarity. It is easy. It is safe. And, the truth is, there are two kinds of people in the world, if you look in the workforce. You see it when you put something in front of your people that they have never done before. There are some who will grab it and run with it. The challenge of the unknown turns them on.

And then there are others who will absolutely panic and come back to you and back to you and back to you a hundred times to check, because they have never done it. They are afraid to break out of their box because they are afraid to make a mistake. They think that, if they make a mistake, they will fail and not have what they had before. The higher up you go, the more you have to lose, both in terms of reputation, the number of people watching you, the financial perspective and more. That always makes it a little harder.

But, when you are confronted with a new challenge, you can always look back and say, "Okay, this other challenge really scared the heck out of me. I have a lot to lose if I blow this, but look at those other challenges. I made it past them." You go back to those old experiences and lean on them for comfort.

If you are not passionate about your work, you shouldn't be doing it because you will do a poor job. It goes back to mediocrity. Maybe there are some jobs you just can't be passionate about, and that is a shame. Life is too short. You spend way too many hours working. If you aren't going to be passionate and turned on about it, why bother? You can see passion in the quality of people's work.

You have to be your true self. I am always myself. I have a board and it is filled with very senior corporate people. That means that, if I am listening to a discussion go down a wrong track, I'll stand up and say, "Wait a minute. What are you talking about? Let's look at this the way we should be looking at it." It comes back to being passionate.

I have had some good mentors over the years. I have sought them out by calling and saying, "I have this issue. Do you mind if I talk to you about it?" They weren't bosses or direct reports because I have always tended to be the most senior person. But, I have gone to people I have met, clients I really respected, and I'd ask their opinions on things. Over time it became a give-and-take relationship. Learn to ask for help and ask for advice. Go to the people whom you think are the experts, whom you think are knowledgeable. Go to the accountants, the lawyers, the people in the field. Go to friends and friends of friends. Pick up the phone and say, "Hey, could you give me an hour of your time?"

People are willing to do that. It builds relationships and, in time, they will come back to you for help. So many times, I will hear from someone who helped me early in my career who now needs information or help with something. The biggest mistake is not asking. Don't think twice about it. Other people can give you experience where you don't have experience. They will make opportunities for you.

People will respect you when they know that you are who you are, that you are authentic and honest. They need to know what you believe in and that you know what is the right thing to do. If you aren't sincere about who you are, you aren't going to be projecting trust. People aren't going to trust or respect you. ■

Judy Spires laughed when she said she was fifty-four years old, going on eighteen. "There aren't enough hours in the day to do everything that I want to do. Everything intrigues me. I want to learn everything and experience everything. I went back to graduate school. I am in a health and nutrition exercise regimen. I want to become a long-distance cyclist. I started taking piano lessons. I love theater. There are so many books to read that I've got piling up. So many places I want to visit and languages I need to learn. There is no time to rest on your laurels or think that life is boring."

Her success has been driven by her passion and her keen understanding that, when things go wrong, you just work harder. Spires started her career with Acme Markets as a cashier in high school, working for extra money for college, where she studied to become a teacher. She recalls the day she went to her father to tell him that she didn't want to be a teacher. She wanted to be an Acme manager.

"Judy, you can be anything you want to be," he told her.

She is now president of the company. "In this day and age, an entry-level person has the opportunity to become the president of the company," she said. "Isn't that great?"

11 Don't Get Even—Get Better
Judy Spires
President
Acme Markets

I have never worked a day in my life. That is what it is like when you find a passion for what you do.

I absolutely knew I had a place in this business. It was in my gut. I was working part-time as a cashier for an Acme supermarket to get money to go to college and I just loved the business. I knew in my heart of hearts that this was where I belonged.

Everybody wants to keep going up, up, up, up with their careers, but there are not always sunny days. There are things that are big disappointments.

I didn't think it made any difference that I was a woman in this business, but I have heard stories now of things that happened that I was oblivious to. Early on, my goal was to be a store manager. I was producing at the top to be the next one, so I was made a store manager by the district manager and regional vice president. A month later, when the senior vice president found out, he said, "There is no way we're going to have a woman doing that." They took the store away from me. That's right. It was 1978, so it was thirty years ago, and that was my first tough experience.

That was a situation where I could have walked out the door, but I have an adage: "You don't get even. You get better." I was right out of college, and I worked harder. Within a year, there was a new regime and I was given a store.

Several years later, I was managing the last store I would manage before moving into merchandising and my assistant manager came up to me and said, "I think there's a boss in the store."

I saw a tall gentleman standing there, and it was the man who had taken the store away from me years earlier—my nemesis. He was no longer with the company. He walked over and said, "Hello, do you remember me?"

I was like, "No, I can't place you." I didn't want him to know he'd made a lasting impression.

He said, "I'm Paul and I need to apologize to you. Years ago, I made a mistake concerning you. I actually work in a different company now and I send all of my managers to this store to observe you and see how a store should be run."

I said thank you, then went about my business. I wasn't going to spend any time with him. I did wonder if he was going through a twelve-step program and making amends.

Later, it was hard for me to advance from store manager to district manager. I had the highest level of education. I was running the highest-volume store and it was producing No. 1 results. But there were so many barriers. Every time I was considered for district manager, they threw up another barrier. First it was that I hadn't managed a store with the new service departments. So I did that. Then it was that I hadn't managed a combo store. I did that. Then it was that I didn't have merchandise experience. I said yes to every opportunity that came along.

I was then told I would get the next district manager's position after going up for it four times. Absolutely, they said. It was going to be mine.

But, there I was at a black-tie event, standing behind the vice president of human resources, and he didn't know I was behind him. Someone pointed at a gentleman a few feet away and asked the vice president who he was.

"That's our next district manager!" he said.

My heart crumpled.

First of all, people weren't being honest with me. I was working and producing and doing all the things I needed to do. My first reaction was, "Well, I am going to leave this company. I am underappreciated. I have worked really hard." But, I thought about it that night and I realized I wasn't going to bite off my nose to spite my face. I loved the business. I had goals I wanted to achieve. I had significant vacation and tenure and savings, and financially, my leaving wouldn't mean much to them—but it would to me.

Again, you don't get even, you get better.

That meant go back and work even harder. And I did. Within a month, they came back to me. There was a new company president who believed in cross-fertilization of high-potential people, so they brought me in to work on merchandising. I wanted to be a district manager, but in a mentoring moment, the president said this would be a much better move for me. So many doors opened up. I could get into sales, human resources, advertising, marketing, and then go back and be a vice president of operations with all of that knowledge.

Much later in my career, we had someone come into the business who wanted to bring his own person in and move me out of my job. I was senior vice president of merchandising and marketing, and it was a devastating experience, being moved aside like that. I'd been a very successful vice president of operations. I'd delivered the numbers and had been promoted to that new position, and to be taken out of something I'd worked so hard to get was very devastating. I cried my eyes out for a night, but again I decided I wasn't going to get even. I was going to get better.

I came back to work the next day with my head held high and decided I was going to support this new regime better than anyone else in the world. I had a welcoming party for the person who took over my role. He had more experience than me, and I learned everything I could from him. I became friendly with him and his wife, and within nine months, he became president of the organization and asked me to be his senior vice president of merchandising and marketing, which had been my job in the first place.

The point is, when you get derailed and think it is the end of the world, it is not. Hold your head high and know you can contribute and make things work out even better in the end. Don't get even, get better. That just plays in my head. I have that fighting mentality. I know my value and I am going to make myself indispensable to the organization I am in.

Have the confidence to know that you know the right thing to do. When something isn't feeling right with you, act on it. That's one of the problems we have in the business world today: People don't trust their instincts. Your instincts are there because of the knowledge and experience you have. You have to believe in yourself.

You have to perform. You have to perform better than anybody else. That's a key. People who try to move ahead strictly through relationships will not succeed. I have so many people who want to be in my shoes tomorrow, but there are experiences they need to go through and things they need to produce for the organization in order to get there.

I have very little tolerance for people who are in one job and can only talk about getting the next job. It's always, "When can I get promoted?" I believe you produce first, and then the next step will come before you.

That said, it is very important to have a comfort level talking to people in the organization. When I go to a meeting or an event, I feel very good about the people who are willing to come up and talk to me. You aren't going to get noticed if you are afraid of people and stay in the background. You need to learn to matriculate at an executive level. There is a difference between self-promoting and saying you are ready for your next position—which I don't like—and talking socially about what you have been working on, or things you have noticed in the business. Those kinds of conversations show me who can be contributors to the organization. I can envision the individuals sitting around the president's table with the ability to communicate openly and honestly.

I have very high standards. I am a perfectionist. My drive has always been to just do it the best.

Don't do anything unless you do it the best. My passion for that gets people to jump on board. It gets them excited. And that feeds my excitement. People want to win. So have the highest standards. Don't judge yourself against other people, judge yourself against the very best you can be. ■

Regenia Stein's story is unforgettable because of where it began: being raised in a segregated world and being mentored by a wildly successful father who believed she could do anything. His lessons were simple and remarkable. His legacy continues through her. Before returning to Kraft in customer development, she was vice president of National Accounts and Sales Planning at the Miller Brewing Co., where she was named by *Consumer Goods Technology* as one of the "25 most influential" for 2004.

She has been accustomed to being the only woman or only minority in the room. Earlier in her career, she said, she would take isolating vacations with her husband where she finally could relax and be herself. She'd been muting her "real self" on her day job.

"That was wrong," she said. "I had to be myself every day. So I started bringing my whole self to the table. I am an opinionated black woman. I am passionate about the business. You have to understand that. Now I don't hold anything back."

Knock Down Barriers
Regenia Stein
Area Vice President – Central
Kraft Foods North America
Customer Development Organization

My dad only went through the sixth grade. He was a self-made businessman, and he owned a number of businesses, starting with a grocery store, then two, then this, then that. He had a number of cafés where you could go for lunch or dinner. He owned a lot of liquor stores, washeterias and a ton of food-related companies. And this was a man who learned to read and write on his own!

Because I was the oldest, I somehow got connected with him. He would teach me along the way. I learned to count by counting dollars, hundreds and hundreds of dollars over the summer. He would take me to the bank and show me his transactions. He taught me to be good with money and how to manage a business.

He taught me to manage the staff. It was all about treating everyone with respect. You need to treat the janitor the same as you treat the president. People taking out the garbage were just as important as the people seating the guests. You can learn from everybody. The janitor sees what is thrown away, and you can learn from that. He might say, "Buy less of this." Those observations are strong, and ninety percent of the time, they are accurate. So, listen to everybody.

He taught me to speak plainly. Keep it simple. Say exactly what you mean so people know what you want to get across. You get better communication when you can be prescriptive and deliberative about what you want to say.

My father told me I could do anything. "You can be the president of the United States if you want to." He would say that daily. He said, "Whatever you want to do, go do." There were no boundaries. He gave me the confidence that told me there were no limits.

When I was young, he had a café. He'd let me come in at night and cook, and I was one of the short-order cooks. If someone would complain I'd go right out there and ask, "What is it about this meal you don't like?" The customers saw it as intimidating. My dad said, "That is not good customer service."

One of the things he taught me was to be down front. That is where things happen. People don't go into a building and look to the back. Be where it is going on.

He taught me to count money when I was three. I was the banker. He taught me accounting. I would ride with him a lot of evenings to meetings.

He broke a lot of color barriers in Texas, where we lived. Without going into detail, I have painful memories of segregation. People think that ended in the 1940s, but in reality, it was still an issue in the late 1960s and early 1970s. It was a part of my life. I remember my mom and dad talking about it. They told us that we were in a segregated part of the world and we needed to do our part to be good citizens. They said, "Look forward. Don't worry. It will all work out." We lived in places where we weren't completely integrated and there were people who weren't pleased that we were there, but my parents told us that we could educate them by example, that we should live there and they could see we were good stewards. It was a trying time.

My dad went into business because he wanted to be able to take care of himself. Segregation was so strong. He knew he couldn't work for someone else and realize what he wanted to realize. He was very, very charitable and always found ways to provide work experiences or funding for other people. He was so good about paying back and helping others. He did that often.

He was the business person. Mother was the soft part of the duo. She was business-minded, but the caregiver. She wanted to teach us the life lessons. One thing she always did—and I hated it—was send us to the farm where she was raised. My brother and I had to go there every summer for three weeks. They didn't even have a bathroom. She'd say, "It grounds you into understanding how other people live." There was no McDonald's. They didn't eat the way we ate or dress the way we'd dress. There was no TV and no telephone. We'd have to hunt our own food—go get the produce from the field, make our own butter. She made us do that for years so we would know there was a different life out there. We could milk cows and churn butter and all of that. Looking back on it, it was fun. But we hated it at the time. The TV thing killed us.

She did that to show us that there is a balance between the worries of business and the fact that there is another part of life that is not business, a place where you could put your feet in the earth. It gave a balance to us to do both things and not be so serious about either one. I came up much more rounded and resilient. I don't make everything so intense.

I felt the family business was too hard and I felt I could make more money working for a company. My father's work involved too many hours. It was a 24/7 thing. Everything was done by my father. He worked all the time and had very few vacations. I figured there were ways to be in business without being in business twenty-four hours a day. If I went with a company, I might be able to have a life.

Everywhere I have gone, my mentors have always been white men. That is the opposite of what you would have thought. I don't act like them and I don't look like them. I don't know what the connection is, but I always say it was a collection of men that made me. They always saw something in me that I did not see. They selected me; I never selected them. They always provided counseling and guidance. They pushed me to do things I never thought of doing on my own. They'd say, "I think you should do this." "You should apply for that." "You should talk to him." "Take on this assignment."

I am in the sales organization, which is really male-dominated. I learned that you are not going to be isolated—but that people will notice you. You do not blend in. You have to choose what you do with that. In many meetings, I am the only woman and, in some cases, the only black person. I have always used that as an advantage. Once they hear me speak and confirm that I understand the business, they start to ask for my opinion. People see me. They are waiting. I am able to use my diversity to benefit the company. I do see things in a different way. I have always been comfortable in a place where there are few people like me.

The most difficult experience for me was working with the Miller Brewing Co. because, for some reason, people really perceived me as a threat and they were worried because I was there. My experiences were broader—running Wal-Mart and Costco and Target. Let's say we were in a meeting and there were six of us presenting. If my boss left the room, they'd find everything about my presentation that was wrong. As soon as the boss came in, they started listening again. It was all old-school, things you would think would never happen anymore. They would slice information to say it wasn't as good as it was.

It was partly because they were men and hadn't seen anybody like me and there was only one woman in the whole sales organization in a management position. But I would be straight with them and they would be scared and intimidated. It was watershed for me. I hung in there for four years. The bad time lasted for the first year, but we got through it. We performed. We got beyond it. People still call me to say they wish I were still there.

Things haven't changed as much as I would like. I still go into meetings and, instead of there being just one woman or one woman of color, there is one or maybe two or maybe three. There is still a lack of diversity. There are still too many blue-shirt men walking around, and there aren't enough yellow shirts or pink shirts or coral.

But that's changing. It really is. ■

Driving Your Career

You get a job, work hard, get recognized, and then move up. You go up, up, up, and then you are there—at the top. How many times have you heard it referred to as "climbing the ladder"?

While there is a ladder for some, for others it is a highway. Or a lattice with vines. You might want to reconsider that straight trajectory that sounded so logical. The logic in moving up comes from taking a few twists and turns.

Many of the women in this book said they steered nontraditional courses for themselves. In some cases, that meant lateral moves and self-demotions that were deliberate maneuvers to give them the experience they needed to broaden themselves.

For example, Janel Haugarth was moving straight up the track to CFO at SuperValu, but she purposely took a demotion—and a pay cut—to get the operational experience she would need to be poised to actually run the company. That step down was so painful to her that she couldn't bring herself to put her title on her business card. It moved her way out into her discomfort zone, but she had to go through it if she wanted to be more than the company's financial brain. The strategy worked. Now she is president and chief operating officer of supply chain services at SuperValu.

Many of her peers in this book did the same thing. They figured out what they needed to know, and then set about charting their careers in new directions that would give them their expertise.

Risk-takers like that spend a lot of time in their discomfort zones.

The discomfort zone obviously got its name because it is not comfortable there. If you need things to be predictable, safe or easy, you will do everything you can to avoid that feeling of discomfort. But discomfort is where we all find our greatest growth and opportunity. It is where we are pushed to grow and redefine ourselves. The good thing is, discomforting challenges get easier and less disconcerting as time passes and as you get experience. And once the discomfort becomes a little too comfortable, it is time to shake things up again. If you dare.

Discomfort means daring to do something you know nothing about, and having the confidence to know that you will learn what you need to learn. It's knowing that your leadership skills will translate in any environment and the people around you will help you to get the expertise you need. Have faith that it will get easier every week until, in time, you have it mastered.

Success is not accidental. You have to drive your career with intention.

While lunching with Caroline Cotten Nakken, I mentioned how interesting it was that so many of the businesswomen I interviewed seemed so put off by people blatantly *angling for promotions and raises.*

Nakken's facial expression completely soured.

"I can't stand it when someone asks for a raise," she said. "Take on other assignments and promote yourself. Do the work, and the raise and the promotion will be there. If the promotion isn't there, you either aren't doing the work or you're not in the right company."

I brought it up while speaking at the NEW Executive Leaders Forum. Almost every woman in the room got the same expression Nakken had when I mentioned people asking for promotions or raises.

Apparently, you should not ask what your company can do for you, but what you can do for your company—if I may take a turn with JFK's words.

If you want to move up, move yourself up by strategically driving your career and volunteering for assignments that demonstrate your value. Don't ask for a promotion. Promote yourself by volunteering for special projects and committees, and expand your grasp and influence just by doing the bigger job you have created for yourself. The official promotions should come automatically because you are seen as a change agent, a contributor, and someone who is competent and deserving.

If you see something that needs to happen, you can say, "This seems to be a problem. I'd like to do x, y and z." Or, "I think this is a real opportunity for us. I'd like to coordinate this." Because they don't cost the company anything extra, volunteer efforts are appreciated. If you keep doing that, you will demonstrate that you are visionary, proactive, productive and increasingly valuable to the team.

When Susan Parker worked for Southwest Airlines, she had a rapid trajectory up the hierarchy before becoming the senior director of marketing. Her title didn't change for six years, but during that time, she significantly increased her influence and expertise by expanding three departments. As she said, "I did not wait for a responsibility to be assigned or a project to be given to me. I didn't wait to be promoted to vice president to act like an officer. I saw business opportunities that needed to be pursued, and I pursued them."

Successful people know how to leave their mark on the right projects and advertise their successes.

It's not about you. It's about the company. Even if it is all about you.

And, if the promotion doesn't come automatically, you may need to come out and ask, "What else can I do to move to the next level?" If that doesn't work, you may be in the wrong company.

But the greater point here is that it is up to you to drive your own career. Mentors will help you map it out, but you have to decide what you want and, ultimately, how you are going to travel to get it.

Are you communicating with your boss so that he or she knows what you are doing and how well you are doing it? At the same time, are you getting the feedback you need in order to know how your performance stacks up to expectations?

The subject of self-marketing has come up again and again. But, remember that if you think your hard work and excellent performance put you on the fast track, you're wrong. It puts you on no track at all. You have to build relationships and market your results in order to drive your career. That is simply the way things work.

Some of the women in this book said it was necessary to make career sacrifices and put their careers on hold for a time while taking care of family or personal concerns. While they worried what the long-term implications might be, all of them said they had no regrets. And, while some admitted they could have moved higher and faster, they ultimately progressed. It was just another one of those off-ramps from the highway.

You are driving your career, so don't count on your company to drive it for you. There is so much you can control by consciously taking charge, deciding what you want and strategizing what you need to do in order to get it. You can't count on company leaders to actively worry about what is best for you. That's your job.

You deserve to have challenging work that calls you. You deserve to be in a company that is a good cultural fit. You deserve to succeed. And, you deserve to have fun in the process.

If you are not in an environment that is letting you do what you dream of doing, it is not the company's fault. It's yours, for staying in a situation that is not working. Don't be afraid of making the changes that will define your individual greatness. Be afraid of waking up two or five or ten years from now, still breathing the same stale air that you are breathing right now.

I have noticed that it often takes the same effort to succeed as it does to languish. Languishing takes so much psychic energy that could instead be used to propel yourself toward something that matters to you.

You can drive in fifth gear, or you can idle away.

It's your choice.

The NEW Rules for driving your career:

- A career is not a ladder, but a highway with off-ramps and on-ramps and turns that will take you to interesting places. You may want to go north, but you can get there by heading east.
- Sometimes, the way to go up is to go down. Or sideways.
- Take on projects that you can put your name on.
- Create a voice within your organization. Have your fingerprint or handprint on something different in the organization.
- Be a change agent.

- Embrace risk.
- Don't be afraid to take on a challenge—even if you fear you don't know enough about it. You will learn it through your leadership of others.
- You are in charge of your own destiny. There is no pre-set path to success.
- Give yourself permission to promote yourself rather than waiting for somebody else to promote you. Don't wait for a promotion to take on new responsibility.
- You can always go home. You can't always reconstruct an opportunity. Have a run at it and give up later if it is necessary, but an opportunity may never come again.
- You are not always ready for a promotion. You are not the No. 1 person until you have the job. You can't practice for it until you do it.
- Don't be afraid to go lateral. Go for the best experiences.
- Always ask what you can do better.
- Work in an environment that has a culture that is consistent with your values.
- Merchandise your success. Don't be humble about your results.
- It is not the responsibility of senior management to notice your results.
- You will be rewarded for your willingness to be bold and go after something.
- Speak up for yourself. Don't always accept the immediate response. Continually push the envelope, but do it in a way that doesn't alienate people.
- Ask your boss and boss's boss how you are doing against your objectives. That way, they know what you are doing.
- It is okay to say no. It doesn't mean you will never have another opportunity.
- If you stay in a demeaning situation or one that holds you back, you will become mediocre.
- Life is too short to do work that you are not passionate about.
- This is a marathon. It is not a sprint.

The thing about the corporate bio is that it is so dry, it never captures the fact that there is a real human being behind the title. Like this: "**Melody C. Justice** is Executive Vice President, Business Transformation, Coca-Cola North America, with more than twenty years of broad experience in the Coca-Cola system..." Well, it does capture her credentials, experiences and achievements, but it misses the big truth about Justice, who is warm, approachable and cares about mentoring others.

I told her I had just done an interview with a woman who asked repeatedly about who else was in the book, as if to make sure she wasn't participating with people less than her caliber. Justice was silent for a long while, and I asked why. "It would never occur to me to even ask that." She knows she has a duty to mentor because she has been mentored.

"To fail to be humble and approachable and respectful of other people would be my downfall," she said. "It would make me something I am not. But humility is a two-sided coin. Too much humility can lead to too much self-doubt and paralyze you. The kind of humility I embrace is wisdom that I don't have all the answers but am going to learn more by asking questions than issuing directives."

13 Embrace Change
Melody C. Justice
Executive Vice President, Business Transformation
Coca-Cola North America

I was ready to graduate from Emory with honors in my specialty, psychology. I was all set to marry my childhood sweetheart, and everything was all laid out. I was going to go into clinical research. The game plan was set, and I was going to lead a very predictable, monotonous life.

I knew something was wrong. It didn't feel right.

So I took an unexpected right turn. I decided to leave Atlanta, go to business school and get an MBA. I decided not to marry the man I'd planned to spend my life with. I had to go out and experience some things for myself, and be on my own.

The hardest thing I ever did was walk away. I had the sense that I had disappointed other people. It wasn't just that I had laid out that path for myself. I'd laid it out with my companion of many years, my parents, my brother, my friends—it felt like I was rejecting them to do something for myself. I learned to trust my intuition and listen to my heart.

It was frightening because I had no money and I didn't know anybody. But I made friends, I learned a new city and I learned I could be on my own. That experience has made me very self-reliant. It has taught me that I can get through the unknown—as frightening as it might be. I can figure things out.

It opened up a whole new set of adventures, creating an independence and faith in myself that has been very valuable. None of this would have happened if I'd stayed on the set path. I wouldn't have had the education that led me to the business world, and I wouldn't have met the man who would be my husband.

That was a long, long time ago, but it was the defining moment in my life.

I have never had a linear career. I've always been putting one foot in front of the other, just doing the next thing. I have taken a lot of side steps, made lateral moves, and just done a lot of things because they were interesting to me. If I needed new meat to chew on, I would do something different. I never felt I was destined to be at the top of the organization; that just happened. I know I am capable and I work hard—but I never felt this was my destiny.

I have had staff jobs and line jobs. I have lived in Europe and New York and Dallas. It has been a great experience. But I have chosen to focus very intently on my work and family and not so much on a lot of hobbies or outside pursuits. I know there will be a "Phase II" of my life and I will have to re-create myself. That's still to come.

I think it is hard for young people to realize that a career or life in general is not a ladder. It is a highway with lots of off-ramps and on-ramps and turns that will take you to some really interesting places. You may have a sense that you want to go north, but you can get there by heading east and west along the way and still get there. I've moved geographically, through functions. I have run organizations that have thousands of people, and organizations that have only a few. I have had a P&L responsibility and jobs that didn't. I think there is something that keeps us fresh about all of that and learning. The set of experiences I had in finance, sales, marketing and management never would have come to me had I tried to go up through any one of those areas.

I left a corporate role at Coke, where I was an officer perceived to be on an upward trajectory, to go into Coke USA, which was a troubled business unit. I did it to get an operating assignment. I knew I could have an impact. I had good mentors and I didn't feel I could get lost once I went. It just made sense to me to get that experience. Another time, I moved into a sales role without having any experience in sales. Again, I wanted to learn on the front line by dealing with customers and bottlers. It worked out great.

Once, I took a bit of a downward move. I'd had a lot of people and a lot of P&L responsibility and gave that up to get some experience in strategic planning. The new job would have relatively few people, no P&L responsibility and was more of an academic kind of job. Traditional wisdom says you don't leave a line job for a staff job, but it was a refreshing break. I learned a lot about strategic planning and consulting and policy, and it helped me when I moved back into a line role to the job that I am in today.

These breaks and transitions keep me energized and focused. They keep me from getting bored. The way I adapt to new situations is to ask a lot of questions. You don't know what you don't know, and since you are a novice, you can ask a lot of questions and observe.

When I come into something truly new, I take advantage of the first sixty or ninety days. I don't worry about producing. I focus on the learning. It leads to somewhat of a slow start, but I have found out that it always pays off later.

For example, when I went into sales, I had people walk me around the stores and show me how to evaluate the beverage sections. I rode on a truck with the drivers who deliver our products. I went to some customers and had them tell me all about their experiences. Being new, I could be the idiot. I didn't know anything for a while, so I took advantage of that and learned. I didn't produce at first, but I did over time.

I've made mistakes. I once took responsibility for a region and didn't get the right people in the right jobs. We didn't deliver. It took too long to fix. This was a big learning experience. People are the key to everything. The business was on autopilot and wasn't progressing, so in this situation, it wasn't like the house was on fire. It was just stagnant. We had ambitious goals and needed to move to faster growth and higher performance, but the team wasn't working well together and the members didn't really respect each other. Everyone had a different view of what needed to be done.

I have found it hard to fire people and deal with performance problems. Over the years, I have learned to do it faster, but it hasn't gotten any easier. I've gotten more familiar with it. It is one of the hardest things to do. Nothing makes me happier than having a great team of people who are performing. Nothing is harder than having a team that doesn't work well together. I can make changes. I have to do that. I've done it numerous times. But it doesn't get easier. I can't hide behind the HR person or find some minion to do it for me. I have to do it myself.

I have learned that direct, plain talk is best. It should be easily understood and not harsh or cruel. Just plain and simple and direct. Say, "You don't seem to be happy." Or, "Things don't seem to be working out. Tell me about that." I try to do that in a candid and thoughtful way.

The three pieces of advice I would have for others are first: Have high expectations for yourself and for the business. High expectations are the key to everything. Not impossible and unreachable expectations, but high ones for you. Stretch yourself. Grow. Mediocrity will sap your energy and strength, so never settle for that.

Second, get with the right people. Find the right people, whether you join the right people or hire the right people. It all comes down to people.

Third, remember this: Be sure you have a life outside the business. The business will not love you back. ∎

Janel Haugarth is, perhaps, the most honest among us because she is the one who will speak a whole truth about the emotional rigors of life at the top.

"I love your suit," I told her the first time we met.

She seemed so relieved by the compliment—and she had a good reason. An employee had stuck it to her in an exit interview and Haugarth had to undergo a major performance review with consultants. Among her alleged "deficiencies" were her wardrobe and her hair. I asked if she could imagine a man being told to do more with his hair and clothes. She shrugged.

The weird thing was, I'd had the exact same conversation about the exact same thing happening to a senior executive with Ford Motor Co.

When you are really alone at the top of your company, it's hard to see that the problems you face come with being the first woman to claim senior executive turf. The fact that she's had these experiences—and decided to so bravely share them with us—speaks to the leadership role she plays for all of the rest of us.

Haugarth is responsible for all aspects of the company's logistics and supply chain operations and for planning, implementing and guiding its growth.

Beyond her titles, she's real.

14 Take Risks
Janel Haugarth

Executive Vice President
President and Chief Operating Officer, Supply Chain Services
SuperValu

Sometimes the way up is to go down.

My background was in finance and accounting. I had my CPA certificate, so my route was up the CFO track. I wanted to make decisions and execute them, and a mentor told me, "You will never be happy just pursuing the financial role you are in. You have to make the jump to operations. If you don't step back now, it won't get any easier." Basically, I had to demote myself.

I had to go to lower-level titles in the organization to pick up the operating experience I didn't have, then fast-track it back up the ladder again. That wasn't an easy experience. I went into a full-time training program and absolutely hated it. It was one of those special-assignment roles, and I'd never seen anyone take one of those assignments and come out with a good story.

I'd been the VP of finance and controller of an operating region. Suddenly, I was an assistant category manager. I didn't have enough training to even be a category manager. The word "assistant" felt terrible. I didn't even put my title on my business cards.

But any time there was a vacancy, I'd get slotted into it. I did all kinds of jobs in interim assignments while the company looked for the full-time person. It was real-time experience. I wasn't just watching somebody work.

I took a pay cut to make that change, and that was a big decision because I was the only financial support at home. After I'd gotten pregnant for the third time, my husband stopped working. It wasn't planned that he would do that, but it came out of our attempt to find decent day care for my newborn and the other two children. I wasn't the kind to stay home and raise the kids, but my husband wanted to do it. That brought emotional and financial stresses. For a while, we didn't spend anything. We didn't eat out, we didn't take vacations, and we didn't travel home to see family.

And there I was, taking a pay cut.

I had to demote myself career-wise to restart myself on my career track. I was positioning myself to become president of an operating region. That was my goal. That was as far ahead as I could see. That was four steps up to a president's job. Now the presidents report to me.

It is a constant learning process.

Not long ago, I had a very difficult experience with someone on my staff who said some tough things about me in her exit interview. She talked directly to the senior vice president of human resources, who wanted me to go through a 360-degree assessment from an outside firm.

The 360 gave me a fair amount of paranoia at the time. I was the only one going through it, and it was big.

In retrospect, it was valuable. It brought home for me the things I needed to work on, and it prioritized them. They interviewed people. If somebody said something, the assessor would ask for an example and an explanation, so the assessor gave me input why people were saying what they were saying. The feedback came a month before I was named to my next job, and that was good because I went to a different environment with different people working with me. It was like I got a whole opportunity to start over again. They may have known my reputation, but they hadn't had me as their supervisor.

The biggest thing that came up in the 360 was my needing to keep my mouth shut in a discussion until everybody weighs in. You have to understand the influence that title has on your audience. For example, we'd be discussing an issue and people would think that, just because I'd said something, my mind was made up and that was where I was. They thought it couldn't be discussed further. I was actually trying to engage them in discussion, but because I'd weighed in, they thought it meant the conversation was over. What I am trying to do now is let them know I want them to speak to me more and talk it through. Sometimes I have to be a very good listener. I can't say anything at all—I have to hold back and not ask a lot of questions.

Another thing that came out of the 360 was that I needed to improve my dress and have a more professional appearance. I'd never heard that. I didn't think that was an issue, but it was, apparently. When I got that feedback I asked specifically, "What does that mean? What am I supposed to do?" Nobody could tell me anything about it. But I took it seriously and went out and found new suits, got a new hairstyle and new makeup. At that point, I was trying to do so much, and I was trying to address all of it. I overkilled it.

You always need to take criticism, whether it is constructive or not, and you need to look at it seriously to adjust things where you can. But you shouldn't obsess on it, and some of it you just have to disregard. This was one criticism I tried to address. I figured it certainly couldn't hurt to get a different wardrobe. But I should find out if this has ever come up in the 360s on men. I suspect men aren't as critical of men as they are of women.

I have to go through another 360 this year—everybody does on the CEO staff. Ever since I heard I have to go through it again, I am almost paranoid that something is going to come out that I don't expect, and I will be judged and not be able to defend myself. I have to have more confidence in myself. I can just see the politics in this.

SuperValu acquired Albertsons in 2006, so we are going through a lot of change at the senior level because we went from a $20 billion to a $40 billion company. One of the things that is still the same is that the executive group is still all men, except for me and the CFO. I cannot voice a difference of opinion in a strong way because the rest of the group will shut down.

I watch the men banter back and forth and have strong words to each other and take strong positions, and, when the meeting is over, they pat each other on the back and talk about going to dinner with their wives the next night. But if I do it, they become very uncomfortable and their response back to me is very abbreviated and short. They avoid me—especially if I get very excited. And they think "very excited" is if I raise my voice a little bit. They will avoid me. It drives me crazy.

I want to engage in the kind of two-way discussions that they have with each other, but I can't seem to get that done. And if there are any harsh words, there is no dialogue going on. I almost have to go up to them and make up. These men haven't worked with women before, and I know I am making excuses for them. But that's the reality. ■

Caroline Cotten Nakken is the owner and founder of... oh, don't let her impressive bio (running Mass Connections and its three sister companies) distract you. She's all about the storytelling, and she makes sure she's always telling a doozy.

Nakken is a master of retail promotional marketing, having built Mass Connections, which takes in more than $100 million in annual revenues through direct-to-shopper intercepts. Her clients include General Mills, Nestlé, Kraft, SuperValu, Sears/Kmart, Target/SuperTarget and Wal-Mart.

She is married and has four children.

She made her mark her own way, as a woman and communicator. "You don't have to behave differently from men," she said. "If you are a good leader, you are a good leader. If you are a good communicator, you are a good communicator. We don't have to apologize for being women. We are women. Many women don't realize how empowered they are."

If you want to see one who knows her power, read Nakken's story.

15 Question Authority
Caroline Cotten Nakken
President and CEO
Mass Connections Inc.

When I go back to my era, 1974, here were the choices: I could be a secretary, I could be a nurse, I could be a teacher, and of course, I could be a mom. Or a flight attendant. Well, I had a Type-A personality and I loved adventure and wanted to travel; what was I going to pick? My intent was to be a flight attendant. That was my big goal in life. But, the oil crisis hit back then and cars were lined up waiting for gas and even though I'd gotten hired by the airlines, they decided there would be a hiring freeze for a minimum of two years.

So I joined the Army.

I joined for helicopter maintenance. It was a two-year program and I would get hours by actually fixing helicopters. But, with less than two weeks to go before boot camp, I got the letter that said the Army didn't really want me for that; it wanted me to go into administration or nursing. I already had my fatigues!

Right about that time, I got the letter from Northwest Airlines saying they were calling me back. I went to my recruiting officer and said, "I don't want to pass up this opportunity." Incredibly, they let me out of my contract and I went out to Northwest Airlines. I was on my way.

Well, I got fired. That is, for me, my biggest failure story. My supervisor at Northwest told me that I was a nonconformist, and I questioned authority too much, and she didn't see that I was a fit there. I was like, "*What are you talking about?*" But, I knew she was going to fire me because she'd handed me a one-way ticket to L.A. and I knew something was wrong. I will never forget it. There are certain moments in time you never forget. I will never forget her telling me I was a nonconformist and that I questioned authority.

And there I was. I'd walked away from the Army. I'd just been fired. I was living in this city and I thought, "I am such a loser. What do I do now?" I tucked my tail, followed my boyfriend as we women did in those days, and I went to Arizona. I enrolled at Arizona State, where I thought I'd go back to school and finish my degree in business. I wanted to pick something I would utilize.

While there, I needed income.

Before that, I had done in-store events. You know, I'd give you the perfume as you walked through the department store. I did a lot of product promotions. I thought, that is something I can do because it is mainly on weekends. In Arizona, I couldn't find any companies that did in-store promotions, because most stores were utilizing friends or family to do it. So, I went down to city hall and said I wanted to start a business. You know how much my first business license cost? Two dollars. So there begins the story.

My boyfriend was a cheerleader at ASU. Who would I get to do these promotional jobs? Why not the cheerleaders? For my business, I started knocking on doors, from major resorts to Honeywell. I was practically the agent for the Arizona State cheerleaders. And the companies were like, "That's cool. We can have cheerleaders at the next unveiling of a product." That was the beginning. I was going to school, working a full-time job at night as a cocktail waitress for the Jockey Club, and starting a business.

My business was just for supplemental income. It didn't interrupt school or cocktailing at night. I started with a few clients, and they told people who told other people. But, the more clients I had, the deeper in debt I got. I'd send the invoice and—you know this routine—I got paid sixty or ninety days later. But the people who worked for me wanted to be paid that week. So, put it this way: My dinner was the food they would put out at happy hour. You live on that when you have no money.

One day, a food broker asked me if I could go into supermarkets for promotions. He said they needed twenty people for a new product. I got them the twenty people, but eight out of the twenty didn't show up. The client called me into his office. There were five men who had to be between the ages of forty and sixty, and I was twenty-three years old and, oh my gosh, that man just blasted me. I mean, he screamed. "*Who do you think you are? Why did you do this? You screwed this up!*"

All I could say was, "I'm sorry."

"*Sorry's not good enough! You know what, missy? Why don't you just get out of the business?*"

I can still hear it. When I left that appointment, I got in the car and, once the engine was started, the tears started. I was talking to myself, "I didn't even want to take that job in grocery stores." But, by the time I got home, all I could think was how pissed off I was. "You know what, buddy? I'm not going to quit. You know what I'm going to do? I'm going to grow this company into the largest in-store sample company in the country." That's what I thought.

Five years later, I wrote that man a thank-you letter. He was ill at the time, and we didn't talk, but I had to find him and tell him that he gave me a defining moment in my life. The letter said, "I don't even know if you remember me, but…" Then I gave him the story and said, "I want to thank you. Five years ago, I did this promotion for you and it did not go well and you were downright mean. You were beyond tough on me, but, that said, I want to tell you thank you. For me, that was the moment that forced me to decide, if I am going to do this, I am going to do it right."

There are so many people whose names you can't remember, but I remember the name of the woman who fired me and the name of that man.

Anyhow, I don't want to make it sound like everything was great as soon as I had that realization. It wasn't. I have to tell you about how I got my first financing.

I got so in debt when I was in Phoenix that I had to drop out of school, get another job, and, you see the cycle. The company would grow and I'd go further into debt. My parents said, "Come home. You are starving to death." I must have been down to less than a hundred pounds. I had a supervisor in Arizona who I thought could run the operation for me while I could go home to California and start one there. She seemed so much older than me. I was twenty-four and she was thirty-two. She was doing a really great job, then one day she called and told me she'd fallen in love with this other guy, he was only my age, and, she was going to tell her husband.

The next call I got from her was, "My God, I told my husband and he parked himself on the railroad tracks and committed suicide." I'm not kidding.

The next call was, "I got an insurance settlement. I have all this money and I want to be a partner in the company. I want to buy into it." The next minute, that woman was writing me a $30,000 check. I was living with my parents and didn't have money to put gas in my car, and back then, $30,000 was like $150,000. I went out and got an office, hired two people, got computers, and it was a real company. I'd been working out of my bedroom at my parents' house, and suddenly, I was a real business.

Well, six months later, she called and said she was broke. She wanted her money back. I asked what happened to the rest of her settlement, and she told me that young guy spent it all and left her.

I didn't know what to do. I found out that banks won't give you money unless you have money. I went to my parents for help, but they lived in East L.A. and didn't have money. My dad refinanced the house and bought her out for less than she'd bought it for. He ended up with her stock, which was thirty percent of the business.

He stayed for two or three years, but had financial problems and told me he needed his money back. I told him I didn't have it. Seriously, for at least ten years, I didn't pay myself. I was so broke, I was driving an old used car and the business kept growing and growing. He finally gave the stock back to me. He said something, and I am sure he didn't mean to hurt me, but he said, "This is never going to pan out. You have been broke. It is never going to be anything. Here, take it back."

He and my mom were going through a divorce, and I gave the stock to my mom. Two or three years later, the business was growing, growing, growing, and I was getting smarter about invoicing. My mother told me I could buy her out. My dad paid $10,000 for the stock, I bought it back from my mother after their divorce for $250,000.

It's a $100 million business. We have one hundred thousand people in our database as employees who live everywhere from Puerto Rico to Alaska. We have chefs, cosmetologists, students—twenty-five different categories of people. We do small projects and big projects. We design the concept and the materials. Now we are big into the online promotions.

I bought my father a home and my mother a home and I bought him a car and paid all his bills. At that point, he said, "I think I was wrong about what was going to happen with this business." ■

About that title: "Executive Vice President, People." What the heck is that?

"Well," explains **Pat Curran**, "I call it 'The People Person of a Million-Three.' I laugh at it. It keeps everything in perspective. It's merchandising, marketing and operations. It's a lot."

Not bad for someone who started in the pet department. She saw an opportunity to grow within the company and, twenty-five years later, rates as one of the most powerful individuals in the company and one of Fortune's 50 Most Powerful Women in Business. She said it is because her father told her she could do anything if she played to her strengths, and Wal-Mart found and nurtured them.

The company has been slammed with sex discrimination lawsuits and negative publicity concerning promotion and compensation of women, but Curran says the company "is a great place to work—for everyone. My experience with Wal-Mart and my being a female within the organization is that I have been given the same opportunities as anybody else. I haven't been treated any differently. In a board or executive committee meeting, there isn't any difference when a female speaks or a male speaks. Our opinion is valued as much as theirs."

Outperform
Pat Curran
Executive Vice President, People
Wal-Mart Stores Division

I've done every role, from hourly associate on up. This all started in 1983 in Killeen, Texas. I was eighteen and thought Wal-Mart was an incredible place to shop. This was my first job after finishing high school. Back then, we had only 300 stores. We weren't as good at training associates, but the orientation showed that we had profit sharing and insurance and pay that was very competitive at that time. That showed me I could do whatever I wanted there. The reason I liked it then, and the reason I am still here twenty-five years later, is the associates. The associates embrace you like family.

My first job was in the pet department, and my sole responsibility was to take care of the animals in the stores. Back then, we had anything that had wings or crawled. No puppies, but we had fish and birds and mice and snakes, and we had bunnies and chicks at Easter time. I woke up every morning and I wanted to be at Wal-Mart.

People often ask if there were anything I'd change about what I did. I often think I would have taken the time to get a degree. I don't know that it would have gotten me any further than I got, but it was a personal goal I'd set for myself that I wanted to achieve. I know that what I got here through experience is a hundred-fold to what I would have gained going to college. I think the more you want to learn and grow—it is all here for you.

It takes hard work. You have to get out there and reach for it, but I think you can be anything you want to be. It is your commitment, your passion, it is your work. All of those things come into play. Whether I have a degree or not does not limit my abilities to grow or do the things I want. At Wal-Mart, you can be a pilot if you want to be a pilot. If you want to do architecture or real estate or merchandising or health care—we have all of that right within Wal-Mart. We have our own experts. And you can do it anywhere in the world.

I've learned a lot about moving a career along. Sometimes you have to take a path that is nonlinear. Don't be afraid to go lateral. Sometimes lateral moves create the best experiences. They may be the biggest game changers in your career. I made a lateral move when I took over merchandising after being in operations for so many years. The experience I got was far greater than it would have been with an upward move inside operations. Most people don't like to get outside their comfort zones, but I like to play in somebody else's sandbox every once in awhile because they have different toys. Learning something different in today's environment is the best thing you can do. As a leader, you make better decisions with a broader understanding of the business. So, keep that in mind. Be open.

My focus was always on the position I had, not the next position up. It was all about doing the job, doing it very well, and doing it to the best of my ability. I did the best I could and hoped it would be good for the company. Your performance will get you where you want to be, so perform.

From a leadership standpoint, your associates will get you where you need to be, based on your leadership skills. There are some people who have a "self" agenda. The person who continues to look up and ask, "Where is my next step?" "What does so-and-so think of me?" is in it for the wrong reasons. I just continue to look at what we are doing together for the company and ask how I can inspire the group I have today to do the things they never thought they could do. If they perform, the business does well.

I was an hourly associate. I know what worked and didn't work from the perspective of an hourly associate. People are not that complicated. Some managers think people are complicated, but people are not. They want the same things. They want to be listened to. They want to be recognized for their accomplishments. And they want to be taught. My No. 1 responsibility when I took this job was to make Wal-Mart a better place to work.

You can't drag an organization with you. Your people have to be inspired and know that the organization they are working for is right for them. It has to be in your gut. People have to feel good about the direction their company is going, and know they are contributing to a larger organization and making a difference. And, "Because I said so" doesn't mean people will be inspired to do what they do. You won't get heart and you won't get soul and you won't get any more than you asked for. You'll get, "I do my job because that is what you pay me to do." That is not what we want.

I am very direct and open and honest with the people I deal with. You have to appreciate and respect everyone, regardless of what role they play in the organization. Leaders have to be able to have a conversation with the lady who keeps our bathrooms clean and be able to have a conversation with the CEO. There needs to be transparency. People forget that it takes everybody inside an organization to make it successful. Some people do very well at managing up. But you have to manage all the way around. That's right. All the way around and be able to sit with anyone and have a conversation that makes a difference in their lives.

My dad instilled in me that I needed to understand my strengths and work on them because those are the things that will bring opportunities to me. He said, "You can be whatever you want to be." He believed you tell people what you think and always ask what you can do better. I wanted to be great at what I was doing. But the management team at Wal-Mart said, "That's great, but you can be more." ∎

Michelle Gloeckler started her career at Hershey in 1988 as a sales rep in Detroit, then climbed the sales ranks until she deliberately detoured herself into a job that she knew very little about.

That decision propelled her upward on the corporate ladder, and now she is Hershey's vice president in charge of the areas of the company that connect directly with consumers.

Gloeckler says she has modeled herself after her mother, who was a working mom in sales for the Wrigley Co. "She was able to work and enjoy a career, and my sister and I never felt mom sacrificed anything that had an adverse effect on us. She never projected a lot of guilt or stress."

That has helped Gloeckler as she has advanced her career while parenting two sons, ages seven and ten. "I don't have guilt. I recognize that I'm going to miss a baseball game here and there, and they understand that. When I come home, I don't do the 'Oh, I'm so sorry I missed your game, I feel horrible' routine. Mom works."

Her husband stays home with the kids, a luxury she said that makes it all work out.

Remember the Details
Michelle Gloeckler
Vice President The Hershey Experience
The Hershey Company

You are in charge of your own destiny and career. Remember that. You don't have to follow some preset path to success.

I was in sales, and that was a much-defined, logical career ladder. You'd go from sales rep to district supervisor to district manager to regional manager. Then, you'd get a bigger region, and so on.

Well, I stopped being logical. I took a huge risk and it paid off.

I was a regional manager, and instead of going for a larger region or a division, I went over to a different department: category management. It was technology-driven, it entailed more computer and analytical skills, and on a scale of one to ten, my technical knowledge was a three or four. This was eight years ago and technology wasn't where it is today. The people who worked in category management were the geeks. The job opening was to manage them and be an ambassador for computer tool creation, data manipulation, and using lines and lines of syndicated data. I was attracted to it because it was going to be the way we did business in the future.

So I posted for the job. I wanted to do it. I was seven months pregnant and interviewed for the job in which I didn't have expertise or background. My manager didn't think I should do it. He wasn't going to be a roadblock, but he expressed that he would prefer that I stay where I was and go for a bigger region. He asked me why I would want to go work with "all those propeller heads." I wanted to try something new, different and scary. And I was doing it at a time when I would have to move from Buffalo, New York, to Hershey, Pennsylvania, during the last term of my second pregnancy. What made it even scarier was that, in my previous pregnancy, I had delivered eight weeks early.

It was scary, walking into that interview, pregnant, with half of me walking in before the other half. But, I got some great coaching from peers telling me to just go in there and tell the guy why I was the right one for the job.

Since my immediate supervisor was not supportive, I sought support from other people I trusted. You have the ability to call on a lot of different folks to help you throughout your career. It is not a completely autocratic society where you can only do what your manager says. It's your career.

It was a very scary move for me, but it was my defining moment. You have to be daring. There is exponential growth where you are unfamiliar. Be comfortable in your own skills and see how they translate in a different assignment. Even if there are things that are risky, that transfer of your skills automatically mitigates some of those risks. For example, if your strengths are in leadership, teamwork and building consensus—and that is what is needed in a particular department—you don't have to know all the details with respect to technology or other aspects. It can work.

One thing I had to learn over the years is to remain focused. When I was a Raleigh district manager, we had something called the "President's Cup," which was a sales competition. My district was first in its group for almost the entire year, but when we got our results in January, we came in second place by two-tenths of a point. It was very, very close.

It wasn't just me who didn't win, but the whole team. I not only let myself down, I let all of them down. It would have been very prestigious to win that, and imagine being in first place all year long and then not winning. We may have been too confident. We'd settled into our first-place status. We didn't look at the details. And that was what went wrong. It was a miss on the analytics on my part.

The lesson from that was detail. No matter how confident you are in your space, you have always got to watch the competition and you've got to understand the detail. You, as the leader, own that. You can have staff people and assume they are doing what they need to do, but at the end of the day, you are responsible. If you let the team down, that bad feeling is yours to keep. That's the price of leadership.

I learned from that mistake. I relocated from Raleigh to Texas that year, and my next group won.

Another lesson I learned had to do with managing people. Everybody has a different motivation, and it's personal. If you are going to manage people, you'd better learn what motivates each individual or you won't build an effective team. My first job as a manager was over part-time merchandisers. They worked outside the home because they wanted to, not necessarily because they had to, and they were not working to get ahead in the corporate world or climb that career ladder. It took me a while to understand that.

As a new manager, I assumed they were just like me. But they were working for completely different reasons than I was. I was twenty-three years old at that time and most of the folks I was managing were significantly more experienced than me—twice my age—and they trained me and took me under their wing. They'd say, "Michelle, I don't have the same goals and ambitions as you. I do this because I like it. If I work my twenty hours and I don't do this or that, it is because I have no desire to be the district manager. I just want to do my job." I appreciated that and was humbled by it.

People are still individuals, regardless of their level in the organization. They have individual motivations. You have to understand that people will give their best if you motivate them in a way that is important to them. Not everybody is just like you.

I am in a position to build my own teams now, and I don't want people who are just like me. I want a more balanced team. Some people tend to hire folks who are just like them and have the same skills set, motivation, style and communication. I would rather have a more diverse team. Have somebody extroverted who talks all the time complemented by somebody highly analytical who thinks all the time.

You have to get to know your people, and that takes time. If you are going to understand what motivates them and be able to motivate them to get their peak performance in whatever job they are doing, you have to know about them. Why do they work? What do they like? What upsets them? How do they like to be managed? Do they need a lot of praise? Are they uncomfortable with a lot of praise? There are thousands of things.

But, the first thing managers need to do is be accessible and care in a genuine way about people's performance at work, and what is important to them in life.

Finally, if it is worth doing, it is worth doing right. I can't tell you how many times my father said that to me. But it's true. It's the foundation for everything. ■

Helayne Angelus is unstoppable when she's on a mission. And she is always, always, ALWAYS on a mission. As president of the Network of Executive Women, she started a cocktail conversation about how great it would be to collect the mentoring wisdom of NEW supporters for a book. Now you are holding it.

At NEW, she has worked to help women and men in the consumer products and retail industry recognize the power of a diverse organization. She's shown how to create a competitive advantage by empowering women and helping companies to achieve best practices. She took her corporate finesse at Procter & Gamble and crafted a position that lets her honor her passion for diversity by traveling globally to build a more diverse and empowered workforce. She cares about legacy—not just for herself, but for all women who are now in a position to mentor others.

18 Have A Mission
Helayne C. Angelus
Vice President, Global Customer Business Development Diversity
Procter & Gamble

Joining P&G sales was like joining the Marines. Most of the managers were ex-military and the first generation of women—including myself—had to prove we were smarter, tougher and could take every challenge given to us. And it all came with a little extra dose of, "Really. Women don't belong here." My goal in the first few years was to survive while still being true to who I was.

I'd signed up for this on an all-male interview schedule at Columbia University, which I wasn't supposed to do. P&G recruiters went to Columbia, which was all male. I went to Barnard, which was the all-female school at Columbia. The interviewer about fell out of his chair when he saw me, and there was a lot of scrutiny and a lot of tough questions.

Then they sent me out on a day in the field in the South Bronx. P&G has a nine-step sales call, and the fourth or fifth step is to check the stock in the back room. New York doesn't have many back rooms—it has basements. They are dark and aren't always clean. I went there with the sales rep and he tried to scare me by telling me how many rats there were in the basement.

He said, "This is a tough part of the job, and not for the faint of heart." He threw a rock down there to make them scurry before we went down the steps.

I didn't flinch. I said, "Fine. I'll go first." It was kind of a hazing, a test of my toughness.

I knew I was born to be a sales executive because I had been selling since I was in grade school, going door-to-door with all kinds of things to make money. I was selling Christmas wreaths I'd made, door-to-door on my Flexible Flyer sled. I think I was getting four or five dollars each, and I probably sold thirty. That was pretty good for a ten-year-old, and I always knew I had sales skills.

After college, I think I had five job offers. I had been propositioned in interviews for two of the other companies. I chose to go to P&G because I felt the ethics of the company—and the people I was in contact with—were far superior to what I saw at other companies.

We had a group interview at the Essex House, and I was a few minutes late because I had to work. I took a cab, which was eight dollars, and that was all I earned that afternoon. I worked three jobs through college to support myself, and I took that cab because I did not want to be late.

I got out of the cab and the hiring district manager was pacing in front of the hotel as he waited for me. I apologized for being late and explained I'd had to work. He asked me how much the cab ride was. I said, "Eight dollars." He knew I worked three jobs and he took the eight dollars out of his pocket and gave it to me, right that minute. That reinforced to me that the values and principles of this company fit my values and principles.

Six years later, I was a district manager in New Jersey and he was in New York, and we were peers. He took enormous pleasure in that. He has been a great friend and mentor to this day.

My first few years, I felt like the Chinese panda at the zoo. You know, "Let's see if that woman can really sell." Women were breaking ground here every day. In those years, we had to be better. We had to be at the job earlier, make more sales calls and be the best to be considered in a world where there were just no women role models.

I was so focused on achieving while developing a high-performing team. The company had only just hired a few women, and they weren't ready for women in the organization. But they tried. In 1977 or 1978 they had their first women-in-sales seminar; it was me and one hundred men. One thing that came up was, what do you do when a woman cries? They all looked at me and I said, "Well, hand her a tissue!"

It was so important for me to be supportive of others—both men and women—to create an open and positive environment for others to succeed. When I first started, I was with men who were twenty and thirty years older than I. I was twenty-four years old and managing people who had daughters that were my age. I wanted to be the best in the business, but I wanted to make sure everyone else succeeded. I've been a big believer in the power of developing other people to create high-performing teams.

One of my strategies always has been to get to know the people I work with and who work with me as individuals—and know their family members as well. Their spouses knew me, knew what I was about and were very comfortable with me as a very young boss. I would take them out twice a year, and in those years, the company didn't pay for it. I wanted them to get to know me and my values and principles. It was an anomaly to have a woman as a first-level manager and I had to take extra steps to create the right environment and support.

I've had some bumps in the road relative to how fast I moved up in the organization. I made personal choices and it is important to note that I had some real goals and objectives in my life that included other things besides P&G. I was goal-oriented, but I never wanted to achieve career success at the expense of my beliefs, my health, or my relationship with my husband, my children, my parents or my friends.

Once I was married and had children, I realized career progression might not be a straight line. I had to create a very different model that enabled me to have a balanced life. When you are single, it is okay to stay until seven or eight at night. But, when you have child care, that's not okay.

P&G is great and wonderful, but it is part of life. It isn't your life.

I became the company's first female sales associate director and was in charge of one of the largest divisions in the company, which was over a billion-dollar business. I got pregnant and my boss—a really big supporter—said, "Well, now that you're pregnant, you don't have to do this job." I said, "Wait a minute. Pregnancy does not affect my brain." So I traveled fifty to sixty percent of the time, all the way into my ninth month. I proved that, not only can a woman lead, but a woman can lead while she is pregnant.

The common thinking was, "Once they get pregnant, they will leave and they won't come back and contribute." I didn't feel like I could fail. I wasn't just doing it for me, but for all women.

Our company promotes only from within. We rarely hire executives from outside. So you only grow. The assignment that helped distinguish me globally was going to Venezuela. I went there to lead a group of 120 Latin men. I had doubts whether I could learn the language and the culture, and whether my family and I could survive and thrive in an environment of revolutions, coups and physical danger.

My father was a diplomat, and I lived in three countries by the time I was eight years old. That really helped shape me. I wanted that for my children.

So we went to Venezuela in 1992. My Spanish was not that good. I studied Spanish every night. Eight months later, I was speaking Spanish, leading the P&G customer business development organization in Venezuela. I was even giving speeches in Spanish. I led the organization from calling on customers with written order pads to multifunctional teams using laptop computers. When we left, the organization was close to twenty percent women.

Where was my angst? It was always with the kids. Would they be okay with all of this? Could I balance what was important to me? That was my angst. I had two children under three years old and I traveled thirty to forty percent of the time. I've had my doubts about that, but, years later, they are independent, good, mature young adults. I may not have been with them all the time, but when I was with them, it was quality time. They are savvy, adaptable, and secure. I never could have done this without an equal partner in the parenting, which my husband has always been.

With children, you never know if you are doing a good job until later in life. We never miss an athletic event, whether it is football or lacrosse. Most of the time we are both there, but one of us is always at the games. We make it a priority. And I was always an assistant homeroom mom. I'd stage the best Halloween party the class ever had.

Whatever you give to the world comes back to you tenfold. The only way to create a diverse organization is to have the right representation of the customers we serve and communities we are in. I've worked hard to do that and the results have been phenomenal. Men and women need to reach out and help the next generation so we can impart the lessons we have learned. We have to make sure the inside tips and the how-tos don't get lost. It is not good enough for women to have one or two seats at the table when sixty percent of the graduating class out of college is female. Half of the seats have to be female. We need to encourage people to take the risks and get the important, crucible jobs and be there to provide insight and coaching when they need it.

As far as my list of how-tos and mentoring wisdom?

First, be clear about who you are, what you bring to the table and what you want. Then communicate that to all the people who need to know: to your boss, your boss's boss, and those key stakeholders who can influence your career.

Second, make sure you have a clear understanding of the expectations of every assignment. Get them all spelled out. Understand what success looks like for whatever your assignment is. "I will deliver x sales and x profit." Get measurable answers on what success is, and make sure everybody who is going to evaluate you understands that is what you are going to deliver.

Third, make your boss your biggest supporter and advocate. It is great to have a mentor, but the greatest relationship you can have is with your immediate manager. Where women fall down is, they don't invest in that relationship. Really get to understand the individual—not just formally, but learn what makes him or her tick. How can you meet the unmet needs? How can you make your boss succeed, and therefore, how can your boss make you succeed?

Fourth, have multiple folks you can turn to for advice and coaching. Have your own personal board of directors. No one individual has everything. Seek out those people who have something you want to learn or something you aspire to, and develop a relationship with them.

Make sure that you ask the individuals who are responsible for your career—typically your boss and your boss's boss—how you are doing against your objectives. That way, people know what you are doing. I think women fall down in this area because they don't want to take the lead in it. Men do it all the time.

Finally, overdeliver. Whatever you said you were going to do, do it better than other people and demonstrate you can add value in a lot of other areas. For me, succeeding for the business is a given. But what else can you do to distinguish yourself as a leader and to support the goals of the company and the organization?

Knowing yourself, who you are, and what is important to you—and being able to communicate that to your employer, to your spouse and to your family—is so important in creating the support mechanisms to help you achieve what you want. I set annual goals. I rate myself against how I am doing against those goals annually, and I track the key actions every two weeks to see if I am living up to what I said I was going to do and be. That has worked for me.

I have had a mission statement for almost eighteen years. "I live a rich and balanced life. I lead change. I role model a happy marriage, a challenging career and investing in others. I believe in synergy, win-win relationships and being true to myself. And, by doing this, I make a difference in the lives of others."

Every two or three years, I reflect on whether this mission still rings true to me. My children have grown older; we all have. But the core hasn't changed much. I really felt, from day one, that I had to make a difference.

And I think I have. ■

Lynn Marmer started her career teaching ninth grade in Cincinnati inner-city schools where she said she learned as much as she taught. Her students and their families taught her plenty about humanity and community. She also learned something that, she now remembers with a laugh, has been invaluable in the corporate world.

"I learned that, if you can explain something to ninth-graders, you can talk in most corporate boardrooms. Any idea, no matter how complex, is more effectively communicated clearly and simply and in a straightforward way." She left teaching for another career—in urban planning. And then law school and then…

Well, she wound up at Kroger as the first female executive officer. It is a great story of what happened in the 1980s when strong women had to surmount the obstacles of stereotype and discrimination to clear their own trail to the top.

19 Do Your Absolute Best
Lynn Marmer

Group Vice President, Corporate Affairs
The Kroger Co.

I was teaching in inner-city schools, but I was working for people I didn't respect. The principals didn't have passion for education; they didn't have passion for the kids. They were simply caretakers. If I wanted to grow in that system, I'd have to aspire into administration. It turned me off.

So I got a master's degree in urban planning, then worked as an urban planner.

After a stint with the City of Cincinnati, I headed a nonprofit agency. My biggest project was developing an apartment building for people in wheelchairs. It was one of the first of its kind in the country—a very strict project, with federal funds, local funds and special architects. What a fabulous place. That's when I became interested in real estate.

I had a couple of job interviews with a well-respected real-estate developer. I was pretty excited about it until he came back and offered me the job. He said I would be his "Gal Friday." He actually said that! He said I would type, do his bidding and run his errands.

I was so insulted. I was an honors graduate from a very well-respected graduate program. I had put together this multimillion-dollar apartment building project on my own, and that guy was offering me a job as his "Gal Friday"?

I turned him down on the spot and told him that it was an insulting offer. As I walked out of that interview, I decided I was never going to be in a position again where I would be asked if I could type. I made up my mind I would go to law school and I took the LSAT. I had enough money saved in the bank for one semester, so it was an enormous risk. I was running the nonprofit and could have stayed there. My LSAT scores weren't great, and I got in just under the wire. But I was at the top of my class at the end of my first semester. I ended up graduating fourth in my class and was editor-in-chief of the law review.

The funny part is that I sit on committees with that developer today. I have never reminded him. I don't want to offend him. But I get a huge kick out of it because I can look at him and think, "Thank you. I have one of the most fabulous jobs in America because of you."

After law school, I went to a law firm and eventually made partner. I was elected to the Cincinnati School Board while I was at the firm. I had a lot of interesting experiences there and met a lot of local business leaders.

Law firms are really collections of entrepreneurs. In the end, you eat what you kill as a lawyer. You have to be able to develop your own business, and I was successful and had a very strong book of clients for the business. After I'd been partner for a couple of years, I noticed I had a strong client base, but my compensation appeared to be lower than it should have been. There was that mismatch between what I was generating and what I was being paid.

So I went to the senior partner and said, "Gee, there is this mismatch here." He said, "You need to bide your time."

I was working eighty hours a week, easy. Bide my time? For how long? And for what? It was one of those times in my life when there was a hand in the small of my back pushing me. I wasn't sure where it was pushing me to, but it was pushing me.

The reality in business is that your measuring stick is your paycheck. That is how you know how you are truly valued. People may thank you for what you do, but the bottom line is, you are working incredibly hard and that paycheck is the symbol of your hard work. It was so discouraging and disillusioning to have believed that this was a meritocracy, that it was based on my merit—when it wasn't. They valued me enough to give me a nice office and expect me to work eighty hours a week, but not enough to pay me at the level I believed I deserved.

One of the business leaders I'd met through the school board was Joe Pichler, the chairman and CEO of Kroger. I went to him and said, "I'm just looking around in the community to see what kinds of other things I might do as a lawyer." He said, "Kroger builds one hundred new stores a year. You are a real-estate lawyer. Why not talk to our general counsel?"

I was hired in the law department to do real estate law and, frankly, that is where I thought I would stay. I never thought I would do anything else. But, a door soon opened that was the defining moment that all those other moments had been preparing me for.

The man who was group vice president for corporate affairs at Kroger announced his early retirement.

I went to my boss in the law department and asked him about the position. He said, "Well, you are going to have a great career here, but I think you need to work a little longer in this department." It was the "Bide your time" message? Again?

I said, "No, I think this is a great opportunity and I'd like to go for it." He fully supported me. He is and has been one of my best friends and mentors.

So I assembled my case of why I was well-qualified for the position. I focused on the work. I asked a lot of questions. Then I was offered the job.

I was in my office and one of the administrative assistants came in and said, "Do you know what this means? You are the first woman officer in this company."

I had not focused on the rank or the politics. I'd focused on the work. I knew going in that I was capable and that I hadn't been chosen because I was a woman. I knew I was not a token. But, I was so fortunate that this administrative assistant took me aside and quickly gave me the dose of reality that I needed. It made me suddenly stand a little taller and realize that I not only had the responsibility as Lynn Marmer, the individual, to do this job, but to do it for the other women in this organization who had, for the first time, a female officer.

I had a lot to learn—I'd only been with Kroger for six months. But the door opened and that little hand pushed me through it. I walked through it because other people believed in me.

You need to do your absolute best work on everything you are asked to do, from the simplest assignment to the most complicated. Every memo has your signature on it and it should be good work. I think people make a mistake in waiting for the big project. They forget that the way to get the big project is by doing a lot of small ones very well.

I applied this same standard to my volunteer work. Being on the school board opened many doors for me. While it was tough—I was a new mom, a junior partner and president of the school board—it was worth it.

Don't ever hesitate to raise your hand. There are opportunities to do different things, learn new areas, broaden your skills base and be seen as a real contributor. Be willing to say yes.

When I was working at city hall, we had a new city manager who asked who'd be willing to do a project. I remember saying, "I'll do that. Sure. I'd love to do that." That raising of my hand brought me to being his right hand for several years. You just don't know. You have to be willing to take some risks and go outside your own comfort zone. If you do the same thing all the time, and do it consistently, that is fine. But to really move in an organization, you have to be willing to take on the tough assignments. That is where you learn leadership.

Another lesson for women is, don't personalize. The guys don't.

When you make a mistake, own up to it and move on. Women tend to want to be perfect and they ruminate about their mistakes. And they want people to like them. When something goes wrong, own up to it. Say, "I screwed up. Here is what went wrong. Here is what I would do differently." Then move on.

You need a certain toughness that only comes from falling down and skinning your knee. ■

In an industry in which many lead from the same place where they began their journeys, **Luci Sheehan** positioned herself as a moving target. An independent, adventuresome, go-for-it gambler, Sheehan has traveled a path of risk and self-definition that began in the 1970s at Procter & Gamble, where she appeared to be on track for a career-long march up a singular corporate ladder. It didn't feel right.

There is no one way to climb or succeed, no one set of rules, no one track that works for everybody. Sheehan proved it. She currently is executive vice president for global sales for Carttronics, a global leader in loss prevention and operational efficiency solutions for the retail industry.

A recent brush with her own mortality taught her that life is too unpredictable to live it on other people's terms. The beauty, she said, is in the ride.

20 Adapt to Win
Luci Sheehan
Executive Vice President, Global Sales
Carttronics LLC

When I was a junior in college, my father ran for governor of Massachusetts. My uncle ran the statewide signature drive to get the ten thousand signatures that would put my dad on the ballot. One day, my uncle went home, took a nap and, after sudden cardiac arrest, died. He was only fifty-one.

It fell to me to organize volunteers across the state and get people to go out and gather signatures. That gave me an early understanding of my leadership capabilities. We got the signatures. The incumbent governor didn't want my dad on the ballot, so he challenged the authenticity of the signatures, but everything bore out as authentic. I still have that adding-machine tape that authenticated the signatures with the secretary of state in my jewelry box.

Even though my dad lost in the primary, the experience validated my capability to organize and run a team. It eliminated fear. I didn't have time to be afraid; I just had to get it done.

I have been willing to take what other people might consider big risks in my career in order to do what I felt I needed to do for me—for my own personal growth. I have always followed my gut and my heart to strike out and create a different path for myself. That early experience gave me the courage to do the things for me.

I was at Procter & Gamble for eight years. I was on the sales management track, and started in New England and became the first female district manager in the company. I have always reviewed and assessed where I am, and in my last year at P&G, I kept feeling like there was something missing. I needed to hunker down and spend time thinking about it, and what I realized was, I wasn't having fun. It was misery. I was doing things that didn't feel important. Clearing deductions was not leading an organization. My manager was the king of C-priorities. He smothered us with administrative overload and that zapped my creativity. That happens in a lot of organizations. There are "leaders" who have been in those roles so long that they don't know another way. If you challenge them, it scares them.

I wanted to learn more about myself. I needed to be in a more sales-driven environment, and P&G is a marketing-driven environment. It became very important for me to strike out and find those experiences that would allow me to use the skills and talents I have in the way I wanted to use them. I wouldn't be pigeonholed there. I wanted to have the experiences that were going to be important to me.

To move forward at P&G, I would have to go back to Cincinnati, and I did not belong there. I found Cincinnati stifling. I was living and working in New York. If I did go to Cincinnati, the division-manager role was a most unattractive job for a woman of child-bearing years who was thinking about having a family. I didn't want to be traveling three weeks out of the month.

Besides, I didn't have passion for what I was doing. Work is central to who I am. You have to look at what is wrong and not working, and then find a new path. One Christmas Day, I analyzed what I wanted. I wrote my résumé.

Then, what I wanted appeared. A wonderful opportunity with an interesting company that did a lot of wonderful things: Whittle Communications. It allowed me to fly higher with my selling skills, and that was important to me.

When I gave notice, P&G put so much pressure on me to stay that I literally lost my voice in the discussions. Some friends said, "You have to follow your heart and do what you want to do." Others said, "You have a good thing here. Why would you leave it?" I have always been an individualist who follows my own voice. In my heart, I knew that I was not where I was supposed to spend my life. If I stayed, I would have been married to P&G.

It was exhilarating to walk out the door. I was happy. I was leaving the industry for something brand new, where I was going to be selling new media. I was striking out in a lot of ways. Overall, I think I felt good. I made a lot of changes in my life. It was my thirtieth year, and I went beyond work and did things that taught me I could do anything. I had been deathly afraid of the water as a child, but I learned how to swim. And I learned how to ski.

I met my husband, set new goals and started my family. I had a very difficult pregnancy and decided to look at doing some consulting, which transitioned me into my next role. Consulting afforded me a little more flexibility. Over the years, I've had so many different professional experiences. I've called on movie studios and General Motors and the Air Force. I worked for one of the largest publishers for the college market. In one instance, I was managing projects one day, and line-managing the grocery division of one of the largest food brokers in metro New York the next day. I felt I hadn't missed a beat. It felt natural. If I had stayed at one company this whole time, the financial picture would have been safer. If that is important to you, then that is what you should do. But, I felt this was a better choice for me in the long run. It was a whole lot of fun—and it still is.

You have to be able to adapt. If you can't, you can't handle true adversity when it strikes. We all have our own individual journeys. Your ability to go into a new situation and figure it out and make it work helps build those bravery muscles so when something does happen, you will have the muscles to get through it.

You don't know how life can change in an instant until it does.

I learned that when I survived three near-death experiences in a ten-day period after going into sudden cardiac arrest when I was fifty-one. I was signing in to take a routine bone scan after my regular physical exam, and collapsed with sudden death. I fell forward, hit my head and face, and then spent the next several days in the ICU. It was a miracle that I survived. I had a defibrillator installed and was discharged after eight days. Less than twenty-four hours later, I coded at home and was rushed to a hospital closer to home. I spent the next five hours in the emergency room and they brought me back to life a second time. Then I went to the ICU and, three days later, I coded again. The next three weeks in the hospital included a week of rehab because I needed to learn to walk again.

The first great lesson was to allow other people to help me. I was the oldest of seven girls and had been conditioned to be a person who takes care of others and gives—not takes. I didn't know how to ask for help for myself.

The second great lesson was that I come first in my life. Not my child and not my husband, not my friends and not my family. Me. I didn't understand that until this happened.

There was no physical explanation for why this health crisis occurred. Actually, I think it was a gift from God. I didn't fully appreciate how much I'd stopped doing self-care.

The biggest lesson was this: Count your blessings and appreciate the moment— every single day. That is the moment of making a sale, interacting with co-workers, cooking a meal—whatever. Just celebrate the moment.

When caught in the details of life, you easily can lose sight of those things, but you shouldn't. Life can change in an instant. ■

Mary Beth West is grounded in her mission and in her essence. She's got the position, heading a more than $3 billion sector of Kraft that includes icon brands such as Maxwell House, Crystal Light, Capri Sun and Kool-Aid. But she's also got the perspective, and that becomes clear when she talks about personal issues that forever changed her view of work.

West is still exuberant about the retail industry. "I mean, you have an idea and then you walk in the grocery store and see it right there. Tell me that is not a cool thing! To have the honor to work on some of these brands that started a hundred years ago and keep them alive today? That is cool. And the people—that is what matters most."

She talks at length about the influence of her father, a man with a genius IQ who awoke every morning excited about going to his job at Kodak. Seeing that made her think that everyone loved going to work.

Growing as a leader meant learning to inspire those who do not.

As the most senior African-American woman at Kraft, West says she bears a heavy responsibility. Senior management has put a heavy emphasis on diversity, but West takes it personally. "I've had so much help along the way, and if I don't put my hand back and help somebody else, it is all for naught," she said. "I put pressure on myself to make sure everyone succeeds, but not everyone will. We have done a terrific job with women here, but we have work to do with multi-cultural folks. There is a wonderful energy around that from senior management all the way down, but you don't turn on a switch and have it fixed. Every time a person of color leaves the company, I feel personally responsible."

Connect with People
Mary Beth West
Group Vice President, Kraft Foods
President, Beverages Sector

I have four brothers and sisters, and four of the five of us are adopted. My dad has a genius IQ and I have a sister at the other end of the intellectual spectrum, and we have everybody else at levels in between. My family was all about appreciating individual contribution and capability within your capacity.

I have one sister who has been a nurse's aide her whole life. My brother was capable of more, but he quit school in the tenth grade, moved to Florida and started sweeping floors at a construction company. He's now the vice president there. My oldest sister—who was the one biological child—has been a music teacher, studied karate and has gotten her pilot's license. She really lives life.

My parents had the foresight to say that everyone has the same opportunity to live up to his or her own potential. And if you asked any one of us how we felt we were valued in the family, each of us felt like we were the star.

It is a lesson that really works in leadership in business. Part of it is understanding just what people are truly capable of, and then helping them maximize their potential within their level of capability. Put them in positions that not only play to their strengths, but also stretch them in areas that are untapped, where you might not be sure if they will thrive. My parents always gave us something to play to our strengths, and they exposed us to a lot of different things we could try because they never knew what would catch. They tried to give us as many different experiences as we could get. But, if we decided to try something, we had to stick with it long enough to decide whether we really liked it, which was generally at least a year.

A lot of leadership is about finding a connection with people. If you find out enough about them, something will connect you. One of the first people I worked with here was Jim Craigie (now CEO of Church & Dwight). We were as different as we could be, but we were from towns right next to each other. We both were inspired to get things done fast. We were both so competitive and we both loved softball. Those were the things we connected on. I worked with him three different times. But, on paper, we were really different. Relationships come down to finding a connection on some level. And the people I have learned the most from are the ones who are least like me.

A piece of advice I got many years ago was that the job you don't take will be more important than the job you do. I think that is true when I think of the jobs and careers I have said no to. One good example happened years ago when Kraft wanted to put me in a marketing services role, specializing in advertising and consumer promotions.

They'd quickly come to the conclusion that I was a good marketer. I was twenty-eight years old, and I really think they thought I was a good marketer based on what I looked like physically. They figured they would put me in a job that played to my "strengths" so they wouldn't have to worry about me.

But my mentor said, "The problem is, you will never get out of there. They won't let you out." It is easier to find the people who want to do the line jobs because more people want to be where the action is, rather than find people for the staff jobs like they wanted me to take. My mentor told me that I was too young to make a decision on what I was or wasn't good at, and that I shouldn't pigeonhole myself. I should try some things.

If I'd gone into that job, I wouldn't be here. That was the pivotal moment of my career. In the short term, I probably would have been more comfortable. But in the long term, I would have had a much flatter career trajectory. If you want to be a group vice president, you do the line assignments. You don't commit to a specialty early on.

You do want to play to your strengths, but you don't want to make a decision on what you are good at too soon. You'll close down opportunities that you could potentially be really good at. If you try golf once and you are not good at it, you can't say, "I'm not good at that. I won't try it again." Plenty of people try it and aren't good at it the first time. You get good with effort.

You make a few mistakes.

Like, I bought a small business for Kraft: It's Pasta Anytime! It was cheap. We bought it for two reasons: as an offensive move, because I thought I could grow it, and as a defensive move, because somebody else could get it and grow it, and we wouldn't want them to have it. I really thought I could grow it, but I couldn't make it happen. I tried and tried for three years, and it was so frustrating. I put the very best person I had on the business because I knew in the last year that if she couldn't figure out how to grow it, we wouldn't be able to grow it. I needed someone in there who I had 100 percent confidence in. She came back nine months later and said, "I don't think this is going to work." So we shut the business down.

I don't think Kraft penalizes you for making mistakes. It's about learning through your mistakes. Afterward, I had a conversation with my manager, who hadn't been my manager when I bought it. I said, "Would you have ever bought this?" He said, "No, probably not. Buying businesses that don't make money before you buy them is not a good idea." We paid $10 million for the business. It wasn't a big investment, but then there was the money we paid for advertising and promotion and, well, I don't remember those numbers—ever so conveniently.

I wish I had put my highest-potential person on the business when we'd first bought it. Maybe we'd have had a shot, but I didn't do that. It is important to have passion for your ideas, but it is also important to know when passion is not going to be enough. To know when it is time to cut your losses and get out.

I remember thinking, "If I get out of this, I am going to look stupid." But, the deeper I would have gotten into it, the worse it would have been. I had to stand up and take responsibility.

It was good for me, and it was good for people to see that I made a mistake and my career didn't fall apart.

It was just another learning experience.

People are motivated by fundamentally different things. For some people, it is money or power. For others, it is legacy. The trick is finding out what each person is motivated by so you can tap into it, and not assuming that whatever it is that drives you is what drives others.

What drives me is family. I have a lot of perspective about this. I lost a baby when I was seven months pregnant. You think there is pressure in business when the numbers are down, but, compared to losing a baby, work pressure is a joy ride. I had never hit a hurdle like that. It was as if my life had completely collapsed.

From that point on, it didn't matter what I faced here in the office. Nothing was even close to that pain. From that, I was able to create a distance where I do the best I can every single day, then go home at night and sleep very well. I have an appreciation for what real drama and crisis are. It is not here. This is business. You want to embrace the business, but you don't want it to smother you. If it becomes who you are, you have a problem.

I have two children, ages four and twenty-one months, and both are adopted. When I walk through the door at the end of the day, they scream, "Mommy! Mommy!" They don't ask me what the numbers were. They don't care. I am "Mommy." That is the most important thing, and the rest of it will wait because it will always be there tomorrow. ■

Jennie Jones's story is a painful snapshot of what women faced once they began to make strides in the workplace. It is an emotional account of the sexual harassment that was once so common, yet now seems so implausible.

Jones tells of sharing the story with her daughter-in-law, an aeronautical engineer who works in a male-dominated environment. "She looked at me like I was smoking crack," Jones said.

That says plenty about how far women have come. Some of our most troubling experiences that were so common thirty years ago seem like fiction to women today. It was way too real way back when.

Jones is one of the founders of the Network of Executive Women. Her involvement originally began as an assignment in her annual objectives when she worked for Crown Central Petroleum Corp. "What happened with NEW went far beyond anything any of us ever expected, and it has been one of the most gratifying achievements in my life—except for my children and grandchildren. I wish I could have had the network to rely on for guidance because I think it would have made me a stronger and better person."

After hearing her story, you can't help but wonder how she could have been any stronger than she already is.

22 Fight Back
Jennie Jones

Vice President Marketing, Convenience Store Sales Division
S&D Coffee Co.

It is hard to tell this story. It happened. It is true. This was the way business was done in the late 1970s and early 1980s as women came into the workplace. It seems so far away now.

I worked for a major corporation in an office where there were seven women who were being sexually harassed simultaneously. I'm not saying verbally. I am saying physically.

None of us knew what was going on with the others—we thought we were on our own, by ourselves. There were physical threats to the point that the boss would back us into the corner and he would threaten us if we didn't give him sexual favors. Once, he told me I would have to have sex with him, and if I didn't, I would have to fire an employee. Another time, we were on a business trip and I literally had to hit him in the head to get him to stop.

The first time it happened, I dropped my husband's name into the conversation and said, "Jimmy would not appreciate this, and I don't appreciate it either."

I will never forget what he said back to me: "Well, you wanted me to be nicer to you."

I was humiliated. I was totally degraded to know this is what would happen, regardless of how hard I had worked. I was a senior buyer. I was in a management role and worked hard to get there. It was just humiliating to be in a position where the person who controlled my destiny was going to do that to me.

I did not tell my husband. I internalized everything and I truly believe it caused me major health issues to the extent of having to have three surgeries. I lost part of my intestines from ulcers.

The first time, I did not go to the division president. The second time, when he tried to stick his hand up my skirt, I did go.

It took a tremendous amount of courage doing that, going to the division president—whom we called "Mr. B." It was one thing when the boss kissed me on the cheek, but when he physically tried to stick his hand up my skirt? There was no way I could stand for it. I stood up, put my hand on the doorknob and said to him, "You are crazy. I am not doing this."

The response I got from Mr. B. was, basically, "You're young, you're attractive, things like this happen; we work in a friendly environment, I'll talk to him but don't you think too much about it."

He told me that what happened was 50 percent my fault because I looked pretty good back then. I was five-foot-two, long brown hair and weighed ninety-nine pounds. Mr. B. made me feel like it was my fault!

The thing was, I had never dressed provocatively. Even today, I wear my clothes too big to cover myself up. He made me question who I was. I kept thinking, "I'm not doing anything! I'm not wearing anything low-cut or short!" I've always dressed professional, like a corporate stiffy. It made me insecure and doubt who I was, and it took me years—and I mean years—to get over it. I did not get over it until I turned fifty.

After my meeting, he came into my office and told me he'd heard I went to Mr. B. I said, "I don't want you to think I am going to tolerate that behavior. And, as soon as I can, I am going to another department. I did what I thought I should do to protect myself." He just laughed and said, "All Mr. B. told me to do was keep my zipper up the flagpole." He had a smirk on his face.

I didn't want to work for him, but I couldn't leave the company. It was the best employer where I lived, other than the federal government. I hadn't quite finished college, I had two kids and it was not a viable option to quit.

Remember, that was 1980. There weren't that many opportunities for women. I could not leave. You have to understand that. Women didn't have options like they do today. If it happened today, I would have choices. I had no choices because the opportunities weren't there. My husband was entrenched in his business for a local bank. He had shares in that bank.

I went to another department head and asked to be moved into a sales position. I kept politicking until I was moved out. I just couldn't work for him anymore. I transferred to a sales and marketing position and was gone for a little over a year and a half. In the meantime, he started a full-fledged affair with his secretary, and it was well-known throughout the building. He was going to leave his wife for the secretary, but his wife got breast cancer, so he didn't leave. And the secretary's husband took a transfer to California, so she was out of the picture and he was back in action again. He started hitting on other women.

There was a huge acquisition coming, and the company was sold to the Japanese. For every woman at the company, that was the kiss of death. My department got downsized, so, if I wanted to keep my job, guess where I had to go? I had to go back to work for him.

That was when I told my husband what had happened. The man also lived right around the corner from us, and my husband was his banker. This was a very small town.

The first thing my husband wanted to do was get a gun. I'm not kidding. Then he said I would not be going back to work for the guy and that we would hire an attorney if we needed to. He offered 150 percent support. He never made me feel like it was my fault.

I went to the HR director and told him I couldn't go back to work for him because I would have a nervous breakdown. HR wanted me to file a complaint, but told me I had to go back to work for him. Because I filed the complaint, they started the investigation. I was assured that they were going to fix the situation, and that was the only reason I went back to work for him.

During the investigation, I was told there were other people who had been harassed, but I should not try to find out who they were. We were absolutely not to meet or have any discussions with each other—or we would be terminated. Of course, we didn't listen to that. Once we started talking, we put together bits and pieces and figured out who the other victims were. There were five of us who got together and we did have a discussion. We never did figure out who the two others were.

One of the women hosted a meeting in her home. We seriously considered suing, because that had not been done before. It just wasn't done back then. Nobody had sued a corporation of that size. And, there was so much philandering going on there. It was rampant. It was a lifestyle. Nobody felt it was a case we could win.

One of the women openly admitted having had sex with him because she felt she would be fired if she didn't. She'd had a tough upbringing, and she thought having sex with that man was just something she had to do. It was like, "Okay, somebody is forcing me to do something else. I don't have any choice. I can do it." During the investigation, HR told her that because she was single, it was consensual.

When the investigation concluded, we were called into HR individually and told the results of the investigation. He was let go. They told us he had been dismissed, that he'd been escorted out of the building and that the problem had been handled. Then, we were told to sign a document that said the matter had been handled to our satisfaction. We were told that if we sought any legal action, we would not work in the industry again. That is exactly what the director of HR said.

I think we were happy that he was relieved of his responsibilities, but he walked out with full benefits, his bonus for the year, his profit-sharing, and a pocket full of money. At that point, you lose respect for the company you work for.

Shortly after that, several of us left. We were labeled as troublemakers. I still maintained a friendship with two of the guys in my old department and they finally got brave enough to talk about the situation. They said they'd known what was going on —all of the guys did. They knew all the graphic details.

If you are truly harassed, you never forget it. I am still good friends with one of the women—and we still talk about it even though twenty-seven years have passed.

Young women today do not believe this could happen—but it did, not only at my company, but at many, many companies. It was not uncommon. These are the strides we have made. ■

What moved **Denise Morrison**'s story into pop culture is the bloodline. Corporate success flows through her family's veins, considering Morrison's success and the achievements of her three other sisters. Her sister Maggie Wilderotter is chairman and CEO of Citizens Communications, sister Colleen Bastkowski is regional vice president of sales for Expedia Inc.'s corporate travel division, and sister Andrea Doelling was senior vice president of sales at AT&T Wireless before pursuing her equestrian career and becoming a champion horse jumper.

The "Sullivan Sisters" grew up learning principles of teamwork, strategy, marketing, planning and execution from their parents. Dad taught them profit and loss; mom taught them that ambition was feminine.

The lessons apparently worked.

In 2005, Morrison was made president of Campbell USA at the Campbell Soup Company. She heads a business unit with more than $3 billion in sales, including all U.S. soup, sauces and beverages. Among other things, she is responsible for the U.S. supply chain, marketing, strategy, finance and sales.

She's tracked fast at Nestlé, Kraft, Nabisco and PepsiCo, and boldly lays out her future goals. She wants to be CEO at a Fortune 500 company.

Like mom said, a woman can be ambitious.

23 Find Your North Star
Denise Morrison
President
Campbell USA

Instead of taking us to Disneyland, my father used to take us to the Stock Exchange on Wall Street. He would take us to New York City to go to work with him, long before taking your daughter to work was fashionable. I got excited about business at an early age and I always viewed myself as a leader. It wouldn't be enough for me just to go into an arena and work. I had to be a leader in that arena. It was my expectation.

My parents literally raised us with the opportunities to achieve our full potential. The choice I made very early was that I wanted to run a company. My dad worked for AT&T and the exposure to marketing plans at the dinner table and discussions about boards and discussions about how his day went were very enlightening to me.

One defining moment involved moving from sales director to a business director of marketing at Nestlé confections. It was an unprecedented cross-functional move. It got me on track for general management, instead of being a function leader. I don't know if women are aware of how important it is to move to different tracks. Once you define what you want to be when you grow up, you have to identify the right strategic assignments to get you there. The move into confections marketing was huge.

It was also significant because it was sponsored by the president of Nestlé. He stuck his neck out and said, "I believe you can do this and you can show everyone that it can work." From that, I learned the value of sponsorship and the value of having a very senior executive believe in you.

But it was also a defining moment for me because I ran into the buzz saw of politics. I didn't have the same background as everyone else there. Initially, it was a little chilly. People weren't lining up at the door to congratulate me or help me. I understood where they were coming from. Seek first to understand, then to be understood. I approached the job with humility, not with arrogance, and I told the people that I recognized their experience was beyond mine in some areas, but mine was beyond theirs in some other areas.

I am not, by nature, an insecure person. I felt adventuresome about it. To me, it was another challenge. Knowing that, at one point in my end game, I wanted to run a company, I recognized the value of the experience. I was going for it.

I had to use enormous influencing skills and humility in order to have a positive outcome. I initiated a self-training program. I said, "This is what I know, and this is what I don't know. I will check into manufacturing plants for two weeks and make product and do two very deep orientations with the ad agencies and..." It was a six-month window that brought me up to speed or even beyond because of that extra initiative. That experience taught me that you need to be creative and go beyond the obvious to make something work. You have to admit what you don't know. Six months after I took that position, it was a nonissue. The quicker you learn, the quicker you add value to the business. That was a vital transition for me in shaping my whole approach to leadership and, for lack of a better term, the corporate climb.

I always suggest creating a one-hundred day plan, and having that be a source of dialogue for building relationships so you are enrolling and enlisting key stakeholders as part of your plan. At the close of one hundred days, there should be a checkpoint with yourself where you ask, "What did I set out to do here? What did I accomplish?" I believe that, if you take that time to plan and dialogue about it, you will have the best tool to become more comfortable over the course of the first six months, and you will be getting constant feedback.

Building relationships is equally important to delivering positive results. Networking is working. It is really important to develop relationships with senior executives. You have to be mindful of how you do it. It would be helpful to just understand what kind of opportunities your company offers for you to network or interact with senior executives. I made it a point that whenever there was a project or task force or committee, I raised my hand and said, "I want to do that." Doing that gives you visibility. And visibility over time and over places gets you recognized, and when you get recognized, you have better opportunities to be sponsored.

Another defining moment came when I became chief customer officer for Campbell Soup Company. I'd been with Nabisco, with Kraft after it bought Nabisco, and was an executive vice president and general manager of their snacks business. I was on the operating committee. When Campbell Soup called and offered this position, it gave me a global orientation. It was an opportunity to fine-tune my influence and executive skills. I would be sitting at the table with the CEO and members of the corporate leadership team.

The skills that made me great at operating a division or a business were not necessarily the same skills that would make me successful at being an executive who had to influence and get things done. That was an "Aha!" for me. Because the design of this position was to be the function leader for twenty sales forces across the globe, I had to learn across the company and home in on strategic skills and conceptual thinking to advance the company's agenda. That was different for me. It was a little uncomfortable, but I accepted that it was a great challenge with a lot of excitement.

I was a total road warrior, on a plane 24/7, and it was fascinating. The skills I had were not, in and of themselves, sufficient to make me successful. The skills I had to enhance were about influence and executive skills, in addition to business leadership skills.

The first thing you do to influence others is listen and really understand everyone's point of view. Have a good grasp of the fact base. You need a crystal-clear idea of what you want people to align with you on. Be very clear about how the situation works, how it impacts them and their organization, and really have a dialogue about it to be sure that you are, again, securing alignment along the way. Not necessarily agreement, but alignment. Have clarity around the benefits of your idea and a plan of action that you want them to agree to.

It doesn't always go smoothly. You might have to go back and forth along the continuum a little bit to get closure. Sometimes, the dialogue gets to a better level because you have had the interaction. You really have to take time and energy to influence and get things done.

It is really important to develop a personal mission statement and define your roles and goals. Remember Stephen Covey's "7 Habits"? He has a chapter on how to create a mission statement and manage multiple roles and goals in your life. Reading that book changed my life. I did everything it outlined and updated it at my different life stages. It's been a real North Star for me.

My mission statement is to serve as a leader, lead a balanced life and apply ethical principles to make a significant difference. The fact that I can say that without even reading it shows that it is on the tip of my tongue. It guides me every day.

Ultimately, I want to be CEO of a Fortune 500 company. I think I am on a good track for that. My focus right now is to do the best job I can as president of Campbell USA. I really believe, if I deliver the business and develop and motivate the people and lead, I ultimately will be recognized.

If you can't get up every day and look yourself in the mirror and like what you see, it is a day wasted. You have to have integrity. If you don't have integrity, you can't lead. ■

Leading by the Rule

*T*here is a Jewish version, a Christian version, a Native American version, a Buddhist version, a Shinto version, a Hindu version...

And, a corporate version—of the Golden Rule.

1. Do unto others as you would have them do unto you...

2. Love thy neighbor as thyself...

It plays out every day with the leaders who know that the only way to create "followership" and build formidable teams is by treating people well. So many leaders in this book said the Golden Rule is their compass.

Think about it.

Do you enjoy being yelled at? Treated as though you are less than someone else? Micromanaged? Undermined? Do you like being second-guessed? Stretched too thin? Reminded of all your shortcomings? Do you like killing yourself to contribute, and never hearing a simple "thank you"? Do you mind being paid less than you deserve? Cheated out of the recognition or promotion you've got coming?

Of course not. Nobody likes any of those things.

And yet ...

Managers do that stuff.

All the time.

How hard is it to realize that people are human beings and want to be treated as such?

You can set high standards, tough goals and precise objectives for your people, but you won't get the buy-in for over-the-top performance by forcing it. If you want extra from other people, give a little extra of yourself. Become the kind of leader others naturally want to follow by treating others well—like you want to be treated. People expect and deserve your respect before they will respect you in return.

Believe in your people

If you are conducting the orchestra, you can't go out there and play all the instruments. Why is it that so many managers try to do that with their people? A lot of us have control issues, and it can be hard letting go. You know what you can deliver. You know you can hit a home run. But, if you stock your team with good, capable people, you also have to know that it is their turn to swing the bat and define themselves.

You had your chance. Let your people shine. As a leader, your job is to create the vision and build the buy-in and alignment to make it become real. Your job is not to do all the work. People grow when their leader serves as a teacher and listener. They *suffocate when the "leader" is an unrelenting, domineering, know-it-all boss.*

You do not have to make every decision, even if you know deep down that you could do it faster or better. As your control expands, so does the need for you to let go of things so others are free to define themselves in their own roles. Which leader is better? The one who is so brilliant, insightful and incisive that she can do everything for everyone, or the leader who has the confidence that she has chosen the right people who can handle things for themselves?

It was so interesting hearing the women I interviewed tell me that they had to silence themselves like watchful parents at the sidelines while letting subordinates make the mistakes they had to make in order to grow and develop into stronger, more reliable performers. It's hard to do that, but if you don't, you'll have to hover over every single employee, directing every single move in an effort that ultimately transforms your leadership into impotence.

Is your role to boss, or is it to lead? Bossing may work at the lower levels, but if you want to ascend to the greater positions of influence, your role has to be to lead. So many of the women in this book took jobs in areas where they had no expertise, and they credit their ultimate success to those risky moves. The way they survived and actually succeeded wildly in those situations was by leading people, not managing minutiae. Once you attain a certain level on the hierarchy, it doesn't matter whether you know the technical details. It matters that you know human nature and have the right people around you who do know the details. It matters that your people want to help you succeed because they know you will help them succeed. It matters that you have a vision and can communicate it and build the alignment to execute it.

Also, share the glory—or just give it away. When your people succeed, you succeed. You don't have to put your name on every victory, and when someone else deserves credit, boost them up by sending notes of kudos up the chain.

Appreciate everyone, from the janitor to the CEO

You can't boss people to excellence. You influence them by valuing them.

Time and again, I was told how important it is to value every single person in your organization, from the janitor to the president. Talk to and get to know as many people as you can—at every level. I keep thinking of the story Sara Lee CEO Brenda Barnes tells about her first post-college job—on the night shift at the post office. The bosses were inhumane, and that taught her everything about how not to lead. She knows she is nothing without every level of employee contributing and serving to their greatest potential.

People want to be heard and valued. They want to know that the organization appreciates them and will grow them.

Do the small things to show how much you value your team. Praise. Say thank you. Remember anniversaries, birthdays, and special occasions. Recognize the "whole person" who is coming to work. Get to know their families.

As a newspaper editor, I couldn't understand why other people didn't behave like me. Why would a reporter start writing a story at 6:10 p.m. if it was due twenty minutes later and there was no way he or she would meet deadline? Why would so many people want to linger an extra two hours at work when they could get their work done and leave? Why would they turn in stories they hadn't proofread? Why would anyone do a lousy job on a routine story like a weather story if it was going to be seen by a million readers and his or her name was going right on top of it? Why didn't people take pride in their work?

That lesson—that we aren't all alike—took a long time for me to learn. Several of the women in this book had the same experience and had to learn that people are motivated by different things and inspired in different ways. Good leaders know that and don't try to nudge or push their people into cookie-cutter performers who will deliver the same thing as everybody else. Doing that requires a great deal of good communication and humility.

Influence, rather than boss

You need a better reason for doing something than "Because I said so," even though there are times when you have to be the decider and drop the illusion of management through democracy.

Listen, listen, listen. You'll see that theme in several of the interviews, because some of the women made critical communication errors—by accident. They thought they were simply sharing their opinions, but because they outranked the others who were giving input, their people thought they were shutting down the discussion and the decision was made. Some admit that they made decisions without hearing their people out—and that was to their peril, because their people already had answers that would have prevented bad decisions and the subsequent fallout.

Sometimes it is hard to communicate because subordinates are intimidated by the people who outrank them. I saw that intimidation during the setup process for this book because some of the assistants and handlers for these great leaders were petrified about what I might ask in the interviews. I asked several of the women about the intimidation factor and they said they understand it, but they don't like it. That intimidation makes their jobs more difficult because their people may not feel comfortable enough to give them important information that may be negative or upsetting. They have to work to break down that intimidation so they can get to the truth. They know they aren't always successful at it.

If you are in a position of leadership, recognize that you may be intimidating others just because of your title. I remember being a new bureau reporter at The Miami Herald and getting nervous every time managing editor Vicki Gowler walked into the office. A chill followed her! I am not kidding. I was twenty-six years old and I was intimidated by her position. She broke that down the day I ran in with a huge story that was due in less than an hour. I had to write the story and type in a large chart—but there was too much to do and no time. Gowler walked over to my desk, asked for my notes for the chart and sat down and typed it in herself. Nearly two decades later, I still remember that gesture, because it said everything about how she valued the newspaper, the story, her team—and me.

Communication is easier when you actively leap into the other person's perspective. If you can understand why that person feels and acts the way he or she does, you don't have to force him or her over to your way of thinking. Just ask yourself what your ultimate objective is, then figure a way to create a win-win situation.

Joan Toth is a master of this as the executive director of the Network of Executive Women. We were setting up a panel for the annual summit when one of the participants insisted I give her a list of questions in advance. I said, "I can give you a list, but I won't use it because my panels are more free-flowing."

Joan knew I wanted the freedom to ask good follow-up questions and make my program entertaining. She also knew that this one executive needed to feel prepared in order to be comfortable. So, she thought about the end result. "Fawn, can you give her the questions and help her be more comfortable? Just ask a few from the list? You can be more free-flowing with the other people on the panel, and I am sure once she sees how much fun everyone else is having, she'll loosen up."

I knew I was being played, but I felt valued, and her tactics worked. The participant loosened up, and wound up doing a great job on the panel. Everybody won.

Mentor others, and they will mentor you

I always tell my audiences to remember that the things they know innately as leaders may not come so naturally to everyone else. Are great leaders born, or can they be groomed into excellence? Some people really are born with it. They instinctively know how to treat others and inspire teams to deliver extraordinary results. If you have those instincts, you are very, very lucky. But, don't be a snob about it. Share what you know and empower others so that our influence as women will continue to grow. Ultimately, it will create greater power for you—and all women.

I laugh at the fact that I have made a lot of money exploiting the worst boss I ever had. I tell audiences, "Some people have a mentor. I had a tormentor." And then I tell how the man sat me down and said, "You've gone as far as you are going to go. All you are now is all you are ever going to be—a reporter." Everyone shakes their head knowingly, because just about everybody has had one of those jerk bosses who has thrown up obstacles and tried to derail their success. Many of us have succeeded in *spite of bad leadership.*

I can't help but wonder why some people use cheap and mean power plays to prove their worth. What do they get out of that "Because I said so" garbage? Do they really think they are going to inspire anybody to do their best? Will anyone want to give anything extra?

Long ago, Nobel Peace Prize laureate Betty Williams told me that real leadership "comes from behind." You don't have to stand up front, claiming credit and dragging people along. You bring them with you by standing behind them. You treat them like human beings. You let them know they are valued.

You follow the Golden Rule.

The NEW Woman Rules for leadership are:

Create Followership
- *The most important management principle is the Golden Rule.*
- *Have a crystal-clear idea of what it is that you want people to align with you on.*
- *Don't try to make every decision. You can't be close to every detail as your span of control expands.*
- *Enable your people to think on their own. Let them make mistakes.*
- *Your job is to listen and teach—not tell. If you lead by giving orders, your organization will only be able to achieve what you can process.*
- *Teach people to fish instead of giving them fish. Unless you build capabilities in your organization, you can't replicate any of the results you are creating.*
- *Once you reach a certain level, it is all about leadership. You should be able to lead anything, whether you are an expert in the area—or not.*
- *Don't assume that what drives you is what drives others.*
- *Knowing what motivates an employee helps you to get peak performance from them.*

Build Loyalty
- *Talk to and value everyone from janitor to president.*
- *Help your people grow and expand. People follow people where they know they will grow. Great leaders make them stronger.*
- *You get more when you show that you value somebody's efforts, acknowledge that their work was difficult and refrain from telling them how it could have been improved.*
- *People want to be listened to. They want to be recognized for their accomplishments. They want to be taught.*
- *Remember small things like anniversaries, birthdays, special occasions.*

- *Say thank you—all the time.*
- *Share power.*
- *You can be efficient and get something done yourself, but are you being effective? You need consensus. You need to get people involved.*
- *As a senior executive, learn to lean back in your chair and hope the answer comes out of someone else's mouth.*
- *When the other person flat-out loses on everything in a battle, you end up losing, too.*
- *You don't have to get an A+ in every subject. Have people around you who get the A+ in the subjects that you don't.*
- *Don't hover and micromanage your people. Develop them.*

Communicate as a Leader
- *Speak plainly, keep it simple, and say exactly what you mean.*
- *You don't have to slam your fist on the table. You don't have to swear. But, you can say you are disappointed—and you should.*
- *"Because I said so" does not win leadership points.*
- *Pay attention to your people and don't cut them off with questions or by giving your opinion before they tell you the information that they have that might help you make the right decision.*
- *Develop the win-win mind-set. Always remember your ultimate objective, and get to that without having to prevail in a conflict.*
- *Break down the intimidation to get the truth from your people.*
- *You are never too high up to ask for help. Actually, you are a fool if you don't.*
- *If people want to offer advice, listen to it.*
- *Put yourself in the shoes of your people and figure out what is on their minds.*

Leadership came naturally to **Irene Rosenfeld**. When she was little, she used to don a blazer, put on a tie, pick up her "briefcase" and play going to work. It sounds a little nerdy, and she laughs about it because she also was treasurer of her Brownie troop and captain of the school safety patrol.

It was a preview of what was to come for the woman who is now one of the most powerful businesswomen in the world. "I always felt comfortable being in charge—not because I wanted to use the power of my position but because other people wanted to follow me," she said.

Rosenfeld called within a microsecond of her scheduled interview and did not rush one bit. She was all about giving back so others can find their own success.

24 Be Golden
Irene Rosenfeld
Chief Executive Officer
Kraft Foods Inc.

The most important management principle is the Golden Rule. You learn it very young and it never leaves you. I always say to myself, "If I were on the other side of this situation, how would I want to be treated?" It is as relevant if you are terminating somebody as it is if you are passing on bad news to your boss.

It always comes back to understanding what is important to people. Put yourself in their shoes and imagine what might be on their minds.

One of my defining moments came when we bought Capri Sun. Kraft wasn't approving any small-scale acquisitions, and Capri Sun was small—only a couple hundred million dollars. I was running the beverage business. We'd looked at taking our trademarks into the ready-to-drink format, but we hadn't been very successful. So, we looked around.

We saw a terrific brand called Capri Sun. It had a strong following on the West Coast and it was a great company to buy. Lots of folks said it would never happen. Against all odds, it did.

That process was my first exposure to the board of directors. I had to pitch them. I will never forget the challenge of watching luminaries like Rupert Murdoch and Roger Penske trying to jam their straws into the little pouch. It reminds me of that idea that "everything you need to know you learned in kindergarten."

The owner of Capri Sun was a German man, so it was a terrific opportunity to deal with him, making the points I needed to about what we could do with this family-owned business, convincing him that we could take his little brand and make it into a large and significant national brand. It was doing $60 million in sales at the time, and today it is over $600 million.

When we bought it, I had to meet with the employees who were shell-shocked that this big behemoth of Kraft had bought the company. I needed to convince *them* that *we* were in awe of *them*, that we needed to learn from them—not the other way around.

Every part of this story is about selling. You have to understand your audience. Put on the shoes of your audience and address the issues on their minds. Presenting to the board meant selling them on the fact that this was the right price, that we would be able to sell the product. I had to show how, even though we weren't able to sell our own ready-to-drink product, we could sell Capri Sun. Then, meeting with the employees, I had to agree that they knew something that we didn't. It wasn't the elephant taking over the ant, but the ant triumphing over the elephant. I worked hard to ensure that the elephant did not step on the ant.

When I bought Stacy's Pita Chips, I talked with the owner and basically had the same conversation I'd had at Capri Sun. I shared with her how my team and I had approached the Capri Sun acquisition and I could make her comfortable that Frito-Lay would not overrun her small company.

Those same skills came to play in the most significant final example: the Nabisco acquisition. I remember that first meeting with Nabisco workers. They were worried whether their company would be relocated and wanted to know exactly what Kraft was going to do. I had to reassure them that we valued them and were impressed by what they had done. I showed them what our game plan was for making integration decisions and worked to put them more at ease so they understood what was coming.

In circumstances like that, there is no way to eliminate the uncertainty, but you can manage it by being open about the timeline and the process. They were wishing we could reassure them that they had jobs and wouldn't have to move, but on day one, we weren't in a position to do that. My goal was to be in that position as quickly as possible because the longer the period of uncertainty, the more difficult it is. It is important to be clear about the process and the timeline because it is easier for them to go home at night knowing they will hear in a month—so they don't have to worry every day that "today is the day." A lot of Nabisco employees said how much they appreciated knowing where they stood.

As far as mistakes, it is ironic that one of my biggest mistakes was actually something I got an award for. I led a program in 1998—quite a long time ago—and it was designed to contemporize Kraft and create a new blueprint for the company. I rallied individuals across the organization and there was a lot of energy around it. Everyone was excited about the opportunity to reinvent Kraft, and there were some powerful aspects to it. But I was trying to run this initiative when I was running Kraft Canada and I was based in Canada.

I asked if I could stop leading the effort.

Over time, the initiative lost its way and the idea that was going to transform our company just morphed into a series of ads. From that, I learned that deep cultural transitions take a lot of time. You can't just convince a few people and expect something to stick. You have to constantly communicate it and show how various pieces of the message are supporting the greater effort. I'd won this fabulous Rolex watch and, as far as the CEO was concerned, the initiative was done. But what I learned was that it was hardly done. It barely had begun and it never had been fully understood.

People want to come to work with their minds—and hearts. A key piece of leadership is your ability to be empathetic and authentic. A key piece of that is your being able to keep your ego at the door.

I'd like to believe that people aren't intimidated by me, but I am told that they are. I do my best to put people at ease, but I am a very driven and intense person and I think, at times, that can be intimidating to others. I work hard to remember that I am doing that and remember to put them at ease.

I talk a lot about building capability. I am a very strong proponent of the idea that we should be teaching people to fish rather than giving them fish. Unless we build capabilities in our organization, we can't replicate any of the results we are creating. I've been asked why the strategy I have laid out for Kraft is different from what we have had in the past, and the answer is that this is about *how* to do it—not just what to do. At the end of the day, execution is every bit as important as strategy.

One thing we have to do is learn to toot our own horns. It is important that you make a difference and that others notice the difference you make. In some cases, you have to be the one to let your good work be known. In one of my first managerial roles, the time came for evaluations and one of my employees walked into my office and handed me his. He'd written it himself. He said, "I've done this for you. I have saved you some time."

In a million years, it wouldn't have occurred to me to write my own evaluation. But he'd done a great job of putting himself in his own words. Of course, I had complete editing freedom, but he did me a terrific service and taught me a lot in the process about the value of helping others to understand the value of what you have done and put it into words.

Right now, we have thirteen women leading Fortune 500 companies as CEOs. That is a giant increase from even last year. That's the good news. The bad news is that it is a minuscule percentage—thirteen of 500. And, if you look at female board representation, that is all very, very low. I don't want to minimize how far we have come. We have thirteen women in these roles and nobody is writing about the fact that they are women anymore. That is great.

But we have to figure out how to increase that representation. That is what we have to do now. We are barely getting started. ■

Susan Parker doesn't run from the stories of the tough workplace lessons that humbled her—she embraces them. After all, she learned plenty from them. "If you aren't making mistakes, you aren't stretching yourself," she said. Parker is comfortable in her self, fully being who she is: on task, visionary and very human.

"We hear a lot about life balance, and I prefer to look at our lives as a blend of personal and professional, she said. "I can't come to work at eight o'clock and turn everything off from home. The challenge is bringing all that you are to every situation. You don't have to turn off your heart when you are using your head, or turn your head off when you are using your heart. You come to work with everything that you are."

As SuperValu's chief marketing officer, she directs brand positioning and marketing strategy for the company's portfolio of grocery and pharmacy retail banners, as well as provides support for SuperValu's independent retail customers.

25 Put Customers and Salespeople First
Susan Parker
Chief Marketing Officer
SuperValu

This first story happened when I was with Southwest Airlines for two months. I came into the marketing department as promotions manager, and, as in any company, marketing runs the show. I developed this program where the gate agents would hand out coupons to our customers, giving a discount on their next flight. It takes less than a second to hand out a coupon, and that was no big deal.

Well, I thought it was no big deal.

Not until I got a scathing e-mail from the director of customer service did I understand that the extra second per passenger was a really big deal. The e-mail was in all capital letters and it was like he was yelling at me. I was asking for one second for each of the 127 customers boarding. That added up to more than two minutes, and they had only twenty minutes to deplane, check in and board customers to depart. That one second ate up more than 10 percent of the time between flights! It made the difference between Southwest being an on-time airline or not.

It taught me that something that has little impact on your part can have a huge impact on someone else's. That whole thing unfolded pretty quickly. The demands of retail should be quick and customer-oriented. That was the business model I understood. But, I could no longer say, "I think this is a great idea, let's go do it." It needed to be designed with implementation behind it. The idea had been a very simple promotion with very minimal impact, but that was my perspective. It seemed very insignificant to me, and that is because I didn't understand it from the perspective of the people responsible for delivering customer service.

I messed up. It took me years to recover and build credibility with customer service. If I had done a better job on the front end, it wouldn't have taken so long on the back end. But, they were waiting for the next mess-up.

Today, it is common business practice to hear about integrated teams and collaborative planning. But, it is not a trend. I learned that lesson more than fifteen years ago by learning you can do more harm than good in cultivating customers when you don't work on the execution.

The next story is a happy one for me. It gives purpose to leading people. A couple of years ago, I received a letter at home from an associate who left the company who used to be on my team. It said, "I never thanked you for your help and encouragement when I was going through a tough time in my life." She was talking about a time when she was trying to figure out what to do with her life, when she ultimately left the company.

To this day, I do not know what was going on in her life, but I know it was more personal than professional. She needed someone to talk to and ask questions of— someone who wouldn't judge her. I had to do what was right for the company and that meant requiring more productivity from her. I did it from a compassionate and caring viewpoint. I think she ended up seeing that was the right thing.

She has since come back to the company. The point of the story is that I did not see my work with her as significant, but obviously, it made a difference to her. Often times you are making a huge impact on someone's life when you don't realize it. You have to approach every person and encounter as if you can make a difference—because you can.

Another story. Earlier in my career, I was right out of college and I'd started as a manager in a department store. I was a graduate and I was smart and I was certainly smarter than anyone in the "better women's" department. But I was managing twenty-year veterans who had been working with customers for twenty years. I wanted to run efficient and strong merchandising and tell them how to do a better job. But, I wasn't going to change them. They were going to change me. They had all managed ten managers before me and would manage ten after me. In a situation like that, they are either going to ignore you or they are going to change you, and unless you establish credibility and truly have a better way to build a mousetrap, you aren't going to be effective.

"Because I say so" does not win leadership points. They weren't rebelling but I felt I wasn't being effective. The truth was, I wasn't. As a leader, I didn't start off by listening to learn. I came in looking at management "textbook style." For example, we would get an especially heavy load of new shipments in, and the rolling racks would roll in from the docks needing to get on the floor. My store manager had a directive that all merchandise had to be on the floor within twenty-four hours of receipt, so I was all about following that directive. The seasoned professionals—and I now say that very respectfully—understood that even though the racks rolled in at 10 a.m. and that they could have been hanging the clothes during lunch hour, they knew we had a heavy flow of traffic and that was when we could best serve our customers. They focused on that, versus hanging clothes.

Your priorities have to be set on what is more important to the company. I don't know when the customers and sales don't come first.

A characteristic of the fast-track professional is that he or she is an intentional learner. In the academic world, that means study a lot, take exams, miss some questions, study harder and do better the next time. We sometimes don't give ourselves that freedom in the real world. We have to get 100 every time. Most mistakes are correctable. And, most of the time, 80 percent right is good enough. If you wait to get something 100 percent right, you'll be too late in this fast-paced business world. Your competition will have leapfrogged over you.

That's been hard for me to learn. My mother would always say that, for my father and for me, perfection was *almost* good enough. It was funny then. To this day, I have to self-manage to seek effectiveness—not perfection.

Especially if you are in an analytical or strategic position, there is always more information you can get or another perspective or another projection you can run or more data that can be collected. But, at the end of the day, you have to get solid enough direction to validate your hypothesis and just do it. In the beginning, that made me nervous. But I have learned to get something 80 percent, then go for it.

I can impact business, learn from it and correct, and ultimately be more accurate and effective than by staying in the analysis-until-paralysis mode. Putting something in the marketplace, seeing how it performs and fine-tuning it from there is far more effective than trying to model outside of the market to project within one or two points of accuracy. At the end of the day, the customer is involved and the market is dynamic. You have to be action-oriented. As an inexperienced professional, there is a safer feeling in the planning and forecasting mode. The risk is in the doing. You make peace with risk by taking it.

Be successful wherever you are. While it is a well-accepted sign of success to achieve certain titles or positions, I think we also need to think about whether we are growing and creating opportunities where we are. That is the greater concern I have for up-and-coming women. They wait to be promoted. They wait for a title to suggest that they have arrived and can extend their impact and responsibility.

Throughout of all my mentoring, I have reinforced the idea that growth can happen wherever you are. That's part of being ready for the next position. It is adding value and creating new experiences for yourself within the job you have. Don't wait for a promotion to take on more responsibility.

I was at Southwest Airlines for almost sixteen years. The company is an incredibly flat organization, and the longer you are in your career, the slower the climb because there are fewer positions. I progressed very quickly the first five years, had a nice progression the next five years, then held the same title for the next six years. Yet I expanded three departments and left spending most of my time with executive staff. The point is, I did not wait for a responsibility to be assigned or a project to be given to me. I didn't wait to be promoted to vice president to act like an officer. I saw business opportunities that needed to be pursued, and I pursued them.

So volunteer. That doesn't mean you go and steal somebody else's job and step on somebody else's toes. It means you should understand your capabilities and resources and how you can benefit the company by seeking ways to add more value by going beyond your assigned responsibilities. That's the mark of a change agent. It is giving yourself permission to promote yourself, as opposed to waiting for somebody else to promote you. ■

The truth about the American Dream is that you have to have the dream and then work it hard. **Michele Buck** learned that by watching her father. "That self-made man taught me that if you work hard, you will get the rewards. My destiny is in my own hands," she said. "I continue to expect a lot of myself and expect to work hard to get what I want."

She started babysitting when she was twelve. When she was fourteen, she got her first job as a waitress. Then she worked to cover expenses and finance her undergraduate and graduate education. "I'm proud of that," she said. "That hard work has played a key role throughout my life."

Buck has also worked hard to make time for her three children, despite the demands of her jobs.

"They forced me to take my 80/20 skills to another level. You achieve most of your benefit in 80 percent of your energy. Let the other 20 percent go."

She wanted time with her children not just because they needed her, but because she needed them. That meant changing her philosophy on getting things done. "I had to decide what I could delegate, what I needed to focus on, and what I needed to let go of in order to balance my life. That meant going through every task, all the things I was working on, and setting some parameters."

If she needed to leave the office by six o'clock, she considered what she could take off her list that wouldn't hurt the business. "Obviously, it was not acceptable to say, 'I won't deliver the numbers.' The right answer was that there were a few things that I was spending time on that wouldn't move the needle on the business. And, if they weren't moving the needle, I needed to let them go."

Buck knows her success is driven by the commitment of others, which has given her a keen perspective on leadership that started formulating on the line in a manufacturing plant at Nabisco, where the company then produced Egg Beaters.

26 Stop, Look, Listen
Michele Buck

Senior Vice President, Chief Marketing Officer
U.S. Commercial Group of The Hershey Company

Managing a plant taught me so much about leadership and the ability to motivate and inspire people. It was part of my first general management job with Nabisco. I had marketing, finance, customer marketing and a manufacturing plant directly reporting to me.

When I took over the plant, all of the key metrics were poor. Efficiency was low, manufacturing throughputs were weak, and basically, the plant wasn't functioning effectively or efficiently.

I went to the plant and saw a lot of employees who were not engaged. So I started working the line.

I would get dressed with the hairnet, the white coat, protective goggles and steel-toed black boots. Then I'd get on the line and do one of the manufacturing jobs. People felt like I really wanted to know what it was like in their shoes—and I did. The fact that I would go there and do that was a big deal to them. I'd ask them, individually, "How is it going? What should we change? What can we do better?"

I partnered with the plant manager to put in place a lot of participative management processes to engage the plant employees to own the plant performance. At the end of the shift, they'd go to a room and talk about what went right or wrong on the shift, what they could improve, how we could make them a part of the solution to improving their own output. After working with them for several months, we totally turned around the plant metrics. The employees really came up with most of the solutions on how to make the plant more efficient.

The greatest award I have ever received in my career came when I left that job. Those employees were Teamster employees and the guys in the shop made a frame and one of their wives embroidered a plaque that said, "Congratulations on your new job. Our loss is their gain." I still have that, and it will always be the most special thing I ever got through my work. Those union employees appreciated me that much.

I didn't have a manufacturing background. I couldn't say, "You need to change where you have this person stationed on the line." The value I could add was not technical in nature, but in helping people leverage their knowledge and help them to help themselves.

The higher you go in an organization, the more your success is dependent upon the people in your organization. You have to bring out the best in them. You can't make every decision. You can't be close to every detail as your span of control expands. What you can do to make the biggest impact is hire the right team, get the right people in the right jobs, then motivate and inspire them to bring out the best in them.

By connecting with people, you can drive your business results.

I made a career move to a job where the culture was completely different from what I'd known. I was from a culture where everybody had come from other companies—it was a very heterogeneous, diverse group with different experiences. There was not just one way of doing things. It was, "Let's all share the way we've seen it done and figure out what would work best."

I went from there to the land of inbreeds, where I was the one outsider. Almost all of them had grown up in that division. They all knew each other; there was one way to do things; that was it. When I would question why they were doing something, they looked at me like I had two heads. That was key learning to me. I had taken something very important to me for granted, and that was the cultural environment where I worked. I stayed in that other environment for one and a half years and really learned how important it is to be in an environment that is consistent with your personal values. When you are not, you will feel you are butting your head against the wall every single day.

Now, regarding some of the things I have learned over the years…

One of the biggest challenges we face in the workplace is merchandising our successes. Women tend to be humble about their results—and I am like that, too. We keep our noses to the grindstone and go about making things happen. We aren't as comfortable as men in taking a proactive stand to merchandise our results.

But that is important. Women expect that it is the responsibility of senior managers in the organization to notice their results. But, if there are men who are self-promoting their results and the women are not, who is going to get the attention? It is something I have been coached on. I am still uncomfortable doing it.

I try to manage it by putting together a document on some of the things I am working on and sitting down with senior executives in the company and saying, "Here is what I am doing. What other things should I be doing? Are there other initiatives or opportunities you see that could be driving the business that I should focus on?" So that is the way I am comfortable with it. I don't gloat or put others down, I don't take credit, but I do touch base and show what I am working on.

Regarding office politics, learn who your supporters are and be sure you cultivate those relationships. In every work environment, there will be some people who will connect with you and they will become fans of yours. That is valuable. It is important for your career because they can advance your career, advance your agenda and help you achieve what you think is important. Leveraging that support at a peer or higher level is critically important. Your supporters can help you see your obstacles and help you work through them.

Concerning image, remember to look the part. Too many times, I have seen that if it looks like a duck, it is a duck. If it doesn't look like a duck, people will not believe it is a duck. I have personally coached two female direct reports on topics that were very uncomfortable for me because it was about their personal appearance and how they didn't look the part. It goes from having big hair, long fingernails and too short of a skirt—the gamut. It was very uncomfortable for me, but those women were very talented businesswomen whose substance was undermined by their appearance. I've also had to coach a man on his appearance. He was sloppy. Appearance is a hard thing to coach on.

But is it a female issue? Bottom line is, it is. It is more of a struggle for women than men because we have to maintain our femininity, but only up to a point. For men, it is simpler. There is the suit and the tie. There is a bigger style component for women, and it is a personal issue. Telling a man, "Hey, iron your pants," isn't as personal as telling a woman, "Your skirt is too short and your hair is a little too big." But it is incredibly important because I have seen image undermine women's success. Their substance is questioned. They don't have as much credibility.

Finally, remember that it is a small world. Don't burn bridges. I am working with people I worked with twenty years ago who I didn't see again until we resurfaced in the same spot. Remember, you may be leaving a company today but run into those people years from now. How will you feel if they walk in the door? ■

Linda Dillman remembers the first time she had a one-on-one meeting with Wal-Mart CEO Lee Scott. He asked her how she was doing. That's when it hit her. She'd grown up in a blue-collar town in northern Indiana. Her father was a mailman, her mother was a homemaker and her life was very Midwestern, all-American and average.

And there was Dillman, sitting there with the CEO of the largest corporation in America. "It was like, 'This is not possible. You get up some mornings and think they are going to figure out what they did. That this can't last because it can't be real.' Sometimes I wonder if somebody will call me and tell me they put me in this role by mistake. It is so hard to believe."

Dillman has been on Fortune's list of the fifty most powerful women in America since 2003. She said she did not realize she was extraordinary until it dawned on her that she kept getting difficult assignments and that she could deliver more than she ever thought she could.

As her career raced skyward, she realized there were significant human sacrifices that she wasn't sure she wanted to make. "I don't know that I work any more hours than I did as a programmer, but there is a completely different level of worry and concern," she said. "The higher you go, the fewer people you have with whom you can share concerns. You carry it internally. Plus, you lose your personal freedom because everybody knows who you are—especially when you are in a small town in Arkansas. I am a very private person. I'll do things that I think nobody notices, and then people bring it up. It makes me realize that everything I do is watched."

27 Let Other People Win Too
Linda M. Dillman

Executive Vice President
Risk Management, Benefits and Sustainability
Wal-Mart Stores Inc.

People always ask me how I was able to succeed. My mom says it is because I am stubborn. I never give up. That doesn't mean I don't lose sometimes, but I persevere.

I liked being able to take a business problem and solve it with a system. The time that was the greatest challenge was in 1999, when Wal-Mart acquired a company that was a $10 billion retailer—the second largest retailer in the United Kingdom. I was asked to take the leadership role in converting its systems over to Wal-Mart systems. That was tough because I was taking its very successful system and changing everything. In fact, it was the most difficult thing I have ever done.

I was dealing with geographic and cultural differences, from country to country and company to company. It was high risk, particularly because half of all system conversions fail. It's a heart transplant.

What made it work? Relationships. It always comes down to relationships.

I had to be the bridge between the United Kingdom and the United States. Both groups had to know and believe we were looking out for their best interests and the best interests of the company. There would be differences of opinion, and we would have to resolve them. The only way was to have relationships on both sides.

One of the guys was in charge of managing conversion from the store perspective—getting merchandise in and processed, getting the schedules right, counting and accounting for the cash correctly. It was the more difficult part and it touched a lot of people.

Early on, we recognized the need for us to stay in contact directly, so we scheduled a call every day. If we had nothing to talk about, that was fine. But it was on the schedule every day for a year and a half. That was a shared idea that demonstrated both sides had a high level of commitment. If something appeared to be an issue, it was so much easier to just pick up the phone and deal with it before it went spinning out of control.

It worked, and it taught me plenty.

I came up through the technology side and was CIO for Wal-Mart when I was asked to take on a completely different role in the company. Now, it is risk management, associate benefits and health care—among other things, like our sustainability initiatives and environmental work. This took me away from what I knew: technology. I knew my team because I'd worked in my division for fifteen years.

Suddenly, I went to work where I knew nothing, had no relationships and didn't know the team. What it forced me to do is rely on my leadership ability.

It has worked out, but I went through a period of time when I wasn't sure how it would play out. I gave myself ninety days and said, "For ninety days, I'm not going to make any decisions." I spent a lot of time talking to everybody. Talking to my folks, to leaders in the organization, people outside the organization, and at the end of ninety days, I laid out a strategy. I will never be the expert in these areas. I was an expert in IT. But this time, it comes down to core human leadership.

I believe you should have the best people working for you. Let your brightest people take leadership roles. My job is to listen and teach—not tell. There is a tendency when you are the leader to think you have to give orders. But if that is what you do, then your organization will only be able to achieve what you can process. If you teach and enable them to think on their own—and sometimes that means letting them make mistakes—then the results you receive are multifold what they otherwise would be. Plus, it is a lot more fun.

It is dangerous to get so committed to what you are doing that you stop evaluating whether you are moving in the right direction. You have an opinion about what is right. Sometimes your opinion is right, sometimes it is not.

Sometimes you may believe you are right and you get too entrenched in wanting whatever you are working on to be accomplished your way instead of just figuring out a way to get where you need to go. Figure out the most effective way. There are always multiple ways to solve a single problem.

Sometimes the most effective way is to make sure other people win. They share ownership for what you are trying to make happen.

The first time you have a big success because you allowed somebody else to win, you understand it is easier to win that way. I have never had anyone ask me if I was successful because something was my idea or if I had done it all by myself. You have immense resources around you that can make your mission easier and faster. Use them.

It is a real struggle when you hear people say women have not been given opportunities here at Wal-Mart. It is frustrating because I work side by side with these people every day. We are not perfect—no organization is. But, I have worked with people for fifteen years who have given me amazing opportunities and invested time in me to help me become successful over and over and over again. And there are many women on the executive committee and in leadership who have been given opportunities. Do I believe that a company with nearly a million-and-a-half people has some managers who aren't doing the right thing? Again, we are not perfect. But I have seen so many women do well here and there is so much effort going into developing all types of people.

The issue is the same as with health care. I got a letter from a man asking why we don't offer our people health insurance. We have a million people in our health-care plan.

I guess that is a great lesson about openness and communication. The good and bad of being a company in a small town in a rural area is that our culture was very "heads down, work hard." We didn't go out with our story early. We waited until people beat up on us, and then we thought it would go away. It didn't. We believe that you do something good and you don't talk about it to turn it into a PR event.

But, the truth didn't come out because we didn't put it out there. We've had to learn to open up.

At Wal-Mart, we are very big on servant leadership. It can be very easy to start believing how important you are when you get in leadership positions in a big company. Your job is to make your people successful and remove barriers that exist for them and keep their morale up and going.

You need to go out of your way to realize that you do nothing without the people who are working on the front line. ■

Someone once told **Maureen McGurl** that if she were going to be offended by sexist language, she should change her last name to "McPerson." McGurl laughed. She is a born mentor with a treasure chest full of great stories that tie together a lifetime of mentoring wisdom. She heads human resources at the Stop & Shop Supermarket Company, which employs about eighty-five thousand associates and operates nearly six hundred Stop & Shop and Giant Food supermarkets from Maine to Virginia.

Former Pathmark CEO Eileen Scott said, "You need to interview Maureen, not me. She's *my* mentor."

Now, she's ours.

28 No Fear Here
Maureen McGurl

Executive Vice President, Human Resources
Stop & Shop Supermarket Co.

My parents taught me to treat everybody with dignity and respect. You don't just tolerate differences—you accept them. You don't speak poorly of people. If you don't have something good to say, don't bother saying it. No one owes you anything. Listen to your gut. Have the courage of your convictions. I remember those words, ever so clear. Those lessons played out from the very beginning of my career.

I was twenty-three and responsible for HR at ten supermarkets. I had a math background, and the company wanted to implement a new payroll HR system, which was critical because the guy who was running the old system had a bad heart. They were worried he would pass away and there would be no one to run the payroll.

My God, we were working sixteen- and twenty-hour days trying to get this thing done and, at some point, it came to a vote whether we would implement it at the designated time—or not.

I was the only dissenting vote. My parents taught me to listen to my gut.

Twenty-three years old, and I spoke up. I said, "I don't think we are ready to implement. The system will be too difficult, too costly and too error-prone. We need to do something to automate it more."

You have to have the courage of your convictions. Apparently, I was convincing enough for them to say, "Prove it."

I brought some people together and showed the effort it would take just to enter some transactions into that system. After a few days, they agreed with me. They gave us three more months and they assigned me and a systems analyst to design a contract file that would maintain all the information and drive the transactions. We did it, and we implemented successfully the following January.

That system is still operating in that company today, highly effective and highly efficient—nearly thirty years later! We kept designing bells and whistles to upgrade it, but it was still one of the best systems of its time.

That gave me a lot of credibility in the business. I was noticed by the principals in the company because they were fully engaged in this project. Within nine months, they sent me to the Harvard Program for Management Development. I was only twenty-six years old.

Three years later, I was one woman among all men in powerful jobs, newly promoted as VP of human resources at Pathmark. My father wrote me a letter congratulating me on my promotion after so much hard work. He said, "You are going to have to find a way to be credible. You have got to make an impact there. How are you going to do it?" He told me to pick someone really powerful, and then do something important for that person. He said, "That will make you credible."

He was self-taught. He didn't go to college, and he had three or four jobs in his life. At that time, he was selling cars and my mother was working in a bakery. But he had a lot of insight, and I took his advice.

I looked around and picked the merchandising guy. He needed to reorganize the department and I said, "I will do that work with you." We were an unlikely pair—I was twenty-nine, he was in his mid-fifties. We spent months together and totally reorganized his department by redesigning jobs and rethinking how decisions got made. I went through work sessions with them and dug down into the detail. In this kind of work, you can either move boxes on a chart or really think about how work has to get done and what causes a change in the business. We really got to that level of detail and changed things dramatically.

At the end of it, he had a great organization. It was very effective. And, I gained a lot of credibility in that process. I made great relationships and I got more knowledge about the business. It helped me to establish a credible HR department, which hadn't existed before, and helped me with my partnerships in the business. I put a great team together and we were able to get into the organization, work with it and make things happen.

Another lesson came early on when I was dealing with a union grievance in Philadelphia. I was talking to a night crew chief from one of the supermarkets and a union business agent. I was telling the night crew chief that he was the root cause of a whole bunch of problems in his store. We had significant problems on this night crew. There was a lot of dissent, productivity was low and the biggest part of the problem was how he was leading this team. We were going to take action against him.

The business agent left the room, and it was just me and the crew chief. He wanted to scare me. He leaned forward and pulled a knife out of his boot. He didn't say anything. He was holding it, but he didn't lunge. He just held it there, and he was angry.

I figured I'd better not show him that I was afraid, because it wouldn't have been good for me. I had to be strong.

I looked him in the eye and said, "You need to put that away, or else you are going to have bigger problems." Now, that involved courage and risk-taking. He put the knife away.

When you are afraid, you have to show confidence. People follow people who are confident in what they are doing. They aren't going to follow you if you are unsure, if you don't have a road map somewhere. Today, I deal with things with a lot of confidence because I have all these experiences behind me.

Life is a series of events. Some things we do well, some we don't. It's important to learn from them. If we learn from them, we get better and better and more confident. If you don't admit to a mistake, then you can never get better.

You have to pay attention to perception. Early on in my career, I got some feedback that I could be aloof. The reality is, I am anything but aloof. I am an introvert. But you can't be considered aloof in my kind of work. You have to be considered approachable. You take any feedback and ask yourself, "What should I do with this? How can I make it different?" In my case, I did a number of things. In my job, I go out of my way to talk to people now, to make contact and be more of an extrovert at work. I get on an elevator and I talk to people. I have learned how important it is that we make connections with people. I don't think people can have a lot of trust and confidence in you if there isn't a connection. I like to know who people are, in terms of their families, what is affecting them in their personal lives. I will disclose that to them about me because if I am opening up, they will open up. People aren't going to trust you if you are not trusting them.

Understand that people may be going through difficult life events and might need some help to get through them. I might offload some work, make their schedule more flexible, make them comfortable during that interim period so we can accommodate it. These are problems you help people work through. They are appreciative of it and, in the end, they become more satisfied with their company and their leadership.

There was a union leader who taught me the value of win-win, and she has no idea how she influenced my life. We were in a termination hearing and she looked at me and said, "You know what? This grievance is very justified, but I need to win this one. Maureen, if you win all the time, it ain't good. I have to have credibility to have power. And my power is important—to me and to you." If she didn't have the power and influence to get things done, she would be expendable and unable to influence the workforce.

She taught me so much. You have to make practical decisions and create more win-wins. Because of what she taught me, we developed a give-and-take relationship. That was important. Regarding the termination, she said, "The bottom line is, if he has done it before, he's going to do it again, and next time, there won't be an issue about firing him." So we walked away from the termination. A year later, the guy did the same thing and there was no issue.

My parents were so strong, and the values they taught me have pulled me through my whole life. They taught me so many lessons.

Work hard. Have a strong handshake. Have confidence. And courage. Do what you are afraid to do.

My parents taught me all of those things.

They were my greatest mentors. ■

Cathy Green is forty years old and the COO of Food Lion. She talks fast—so fast that one can't help but wonder if she is in a real hurry. Seriously, COO at age forty? She laughed at the question. "I don't feel like I'm in a hurry. I'm having a blast. I love what I do."

It is obvious. When she was fourteen and too young to get a job, she started her own business: "Clippings by Cathy. Lawns Mowed and Clipped."

"I was always creating opportunities where they didn't exist," she said. She remembers walking neighborhoods and passing out business cards for her little company. Soon, she had more work than she could handle.

"I worked long hours and I learned then how the customer experience was paramount. I'd surprise some of my customers by planting a flower or doing something nontraditional that differentiated me from the other people who mowed lawns."

Green started working in a Hannaford supermarket as a bagger in high school and stayed in the business as she found her footing in leadership.

29 Stretch Yourself
Cathy Green
Chief Operating Officer
Food Lion

The retail industry is more and more peppered with women leaders, but the supermarket industry is traditionally male-dominated. It's ironic, because 72 percent of our customers are women.

I have always liked to lead. At age seven, I was elected president of the "Kids Only" group in our neighborhood. There were ten boys and ten girls. I don't like to think that I was elected because the clubhouse was in my backyard, but maybe I was.

I started as a bagger in a supermarket when I was sixteen years old. You couldn't be a cashier until you were seventeen, so I bagged for a year. I never forgot what it takes to be at the grass roots of any organization. Everybody wants to contribute, whether they are the bagger, the selector in the distribution center, or one of the top leaders in our company. One of my major roles as a leader is to be able to unleash the best in people and create the environment where everyone can contribute.

I was always looking for opportunities to stretch myself as a leader. You can learn the technical aspects of any role, but I took risks and wasn't afraid to assume different positions of responsibility even though I wasn't the best technical expert. I looked to surround myself with people who were, quite frankly, better than I am. People get tripped up thinking they need to be the best technical expert in order to assume a leadership role. Actually, leadership is being the maestro of a lot of technical experts. You need to know your business, but not every single detail. I am a generalist. I don't know every single aspect of the business, but I rely heavily on the people who do have the technical answers.

Part of being able to fast-track is your willingness to take risks, and part of that is your willingness to take on projects that you can put your name on. Create a voice in your organization. You need to have your fingerprint or handprint on something that is different in the organization. Be a change agent. You will be rewarded for your willingness to be bold and go after something.

When there was an opportunity, I jumped on it and continued to learn and grow and ask lots and lots of questions. I am very curious by nature. I wasn't afraid to ask for help and I wasn't afraid to take a stand and make a commitment about something I was passionate about.

I started with Hannaford and spent my first twenty years on the operational side of the business. When Food Lion acquired us, I was asked if I wanted to move back down south. Hannaford was a great organization, and for me to go from a 100-store chain to a 1,200-store chain in the merger was a complex challenge. I came down in a role that was responsible for merchandising and distribution—and I hadn't spent time in either of those areas. Not only that, but I was going into an organization three times the size of my company and doing something where I clearly was not the expert.

But, once you get to a certain level in an organization, it is about leadership. You should be able to lead anything. You have to be able to inspire people and create followership. I believe that part of the reason I am in the role I am in today is my genuineness, my honesty, and my integrity. I care so much about seeing people grow and expand. You will see that people follow people when they know they will grow. Great leaders make them stronger.

I am an only child. Only children excel on every dimension except power. I never had to negotiate at home because I didn't have brothers and sisters. It was a learned behavior for me.

My growth opportunity has been to create "demand with edge." In order for me to bring my full self to work, I had not only to be genuine and caring and passionate, but people had to know when I was disappointed and when they hadn't hit the expectation. I used to care too much about what other people thought, and I wouldn't do anything to damage the relationship with people. But I have gotten more comfortable with the fact that the worst thing that is going to happen is that I will have to clean it up later. It was holding me back before. You have to balance being demanding with being inspirational. You don't lose anything by bringing both of those into your leadership.

I don't have to slam my fist on the table. I don't have to swear. But I can say I am disappointed. Before, I was almost paralyzed by what other people thought. Once I started to try it on and demand with edge, people expected me to play in that space.

You want to be confident, you want to be strong and you want to be aggressive. But, you don't want to be over the top. Try to strike that balance. Relationships are critical to me. Before I learned that, I didn't want to do anything to hurt anyone. But I wasn't creating all the possibilities for the business because I was holding back.

I don't see failure in my career. You could look through my life and say, "You failed there and there and there," but what constitutes failure? If you take what you learned and apply it to the next challenge, is that a failure?

I was a store manager in Wells, Maine. We would triple our business in the summer, and I joked that I needed a "store stretcher" because we were so busy. I could have used a store twice the size. I kept thinking of ways I could drive more sales, and I had this idea. If I couldn't do it in that building, couldn't I put a big circus tent outside and sell products inside the store and out? I was a twenty-four-year-old first-time store manager. I had to get a permit from the town council. I had to put in a $15,000 sidewalk, Muzak and lights and shelving. I had great support from my district manager. But, at the end of September, when we added it all up, well, I say we made a hundred bucks. It's debatable if we even made that.

Someone looking in might say it was a failure. But it gave me broad learning about working with town politics, driving business and bringing a vision to life. You learn from everything. Failure is not an option.

Just learn and grow from experience. ■

Joan Toth stokes the engine for the Network of Executive Women. Her job description says she positions NEW for growth through membership, corporate sponsorship, programming and event execution. In practice, she has grown NEW into a powerhouse, with forty-three national corporate sponsors and eleven regional networking groups. NEW will produce more than fifty events, teleconferences and white papers this year—because Toth is a master at bringing people together and making big things happen.

"Joan was—and is—an industry icon," said Jennie Jones, one of NEW's founders. "She never takes credit. But, in the convenience-store industry, she is still one of the most highly respected women in our channel."

Toth said she preferred not to be interviewed for this book because she didn't think it was her place to stand out front, claiming credit for anything. I asked her, "Joan, would any man ever say that?" And she agreed, no man would. So she agreed to be in the book. I wanted to include her here because I never have seen anyone more adept at handling conflict or difficult personalities. When she leads, people naturally follow.

30 Trust Your Intuition
Joan Toth
Executive Director
Network of Executive Women

When I was in college, I knew I wanted to sell ad space for a living. Coming out of school, I worked on a very small trade association magazine for three years, and then went to *Convenience Store News*. I loved it. I loved the market, the industry, the world of retail and packaged goods.

I have worked with my share of difficult people. You talk about mentors and tormentors? I had a tormentor and I refer to the story as, "The Job I Forgot to Quit." Looking back on it, I don't know how I lasted or why. I learned a lot from that boss, who could be emotionally manipulative, personally offensive—and cruel. My boss really knew how to work me, saying things that made me think I wasn't doing enough, that my standards were low and that I didn't have talent.

At the same time, I was doing really good things. I got recognition from the outside. Women would come up to me at trade shows and say, "I just want to meet you because it is so unusual that you are a woman in this industry and so accomplished at such a young age." I never really took it to heart, but the more I learned about my industry—retail and packaged goods—the more I realized I was an anomaly.

I was promoted several times and, finally, I was publisher of the magazine. I built it to a place it hadn't been before. It was one of the top fifty trade magazines. The year I left, we had record revenues and profits. Publishing is a great, high-margin business to be in—if you are doing it right.

The magazine was acquired three times during the years I was there. After the third time, I couldn't help but be very cynical because all of the acquirers paid top dollar for what we'd created, but they came in acting like we knew nothing about the magazine business. They supposedly automatically knew how to do things better, and I kept having to learn their ways. That was fine. They were the ones with the money who wrote me the check every week. But I couldn't help but wonder: If I had been a man, would it have happened that way?

After the third acquisition, it was the same old story. It was right before Christmas when the magazine was sold and we went to sit down and get our new jobs within the structure. The division president told me I would have a job, but I would have less responsibility. The group publisher job—which is the job I should have had—went to a guy who had been running other industry magazines into the ground. He would be my boss.

I asked why he got the job instead of me and I was told, "We don't know you."

I said, "You know that I have built this business to x revenue and x profitability."
He said, "You clean up nice, but we don't know anything about your performance."
I clean up nice? I was so shocked.

I said, "You know my performance, because that is what you are buying. My performance is this magazine, and you paid top dollar for it. That's my performance. That's what you know."

They didn't know any more about the other guy than they did me. But he was part of the old-boy network, and suddenly that guy was my immediate boss.

I clean up nice. I can still hear those words. Those words marked a turning point in my life. I gave myself permission to take my time and try to figure out what I wanted. All those years, I'd bided my time and worked like a dog.

I stayed on for a year and spent that time busting my butt and delivering gigantic numbers—and clashing with my boss the entire time. After a year, I decided to move to Chicago to be with my then-fiancé, who is now my husband. I told the powers that be that I was leaving, but they wanted me to stay. They gave me a very lucrative but unrewarding position. After a year, I finally realized I just didn't want to do it. It was time, and finally, I said "Adios."

I wondered why I stayed in that job all those years. I asked myself that all the time. It is a very difficult thing to know the difference between moving on and giving up. It is hard to know whether you should continue to stay and fight, or if it is better for you mentally—and career-wise—to leave. What you really have to learn to do is listen to what your gut says.

You have to have a good awareness of what your skills are. It's okay not to be great at everything. Nobody is great at everything. But, you have to know and understand what you are good at, and work as much as you can at what your opportunity areas are. That gives you the power to make changes.

Mind your intuition. *That* is your best mentor.

It pays to develop a highly intuitive sense because you are the only one to whom you are truly accountable. You have to lay your head on your pillow at night and go to sleep. You have to face yourself in the mirror. You have to know, every day, that you are proud of what you did. When the point comes that you aren't happy with your work, you may have to make the hard decision to go. Listen to your gut.

I finally got the power to leave when I realized that my talent was transferable and I had something to offer. Because of my work ethic and my desire to be economically self-sufficient, I knew I was employable and wasn't going to starve. I wanted to take some time off. I had been working nonstop with no more than a week of vacation for eighteen years, and you know what? I wanted to take a break.

I sent out a letter telling my contacts in the industry that I was leaving, and the phone rang the next day with a consulting project that kept me busy for the next year.

So much for taking a break. While I was consulting, I started volunteering for NEW, which had just started up at that point. I was on the first board of directors. We were looking for an executive director and it hit me. I could do this as well as anybody else. Actually, better. I knew the industry, and I saw the parallels between what I was doing as a publisher and what I do as executive director.

The skills sets were exactly the same. I have sales. Selling sponsorships is exactly the same as selling a magazine. You are selling an intangible. Then there is content. The content of a magazine is exactly the same as the content for a conference. And, you have difficult personalities, because you are balancing readers or members on the one side, and the business needs of your sponsors or advertisers on the other.

It was a perfect fit. My heart wasn't in publishing anymore.

My first job at NEW was to get us fiscally sustainable. That was Job One: to get us self-sufficient so we had money to do things. We had plenty of ideas, but unless we had the money—forget it. I was selling a dream for a long time. Now, six years into the process, we really have made tremendous progress and impact.

Over the years, I have learned plenty about working with people and bringing them into the team. Again, it comes down to gut and intuition. You have to ask yourself, "How can I get to win, win, win, win, win with as many different parties as I can, while still being true to myself and having that gut intuition say, 'I can live with this. I can sleep at night—and sleep soundly—knowing that I did the right thing'?"

Selling is all about getting to that win-win point. The reason I have a good reputation in the industry is that I don't sell people short. I make sure that negotiations are win-win and there is benefit for everybody. I have to live with it. I am a firm believer in the Golden Rule.

I also am a firm believer in the saying that, "The toes you step on today may belong to the ass you have to kiss tomorrow."

Just look at a situation. Consider first what you have to do for the business. Second, you get people to buy into that right solution by focusing on what is important to them and what their "win" is in the outcome. You also appeal to them for the greater good, knowing the right thing to do for the business situation at hand.

Validate the players. That means listening to them and trying to incorporate their needs into the solution. I am pretty democratic. People feel they can get heard by me. They may not get their desired outcome, but at least it has been incorporated. The hardest thing happens when you get to the point where you finally have to say, "Okay, there is no more decision by committee here. I'm making the decision and it is standing."

Listen to people and connect. Let them vent. That builds trust and relationships. The higher you rise in your career, the fewer people you will have to do that with. That's the power of NEW. You might not have someone you can shut the door and whine with, or someone you can go to lunch with and complain to. But sometimes you need that. You need a sounding board, even if it is to just express frustration.

One of the nicest compliments I ever got came when one of my employees handed me the fortune from her Chinese fortune cookie. It said, "You never hesitate to make the difficult decisions." She said, "This is you." So, while I never like giving bad news, and I don't like to be the heavy, there are times when that is my role. I think it is easier because I follow my principles. I follow my gut.

And I clean up nice. ■

Sonja Hubbard grew up in the family business, the daughter of a strong, visionary man who made her earn her place on his senior staff. She remembers her last morning with her father, how he guided her through a review of the business, and she wonders if he knew what was coming.

He had to know.

He made sure she was ready. They'd never spent so much time talking about business details, and when he finished, she truly was ready to take charge.

After that day in 1998, Hubbard became CEO of E-Z Mart's 311-store chain. She has had her ups and learned from her downs. She hasn't always done things the way her father would have done them, and she wonders what he'd think. She really wonders.

31 Expect the Unexpected
Sonja Hubbard
Chief Executive Officer
E-Z Mart Stores Inc.

My dad started this business. My dad was a hard worker who raised us to earn our way. He taught us to pitch in and work hard. He taught us business ethics. I don't know what other work I would have done, although I did want to be a Rockette for a while.

I worked summers for him, starting the day after I turned sixteen. I was a receptionist, and he wasn't easy on me. A couple of times, he really hurt my feelings. It took a while to realize that it wasn't a daddy disappointed in his daughter, it was a boss correcting something that didn't go the way he thought it should. But it hurt me more than if he would have just been my boss. I had to just buck up.

I got some of my reprimands publicly—a little more than I should have—but I knew what he was doing. He wanted everyone on the team to know that I'd gotten it just like they did—and they respected that.

There were times when he would demand things that were impossible. We couldn't hit that deadline or reach that goal he'd set, but he insisted, and maybe we didn't quite get there but, because of his pressure and requests, we would get a whole lot closer than if he hadn't pushed us. That's a lesson.

I remember reaching the point where he would call me up and ask me what I would do about a certain situation, such as how I would handle a bank loan. He would truly listen to me, and we were working together as business partners. He didn't always agree with me, but it was rewarding to know that he trusted my judgment.

My father was a private pilot. The morning he went to pick up a plane that had been in the repair shop, he and I reviewed the financial statements. We talked about what he saw as the future of the business and he even told me, "If anything ever happens, this is what I'd like you to do." I was CFO of the company at the time, and it always was his intent for me to take over. There were so many things we went over that morning. We were in the middle of two acquisitions and we talked about how to finance them and make them happen. He talked about an offer to buy the company and said that, if I ever wanted to sell, I shouldn't take the offer. We spent more time going over the future that morning than we had in the prior six months.

And then, he left.

The sheriff called and told my assistant that my father's plane had taken off and it had gone off the radar. They were trying to locate him. She told my husband and he called me over. It was so surreal.

My God, it couldn't have been true—but it was. Two hours passed before they located the plane.

Witnesses said the plane pitched high up and then rolled over and crashed into the ground. There was no attempt to lift the plane up, which suggests he was unconscious. That is kind of a comfort. We really think it was some sort of aneurysm.

He died on a Wednesday.

On Thursday, I was asked what we should do about the acquisitions.

I said, "My father and I talked about that yesterday. We are moving forward."

We had the funeral on Friday.

Monday morning was the day I had to walk in and be strong. We start every Monday with a staff meeting, and I remember putting on one of my most professional suits and thinking, "You've got to be tough." I couldn't sit in his chair. I sat in my chair and told the team, "I appreciate your support. I know where your heart is. We are going to make this work. We are a great team and we are going to continue on."

And, we did. Everybody stepped up to the plate.

It took about a month for me to move into his office. I sat in his chair and we evolved from there. There were several decisions early on—things I knew I was doing that he wouldn't have done or agreed with—but it got to the point where I was comfortable with that.

I am a different leader than he was. Times have changed.

One of those decisions involved closing a store. It was store No. 10—which tells you that it was an early store, and our first store in Texarkana. It was a home-based store, and the people there knew my father. We knew the community. But the store wasn't making money and hadn't for a long time. My father didn't quit. He wouldn't give up on anything. It was, "If we are doing something wrong, let's fix it." But, in my opinion, we'd done everything we could do. The traffic pattern had changed, people had moved and it wasn't going to turn around. I'm a numbers person, and the whole team said there wasn't anything we could do to fix it. Closing that one store was the hardest one for me.

Business turned and got very difficult. We actually went from 525 locations to 311 today. My father would not have liked that, but we have stronger networks, we are much stronger financially, and I think the circumstances would have pushed him to the same place where we are. I don't think we reacted too quickly and, in fact, I wish I'd reacted earlier. I hung onto his philosophy. But I'd close stores and it was like, "Oh we're 100 stores less…" "Oh, we're 150 less…" "Oh, Daddy would not like this." But we've become a different company than we were.

I always look back at what I did wrong. After my dad died, we acquired 125 stores in a period of three months. It was the largest acquisition we'd ever done. We spent a lot on the new stores and needed to go back and reimage our existing locations. If we hadn't updated the stores, I am not sure we would be here today. But I didn't know where to stop. I relied on relationships with some bankers who said, "No problem. We are going to get you money." That was when competitors started selling gas at a low price and the economy tightened. We were leveraged and I was spending a lot out of cash flow based on promises those bankers made. But none of that came to fruition.

I learned very hard that cash is king. You make sure you don't spend money before you have a sure thing. It forced us to sell off some stuff and get rid of some stores. The key mistakes were overleveraging and overspending. And relying on people to keep their word. In business, you should know you don't do something because someone else says they are going to do something—especially if it could jeopardize your financial viability.

In this case, it was a banker we had dealt with for five or six years at the lead bank who had always come through. But the bank had been bought out. This banker was answering to new people and new rules. I should have recognized that. I truly believe he wanted to do the deal. He said, "Go ahead and spend the money." He was going to get me close to $20 million. We spent the money, but the loan didn't happen.

It was awful. But, we had a lead supplier who did our groceries who we'd stopped doing business with—except for the money-order piece, which was small. We needed money and they were the ones who came through for us. They were banking on getting our business back, and they'd been in our same situation themselves. They stepped up and helped us. They gave us the temporary loan, and we would not be in business today if it hadn't been for them. Obviously, we are back doing business with them.

I think, overall, my dad would be pleased. He'd probably say, "I wouldn't have done it that way."

Mentally or subconsciously, I still talk to him. I bounce things around in my head. "Okay, yes or no?"

I had a dream, and in it, he was so real. He said, "You know, I think you need to eliminate some of the review processes in accounting." That was not something he typically would say. But, in the dream, he said we have such good computer analysis now, we could take the data from the store level, analyze it through the computer and find the key errors we need to investigate. The way it is right now, everyone is busy getting data into the system instead of critiquing what the problems are. Well, what he said in the dream makes perfect sense. Did my father really come to tell me that? Or do we do that ourselves—figure things out in our sleep?

Anyhow, we are going to look at doing it.

In the dream, I said, "Where have you been? Why aren't you on my board? I need your input."

It was the most bizarre dream. It is still spinning in my mind. ∎

When **Rosa Stroh** said, "I'm still growing," it was quite clear. The woman really is.

She is honest and open about her own challenges and struggles, sharing her hard-won wisdom because she doesn't want others to have to learn everything the hard way.

During more than two decades with Hershey, she has pushed herself to try things she knew nothing about. She's encountered good bosses, bad bosses, her share of successes and a few mistakes. She has grown into her role as a leader by listening to feedback that might make others cower. It's all a part of the growth process, she said.

"Integrity counts," she said. "I come here to work and I am a good person. I don't like to politick. I don't like to stab anyone in the back. Integrity is the most important thing."

32
Don't Be Afraid to Make a Mistake
Rosa Stroh
VP and Treasurer
The Hershey Company

Things don't just come to you. You have to go after them.

Some people work their entire careers and don't get where they want to be or find a job they want to do. This journey requires character. Disappointments can't destroy you. You can't give up. Some people have it and some people don't. I've had my share of disappointments in my life, and they taught me plenty.

I did not come into the business world with connections, so everything I have done has been by working hard and doing the right thing. I did not know anyone.

I grew up in Ecuador, which is a small country in South America. I never treated myself as a minority because I was fortunate not to feel I was treated that way. I had the same opportunities as anybody else, whether I was Hispanic, white, black or whatever.

I am a bit of a risk-taker. I started in the banking industry and then came to Hershey to work in pension asset management. I had no experience in it, but they hired me, assuming I would grow into it. That's where I tested myself. I knew I had a lot to learn, and even though Hershey did take time developing me in that field, I had to go the extra mile. I wanted to learn quickly and be knowledgeable, so I had to put in the extra time.

I've had a few people whom I didn't enjoy working for, and what I learned was, I didn't want to be like them. I've had more experiences like that than I have had with good mentors, because in my earlier career days, Hershey didn't have a good mentoring program. Now the company has it. I wish I'd had some mentors earlier on, but I worked for some people who were not good bosses, who were so close-minded that they really put you in a spot if you crossed them. It wasn't a good environment. At least it has gotten better.

Some people take risks easier than others do. In the early part of my career, it was hard to make risky decisions. I didn't have any experience, but I had to make the call. I didn't have anything to go on. When things worked out, I felt good that I'd made the right decision. When they didn't, I would second-guess myself. But, we all learn from our mistakes, we learn from our bad decisions, and hopefully the consequences aren't too bad.

Watch what you say. Often times you will talk to peers and people around the company, and remember: Things do travel very fast. Do not talk to anyone about confidential stuff, especially if it is business confidential. Keep it to yourself. People chitchat.

Learn your boundaries and responsibilities.

I've had situations where I solved problems or suggested solutions or needed support in terms of staff—and the bosses didn't want to go along with it. They wanted to put time, money and effort in other areas, and I couldn't do anything. I was carrying a big load, trying to be better, and I needed support and wasn't getting it. You either have to chug along, be patient, or quit and go somewhere else.

I had to learn that it might take longer than I want to achieve all the things I want to achieve. I've had years where the area in which I worked was not valued and we didn't get the support we needed. I had to pull the team together to do more with less. It was a disappointment to see how management perceived us, and it took a lot of time to change things.

I'm naturally impatient, very energetic and want things done yesterday. I had to learn patience the hard way, because there were times when I did not listen well and get all the feedback I should have gotten before making a decision—and the decision was wrong.

I wasn't a good listener. I didn't give the people who worked for me or with me the opportunity to tell me things that would help me, so I made decisions that were not the best. They'd say, "We had it all there for you, but you didn't read it." Instead of letting them tell me the information they thought I needed, I would interrupt and ask ten million questions. I could have made better decisions if I had paid attention to all the information that I had, rather than being in such a hurry. I wanted to be energetic and proactive, not let people come to me and tell me things.

The company gave us tests and evaluations to be better managers. Once, we had to fill out an evaluation and needed to get feedback from subordinates, bosses and also our peers. That's where I learned that my desire to learn so quickly came off as abrasive. It was good for me to see the forms because I needed those around me to support me.

It wasn't that I was rude; it was the way I went about things. So I had a lesson. I was disappointed because it wasn't my intention to be seen like that, but I paid attention to it. I tried to correct myself and be mindful of it because the company gave us those tests to make us better managers of people. Managers who didn't want to make an effort didn't change. But, I knew I should do better and could.

I've learned a lot in this whole growth process, and I hope it helps others.

Don't be afraid to make a mistake. I have people I deal with on a regular basis who are afraid to take a stance because they don't know if it will be popular. They feel uncomfortable if they have to deal with a difference in opinion. We can't all be alike and think alike.

Let other people know what you are doing. You can work so hard and be in your cubicle and nobody knows what you are doing. You have to develop the skills to let them know.

If you are down in the ranks, you have to make a good impression. You want to be yourself, but you have to look at your surroundings. There has to be a match. If you are very casual and your work environment doesn't allow that, you have to change your looks. And you have to ask if you are going to be happy doing that. But you have to worry about appearances.

I make tough decisions, but there is the part of me that says, "Help this person." Help others grow. You don't have to help others, but take the time to do it. You've got to care for the people you work with, and they will care for you. ■

Mary Gendron fought her way as one of the few women in the mechanical engineering program at McGill University in Montreal, doing what her father had done, where he'd done it, just thirty-eight years later. In her third year of the program, she felt ambivalent about what was ahead.

Did she care enough about it to throw her life into it? It didn't feel right.

But she heard a speaker at a conference of the Canadian Engineering Undergraduate Society who changed her life. Industry needs engineers, but society needs translators. The "techno-propellerhead" engineers had immense knowledge, but they couldn't communicate it to anyone else. The speaker said society needed people who could translate what those engineers did and break it down into language that made sense to the business world, lawyers and politicians.

"I thought, 'That's me. My gosh. Thank goodness. I am in the right field. He is talking to me.' "

And that was that. Gendron became the translator of all translators.

33 Remember Your Intent
Mary Gendron

Senior Vice President
IT Infrastructure Shared Services
The Nielsen Co.

I used to figure skate as a kid. I coached as well. You never tell someone, "Don't bend your knee." You say, "Keep your leg straight."

My best experiences have been pulling together a team and putting a challenge in front of them that the company couldn't have gotten over without them. Synergies don't happen by accident. You have to do something.

I have a participative leadership style, which is an attribute that I haven't seen in a lot of male leaders. I think it has a lot to do with confidence and security. How can you capitalize on the strengths of your team so that the team is more than you or they could be individually? It is not all about the leader. It is about getting to the solution that can only come by putting all the people together around the table.

That is a female strength. Men need to know the answer. What I have seen a lot of male leaders do is say, "This is the answer. Tell me why I am not right." They break it down, rather than pulling together as a team to find the outcome.

My approach is that, by my leading and culling the contributions and knowledge and participation from around the table, I can draw out the strengths from everybody. We can draw all that together and get a better outcome. The team always comes up with a better perspective than I possibly could have on my own.

Men feel they win only when others lose. I see the difference in my daughter and my sons. If you bring that into a completely male-dominated corporate culture, it is all about win-lose. But there is another way of doing things. It is hard to introduce that new philosophy when there aren't a lot of women in leadership positions.

But there is an art when working with people with a win-lose mind-set. What I try to do is come back to the intent or the objective that has put us across the table from each other. I really, really work hard at seeing what we are trying to achieve. There is often a second agenda or motivation at play, but if I can get it back to the original intent, the second agenda gets muted. You always have to remind yourself of what your intent is. What is your objective?

I'm in IT, so I am always negotiating something here. I am always negotiating with hardware vendors, software vendors and system integrators. A lot of our reliance is on third parties, so when I go in, I figure out what my organization needs, what I am trying to achieve from the outcome. I go in from the position that the guy across the table gets something from it as well. I can't drive a price to the point where I am his worst contract, because that doesn't pay me at the end of the day. Sometimes, he will put something in that I don't need, but it does not take value away from my company. It doesn't do us any harm. And then it makes it a good deal for him and for me.

I've seen other negotiating tactics that are all about one side of the table, and I've probably done a few deals like that. I've probably gotten to the point where the vendor is losing. When the vendor loses, believe me, you end up losing, too.

What I expect from everybody is intellectual stimulation, courage, dependability, judgment, initiative and respect. Above all, you have to respect yourself and others.

I am a big believer in diversity—not just about race or religion—but in thought. It is creating an environment that allows for constructive criticism and differing perspectives. That is the ultimate in making diversity work. People who understand that get more value out of their teams. Diversity means engaging different perspectives and experiences, and bringing those differences together to produce something of value.

Be forthright. Make real connections with people. Those are huge strengths. Men like to keep it cold sometimes, but I'm not afraid to connect. People are not machines. I always remember that the people around me have families in the community and values that go well beyond their 8-to-5 jobs.

We are all so much more than our jobs. I have had to learn about balancing all of that in my own life.

I was lucky to hear Coretta Scott King speak when I was pregnant with my first child. I love my work—I am passionate about it. I was eight months pregnant and was still working eighty hours a week. I didn't know what I was going to do after the baby came. How was I going to handle it all? Baby? Mother? Professional? Wife?

There was a question from the floor asking Mrs. King how she balanced "the cause" with being a mother and a wife. She said something like, "I am assuming you are defining balance as equal parts and separate parts. I think that is a mistake. I never think of myself as separate parts. For me, I am made up of things that support the cause, being a wife and being a mother. Balance is learning how to live with all of these dimensions."

That was beautiful to me. I realized I didn't have to figure out how to switch on and off how to be a mother, be a wife or be a business person. It was all me. I just had to extend myself to include being a mother. I'd felt like people were forcing me to make a choice, one or the other, this or that, right or wrong, bad or good. She framed it so I didn't have to choose. I could figure it out. I could be who I wanted to be and my children and husband would love me for who I am. If that sounds easy, it is not. But the idea of switching it on and off left me on that day.

This notion of quality time is a bit of a joke. Yeah, I spend quality time with my children, but I want to spend the "not quality" time with them, too. As a working mother, that is hard. I want the normal time. I don't want to just show up at the math awards and performances. The regular time is easy to undervalue. The special times are the regular days. But, what I have come to learn is that my presence in their life is there all the time. The issue is my need to interact with them more. That has a stronger pull.

My work is very demanding, and my guilt over the children is mine—not theirs. My husband is a stay-at-home dad, so I don't feel that my children are missing out. But sometimes I feel guilty about me—I want more time with them—for me. But, when I see how happy and healthy and blessed they are, I don't have second thoughts.

I make decisions, and if they turn out—great. If they don't, I move on. That goes for my personal life and my professional life. I don't live with regrets. Why bother? ■

Networking *Is* Working

Okay, I have to confess that I stole the title of this section from Campbell USA President Denise Morrison, who knows something about this.

Networking is working.

How right is that? It is a part of your job—a critical part of your job if you want to move ahead.

In almost every interview, the leaders in this book said performance only gets you in the game. Relationships make you a player.

You must deliver results, but you can't maximize the return on your performance if you aren't connecting with the right people and advertising your results so they can be leveraged.

Deloitte's Tara Weiner has made up a profound parable about how men bond in their tribal dance and women are too impatient to learn the dance and do that kind of bonding. The point isn't that the dance makes rain fall from the sky. It doesn't. But the dance leads to the bonding, and that is where the power is. We have to learn to do the dance by doing the bonding.

You can go through most of the interviews in this book and see how some people have learned that lesson the hard way. They didn't treat networking as part of the job, and they suffered for it. Those who knew they had to hobnob enjoyed the benefits of their mingling.

It's not what you know, it's who you know.

That tired old cliché was true the first time somebody said it and it is true a billion times later. It will always be true.

How many times have you seen a less capable and less worthy individual get a job, assignment or promotion over someone far more deserving? It happens all the time. Why does it happen? Because somebody knows somebody. People go to the people they know, time and again. They may just be doing a favor. But, often times, they do it because the person they know gives them a level of comfort and security that they can't have with an unknown player. Plus, they tap the person that is right there in their mind, and that is often the person they know best.

Beyond the fact that networking is working, networking is also work. It is hard. It means starting conversations with strangers and building connections when you would rather be doing something more enjoyable somewhere else. This kind of work is often done on your own time, and because you don't have that much free time, you might not want to make the sacrifice.

Sometimes it is very easy to click with an individual and bring them into your network. You have a lot in common, your personalities jell, and it all works just great. But there will be occasions when you have to build relationships with people with whom you have nothing in common.

Kraft's Mary Beth West tells of working with a man who was so unlike her that they shared only two things in common: First, he grew up in the town next to hers, and second, he liked softball. She built a relationship with him based on those two little things, and she wound up working with him three different times. The lesson there is that you have to make the effort to connect if it doesn't happen naturally.

I bonded with Bacardi's Jeri Dunn when she told me that she would rather give a speech to two thousand people than make small talk at a cocktail party. Small talk is painful to some of us.

Fortunately, Bobbie O'Hare's interview is chock-full of tips (and even a script you can rely on) that will help you to start and build the relationships you need in order to expand your network. I've been practicing what she taught me, and now I feel like the prom queen.

Finally, as you build your network, learn to lean on your sisters. Let your sisters lean on you. Look how far we have come as women. There was a time when many, many women saw other women as their competitors.

It was as if women were allotted one slice of the success pie, and if you got that slice, I wouldn't get any. So, instead of banding together to create more pie, we fought against each other to get that one slice for ourselves.

But, as more women advanced higher and higher, our share of the pie did grow. In the past decade, talk about women competing against women has really diminished. We are now positioned to create more opportunities for success for each other, and we are starting to really see and mine the power of our network.

Don't be intimidated as you do this. Being a journalist, I am never intimidated or even awed by title or position. That helps me to connect and build relationships with successful and famous people, because I don't view them as any better or worse than I. It frees me to tell good jokes. To ask them to lunch. To send them personal e-mails or hug them. I remember the first time I interviewed General Claudia Kennedy (the U.S. Army's first female three-star general) in the Pentagon and turned her into my friend. She invited me to her wedding and visited me in Florida. And yet, think of how many people missed out on this great woman's friendship because they were too chicken to seek it out. Try to operate in an intimidation-free zone. You can show respect for an individual's position and accomplishments without falling all over yourself and sacrificing the dignity that comes by knowing you are equal to everyone, regardless of what they have accomplished.

Granted, that will take a little practice. But remember this: People in positions of great power also are in positions that leave them isolated and lonely. I am thinking of four senior, senior executives who have confided their troubles to me and told me that they don't have anyone to talk to. Well, they can talk to me. I'll listen. And put yourself in a position where they can talk to you. They might not share work-related confidences, but they will appreciate the chance to talk to another good human being who isn't all giddy and gooey about meeting someone of their stature.

It's all about the network.

We used to complain (and still complain) about the Old Boys' Club, but that old network was pretty effective. It guarded an ugly status quo for way too long, and effectively shut women and minorities out of opportunities for generations. Well, the sisters have moved up and are diversifying the ranks. Still, you can't take advantage of the opportunities they can create for you if you a) don't know the right people, b) don't cultivate those relationships and c) don't tell them what you need from them.

We were raised not to make others uncomfortable, so we fear asking for favors because we don't want to put anybody out. But, people like doing favors for other people. It makes them feel valuable and worthy. It's almost like you are doing them a favor by asking for a favor.

Seriously, what is the worst thing that can happen if you ask someone for help? They won't help you. But, for all the times I have asked, I have only had one person shut me down—and that experience said a whole lot more about her for being nasty than it did about me for asking for an assist. In every other instance, I have been blessed with mentoring, great advice, a hand up and a push forward. Every single time, it created a greater, stronger relationship with the person who helped me.

So if you need guidance, ask for guidance. If you need a recommendation, ask for a recommendation. If you need a job, for goodness' sake, ask for a job. Why did the Old Boys' Club work so well for so long? Because the old boys worked it. It is time for us to start working our own network. By leveraging its power, we create power. By giving other women opportunities, we clear the way for our own opportunities to grow. By supporting others, we gain their support.

It is all very, very simple.

The NEW Woman Rules on networking:

- Networking *is* working.
- Remember who helped you advance in your career. Maintain contact and continue to thank them for their help.
- Because so much comes down to getting with the right people, figure out who the right people are and network them.
- You can build a connection with any individual on some level, even if it seems you have nothing in common.

- It is critical to spend time with colleagues in an environment that is not work-related. You probably have other things you'd rather do, but you have to do this.
- Visibility over time and places gets you recognized. The more you are recognized, the more opportunities you have to be sponsored.
- Practice talking to strangers and make connections.
- As you meet people, collect their business cards and keep those relationships active with e-mail. Send them updates about what you are doing.
- Recognize that other people are uncomfortable in some networking situations, too. They appreciate your approaching them or inviting them to join you at the table.
- Inclusion gives you exposure. Inclusion gives you opportunities. It is what makes you grow and moves you along.
- You have to toot your own horn because your managers won't notice everything you do, and other people will take credit for things they didn't do.

"Tell me about your year." **Tara Weiner** wasn't prepared for the question from the partner in her performance review at Deloitte. Why did he want her to tell him about her year? She figured he should have already known what she'd done. She made her thoughts known.

"I was fired up about it. Later that night, we were having a party and I heard that partner wanted to see me. I thought word had gotten out that I'd been insolent. When I saw him, I asked if I was fired. He said, 'You made me think. I spend a lot of time putting out fires. I'd better make sure I know who my contributors are. So I should know who you are. But with several hundred people as part of my group, I don't have the opportunity to know you as well as you do. My advice to you is to know yourself best. Be your best advocate, and be ready to communicate to me your contributions.' That was such an important lesson."

Weiner says she will talk to a group of women and ask them to raise their hand if they think that they will be recognized if they keep their heads down and do great jobs. Ninety percent will raise their hands. Then she will ask how many have seen a colleague who hasn't done such a great job be recognized and rewarded— even though he or she didn't deserve it. The same ninety percent will raise their hands.

Then she asks the women in the audience how many of them have taken time to communicate their contributions. They don't raise their hands. That is a critical error, she said. "People don't have time to focus on you 100 percent of the time," she said. "You have to communicate your value. You have to say what you want to be considered for. It is not just going to happen around you. That is how it works."

34 Build Strong Relationships
Tara Weiner
National Managing Partner, Philadelphia Office
Deloitte

I think about the visual of men in a tribe, standing in a circle and doing some type of dance. They are dancing and bonding and the women are off to the side, cooking or nursing a child. All of a sudden, a woman says, "I can hunt. I want to break into the circle." The men say, "You have to put on a loincloth." The woman says, "I can't do that. I have to be covered up on top."

The story is not about the tribe. It's about us, making our way.

Remember us in the '80s? Remember those bow-tie things we wore? We were dressing like men. We put the suit on, and the fabric was horrible. For a while, we could do that to fit in. But then we said we couldn't.

So, women watched men in that circle doing their dance for a hundred years, and they hadn't made it rain yet. We watched it for so long and figured it was a waste of time in that rain dance. We figured, "I don't need to be in this getting-ready-for-the-hunt dance, or make-it-rain dance. I can go hunt and get something and, while they are still in their circle, I can come back with what I have hunted and feed the kids while they are still in their circle."

Then it hit us. We missed what was really going on in the circle. The elders were putting their arms around the younger men. In that ritual, they were bonding. They were teaching them the dancing, the rituals, the rules. It was all unspoken, but a very natural thing for one generation bringing up the next generation, teaching them bonding and making them a part of the circle.

Women trying to do it all were not recognizing what was occurring in that bonding ritual. We had to give time for bonding and blending of those rituals. It was not a waste of time.

How many times do I want to skip a meeting because I know we won't get anything done? We forget that, in that waste of time, we might be spending time with key people, building relationships with key folks. Those relationships are critical. That's a natural network for which women have often neglected to make time.

The other thing going on in that circle was one generation automatically bringing along the next generation. That has been done forever by men, and it is something women are now doing. Not only am I a mentor, but I am particularly focused on my role as a more senior woman because, if not me, who? I make sure I am reaching out and putting my arm around the next generation of women to help them in that tribal dance so they can see past the moment and see through their passages so they can have it all over a lifetime, and not have mutually exclusive choices in front of them.

I challenge myself to pay heed to that. I'll say to myself, "Tara. Tribal dance. Get to that meeting."

My perspective comes from an organization that has had a very male-dominated architecture. I had a much-accelerated path to partner. I worked double-time on my career, with a singular focus and dimension in my life. During that time of rapid advancement, my stepfather had a heart-related ailment. I would fly back and forth to my family from different parts of the world to see how he was doing. I made partner shortly after he passed away.

I was thirty years old when I made partner. My stepfather was sixty-two when he died. It made me realize how life can go too fast. I didn't want to look back and say, "I wish I'd realized how important the rest of my life was." You can't just turn your life into a career in pursuit of a career.

That was a defining moment for me. I needed to take stock of my life and where I wanted to be in the next ten years. I told myself, "Tara, this is a marathon. This is not a sprint. If I am going to be whole and have all the dimensions of my life be meaningful, where am I going to spend the next seven or eight years?" My family connections were very important to me. I made a personal decision to give up everything I had built and be a part of the team to develop the Philadelphia marketplace. I would give up the comfort and stature I had in Boston, and if the firm would not support my decision, I would make changes. I was going to be near my family. I'd made up my mind.

Telling the partners was like an out-of-body experience. It was, "Thank you for making me your first female partner after eight years on a track that is normally twelve. I think there are needs in Philadelphia where I can be of great value …" They looked at me and it was, "What are you doing? Have you given this the right level of thought and consideration?" They were forming a new team in Philadelphia, and I knew it would be the best time for me to start over, rebuild my credibility and rebuild my relationships with the marketplace and clients.

After that meeting, they didn't get back to me. I asked what was going on and they said, "We were hoping you would get over this."

I said, "This is a decision I have made. You need to help me achieve this." And Deloitte did.

It was difficult. I was in Boston, a young woman, breaking all the rules, someone they could put on their largest, most demanding Fortune 500 clients. I was on planes going all around the world. I felt different. Special. There were all these accolades. Female partner, fast track. And then I opted to go to a practice where the last thing they wanted was another partner. It was in rebuild mode.

One of the senior partners in Philadelphia took me to lunch and said, "I've heard good things about you nationally, but we have a pie here. We have very little interest in slicing it thinner. What matters now is purely your competence as a partner and what you put on the table. You have to get in there and deliver with the best of them."

He was right. I told him, "Don't give me any of your existing clients. Let me go out and build and add additional resources to the firm. If it doesn't work, it doesn't work."

I am still here in Philadelphia in this practice. Now I am the managing partner. All careers have elements of both sprint and marathon; it's important to recognize and manage what stage you're in, and recognize that the tribal dance will be critical in different ways during each phase. Sometimes you want to be a trailblazer, and other times you need a smooth, open road. But in either case, choosing organizations that get it, support it and advance it are critical to our success as professionals, and as women. ■

Bobbie O'Hare likes to call herself a "connector," because that is exactly what she is. She is a networker who knows how to reach out to one side and connect it with the other in order to make her vision come to life.

O'Hare is the force behind the Network of Executive Women's startlingly successful regional effort. She was the one who wondered why the infrastructure wasn't in place for regional meetings in New England. She made it happen there, then started reaching out and connecting one side with the other so NEW now boasts eleven regional groups. By the end of 2008, that number is expected to reach seventeen, with one international chapter.

It was all about the networking, and O'Hare—who is chair of regional development for NEW—knows how to network.

She joined her husband's family business—Johnson, O'Hare—in 1987. She was named vice president of business development for the independent sales and marketing organization in 2002 and is responsible for strategies for business development and public relations.

35 Have a Plan
Bobbie O'Hare
Vice President of Business Development
Johnson, O'Hare Companies

I love people. I love connecting people and I love giving back. Networking was a really good fit for me. It is innate. It is in my DNA. It's who I am.

I talked to a woman at one of our events who told me, "Bobbie, I'm not good at networking."

It surprised me because she was gregarious. I said, "You have three children?"

She said, "Yes."

I said, "Who do you know at your children's school? Do you know the principal?"

She said, "Yes."

"The teachers?"

"Yes."

"The school nurse?"

"Yes."

"The librarian?"

"Yes."

"The janitor?"

"Uh, yes."

"See? You do that at the school, but that's not what you are doing at work. You do that for your kids, but you now need to do that for yourself professionally. Networking is work."

I am willing to go up to a stranger and stick out my hand and say, "I haven't met you yet. My name is Bobbie O'Hare." You learn to do that over time. If you can become comfortable with doing that, you will meet a lot of really fascinating people.

Mostly, you need to understand that a lot of people are uncomfortable, too. You may not enjoy parties where you don't know many people, but those are usually safe environments because the people there must be nice or they wouldn't have been invited. So reach out and meet someone new. Do it on a personal level, which is not threatening. Ask, "Where do you live? How many sisters do you have?"

The six degrees of separation really exist. So, it is a matter of taking the risk and putting your hand out there and saying, "Hi. I'm Bobbie. I live down the street." And you need an elevator speech.

When I go play golf, my intro is: "I am not the best golfer in the world, but I'm a really nice person. I understand the etiquette. I play fast."

We just went to a wedding in San Francisco. It was: "I'm Bobbie O'Hare. We are family friends of the groom and we are from Boston. My son grew up with Carson and Jennifer." That opened the conversation and gave them some context.

Getting out of a conversation, that's harder. You need to be honest about it without being hurtful. You can say, "I need to run to the ladies' room," but that is kind of cheap. It is better to say something like, "It was great talking with you. I'm going to try and catch up with the people I came with." If you are nice, people totally understand.

Also, I never leave anybody when they are by themselves and don't know anyone. I will say, "I am going to run over here and talk to so-and-so; would you like to come with me?" That way, if they don't know anyone, you included them—which is important. You haven't left them standing on their own.

Extend yourself. Give of yourself. Give and don't expect to get. It's about sharing and making a connection.

There are a lot of people who are uncomfortable with it. You may be at an event with your friends, but reach out and meet somebody new. It is an opportunity. If you see somebody who is not talking with anybody, go up and introduce yourself. It is all about extending yourself and making the effort. You want to make them feel good and they want to make you feel good because you have reached out to them.

I played golf at the GMA (Grocery Manufacturers of America) and the three people I was to play with didn't show up. I was assigned to the group on the first hole because they needed somebody there. So, I went up to them and said, "You must have pull, being on the first hole." I started talking with one of the guys and I mentioned I was one of six girls, and then he said he had three daughters. In those situations, you just keep asking questions until you find one commonality. I finally asked, "Who do you work for?" And he said, "I work for Safeway." "Oh, what do you do there?" "I am the CFO." And the two men in the foursome? They were the CFO and the CEO of Kellogg's.

We had so much fun that day. When we came back, my friends were like, "You played golf with them?" You make connections on a personal level. Everybody is a person before they are a title.

The story gets better. The CFO at Safeway showed up at the cocktail party later. I saw him and said, "Do you have anybody to sit with?" He said, "Actually, I don't." I said, "Why don't you sit with us?" And he did. We had a wonderful time with him and his wife and the rest of our guests.

People want to be approached. At another event, one of the most senior-level women in America came in and I said, "Do you have anyone to sit with?" She didn't. "Sit with us." She and her husband joined us for dinner.

See, when you are a nice person and reach out, people appreciate it.

Women expect to be noticed for our hard work, and we don't shine our own light as much as we should. I don't mean you should brag or be self-serving, but let people know what you are doing.

If you are in finance and you are interested in moving to marketing, you need to tell somebody. Because, when the discussion comes up in the boardroom or the executive suite, someone needs to say, "Oh, Sally Jackson says she would like to do that." Nobody will say that if they haven't been networked.

One thing we do as women is think we have to do everything perfectly, and I think this creates obstacles for us. Because of that, it makes us less likely to have a "reach goal" or accept a challenge. We think we have to be the best, but we don't have to be. We can learn really well as we go.

Mentors are so important because they get you to the next level. It is so huge to build alliances and relationships. Having vision is huge, too, but you have to have goals with it. Lots of people have vision, but if you don't have goals and an action plan, you won't go anywhere.

I left college in my junior year because I had a great job offer with Senator Lloyd Bentsen on Capitol Hill in Washington, D.C. I kept planning to go back to school, but I didn't—not until I was fifty-one years old. For all those years, it was always in the back of my mind as something I hadn't finished. I had the vision that I would do it, but I didn't.

Finally, I made up my mind. You've got to have the action plan.

I didn't have a formal financial background, and I wanted it. I hadn't taken economics and I felt that was a part of my background that was lacking. I wanted to complete my education, so I got in an MBA program without finishing my undergraduate degree.

I was the second-oldest person in the class, but I learned you really can compete with all ages. Age is only in your mind. Experience counts in the long run. The combination of naïve enthusiasm and experience in the classroom is a win-win for all. However, staying up at two and three in the morning is much more difficult when you are fifty-one. It is a different mind-set to suddenly be a student and write papers.

One of the formulas in the finance textbook was complicated and very hard to understand. I was working with a tutor and decided that we should rewrite that section, which we did. It finally made sense. I went to the finance professor and shared it with her and she said, "You're right. This is much better." I said, "I am happy to share this with the class," so she did.

Some of the kids came up to me and said they were surprised I'd share it. I asked, "Aren't we all here to learn? Isn't that what it is all about?" For some people, an endeavor is all about themselves. For other people, it is not. Leaders are the ones who know that when they have the opportunity to help others, they should.

Later on, I was awarded the Pat Miller Memorial Award from my classmates, as a student who demonstrated leadership qualities by making a difference in the lives of other students.

That meant everything to me. Everything. ∎

Sandy Grimes has studied the science of the business model and turned it into an art.

She figures it works just about anywhere.

Her college-age daughter needs to get a professor's recommendation into a special study-abroad program, and Grimes has mentored her to use the model to build trust and alignment to make it happen. She told her to figure out the professor's goals for the class and learn what papers he is working on. Is there anything he is doing that aligns to the program abroad? Then she advised her daughter to tell the professor, "I heard you say this. I know this is important to that project abroad; can I help you on your project?"

Grimes goes on with the example, but it proves her point: The business model is not complicated by any stretch. It works at any level, in any environment.

Learn it, then win.

36 Sandy Grimes

Never Count People Out—Especially Women

Vice President, Sales
Johnson & Johnson

The business model is a simple model. You just have to learn it—then use it.

Figuring it out was a turning point for me. It really is easy. It is this: You build trust, use good communication skills, and create alignment with the goals and objectives of others. Know what they need to accomplish and what you need to accomplish. Find the sweet spot, and know how you will grow the other person's business or career, then execute and follow up.

I have used it as a rep, as a manager, district manager, regional manager, national sales manager, vice president in three different VP jobs. It works everywhere.

Every person I deal with is looking for certain things from me: that I am consistent, I'm honest, and I do what I say I am going to do—good and bad. Following up is incredibly important for building trust.

You don't say, "Trust me." You earn it. Then have a group that will take the hill for you. There have been a number of people who have come with me, no matter where I have gone. They enjoy working with my leadership, feel that I help their careers grow and that I expose them to the right people. That type of trust is earned.

I have been here at Johnson & Johnson for thirty years. When I got here, there were some women who used a different style to be successful. I don't want to call it sleazy, but the women who succeeded were articulate, very pushy and very attractive, and usually flirtatious. That wasn't my style.

I went to Catholic schools all of my life. I still have trouble dressing. About the time I came in, there was a class of us dressing like men. We'd wear those stupid bow ties, old polo shirts, and khaki skirts. It was the same look the men had, only it was in women's clothing. I had as many khaki skirts as the men had khaki pants, and just as many blue jackets. That was how we modeled ourselves. We were all trying to figure out what to wear—because we didn't know. It had to evolve. It finally got more relaxed and we got more stylish, fashionable and attractive.

I learned to play golf and I learned to play tennis. While I wasn't great at them, I learned that if I wanted to be included, I needed to assert myself. In my time, it was the only way to be—I hate to say this—one of them. I wasn't the Gloria Steinem "Let's do it our way come hell or high water!" I was more, "If you can't beat them, join them. I will find my own way of being successful by at least being part of the group."

I can remember pushing my way in. It wasn't all totally calculated because I am a social person anyway. But I enjoyed hobnobbing. When you have a lighter level of relationship—a social relationship—and you can combine that with your business acumen, you will be more successful.

I wasn't a core member of the club, but I sure was an invited member. I somehow worked my way in. It wasn't easy.

During the '70s and '80s, the question was, who among us was going to win? I had many disappointments when others—who happened to be men—were promoted over me. I don't think those situations were discrimination as much as they were people making assumptions that I would not move because I had a child. They didn't even come to me and offer me the opportunity.

The truth was, I was not relocatable for a while. My husband had a business and we couldn't relocate. I threw myself into projects, volunteered for projects no one wanted to do, and I traveled. I was constantly in people's faces as a very strong leader with very effective results. And the day came when I told my boss, "I can relocate, and do you mind if I call your boss and say I will go anyplace in the United States or to any other country in the world?" I had to let them know. About thirty to forty-five days passed, and then I got a very large promotion.

What I learned from that is, never count people out—especially women. I understand if they tell me they can't move. But I tell them, "You need to tell me when you are ready to move, or what type of event would get you to consider a relocation." In sales, it is so important to relocate to grow your career. You can't get the experiences you need to be an effective general manager in one location.

Over my career, I always have been diligent to figure out a way to be included so that when they were thinking about who might be able to do this project or that work, they thought about me. Was it because I played golf with them? No, but it was because I was someone they knew, and they knew they could value my intellectual ability, my results, my business acumen, and what I could do. And they knew I was part of the team. I'd become part of the group.

Inclusion gives you exposure. Inclusion gives you opportunities. It is what helps grow people, and it is what helped move me along.

The women moving up now have changed so much. In the last twenty years, we have moved to a much more progressive woman who is balancing a lot. She isn't babyfied or flirtatious. She is a very driven, professional individual who is typically well-groomed, doesn't follow any particular style or fashion, is comfortable with herself, is somewhat conservative, but is comfortable in who she is and is, therefore, very social. She gets along with her peers, subordinates and bosses. It has evolved.

As far as good mentorship, I think that, more often than not, if you ask women who their mentors are, they are men—not women. I am sitting here thinking of all the women I've taken from vice president or director level. Almost every one of them felt her No. 1 mentor had been the CEO or president of the company, who was a male. They had women they were close to, but the people who helped guide them were men—myself included. I had three discussions last week about what I want to do about my next move. All three were with men. All three had been my boss at some point in my career. There aren't many women CEOs or presidents, so as women in leadership changes, so will this.

As women, we have to keep pushing. I don't think we are in a position where we automatically will have diversity and representation. The glass ceiling hasn't been lifted. Everything is not fine. We have to be realistic and stay on top of it. When we set diversity as a core value, it helps raise the bar. It really is up to us to continue to focus on representation.

If we stop what we are doing, we will end up with a very male-dominated organization, once again. We sure don't want that. ■

Carolyn Carl means it when she says she wound up at Coca-Cola by happenstance. There was no big plan. It wasn't a natural fit. She's not a salesperson. She's not a marketer. Those are the core parts of the business, and neither are her strengths.

"The things I bring to the party are not part of the mainstream of what the majority of people in this business do. That's okay. Be clear who you are, yourself. Know what strengths you bring. Figure out what you like to do and move forward with it."

Carl recognized early on that she was not the best consumer marketer there ever was, because she did not enjoy that kind of work. "Don't ask me to come up with the next promotion and advertising campaign," she said with a laugh.

Ask her to figure out how a system works. Here is a woman with a major in biology and a keen sense of how the parts make a system run. That knowledge does matter in the business world. Mining her own strengths, she's made her mark.

37 Take It One Step at a Time
Carolyn Carl
Vice President, Management Systems
The Coca-Cola Company

graduated from college and spent two years ignoring reality. I worked in Yellowstone, went to Europe and suddenly I was hit with the "Oh my goodness, what am I going to do?" moment. I'd been putting off the inevitable and it suddenly dawned on me that I had choices to make about my future. I had to home in on what I wanted to do.

I was putting so much pressure on finding the exact right thing that in the process I was doing nothing.

I was the youngest of four children in a high-achieving, medically oriented family. My father was a doctor, my mother a dietitian, my sister and brother were both doctors and my other brother ended up marrying a doctor. I'd majored in biology and, looking at my future, I did think about medical school. But I didn't have the higher calling you need in order to take care of people.

I will never forget a conversation I finally had with my father. I was distraught because I didn't know what to do with myself. He told me, "It doesn't matter what you do. You just need to pick a path. You can even join the merchant marines. That would be fine." I had ignored it for so long and put so much pressure on that decision. I had thought that one decision would determine everything that would happen in my life. It was as if any decision would be permanent and would affect everything else that would follow—everything.

I should have just stepped down the path of life. You only do it one step at a time.

After we talked, I decided to get my MBA from the University of Virginia. I wanted to help in the health-care arena from a business standpoint. But, back then, there weren't many jobs for MBAs. I had to find a role and a job, and wound up working for a consulting firm. I didn't want to do that because consultants end up selling. I didn't want to be a partner; I wanted to solve problems.

I wanted a change and I had connections through graduate school. You just take a step before waiting to find the ideal situation to do something. Just take the steps, and don't spend energy trying to figure out what other people expect you to do. That was how I wound up at Coca-Cola. It was by happenstance.

Be clear who you are, what strengths you bring and figure out what you like to do. Then move forward with it. My competency is in building organizational capability. If you think of capability as a combination of how things work through a system or process, what people you have and the technology you have to enable it, you see what I do. That is the sweet spot of what my strengths are.

I came to Coke in the fountain side of the business. I found myself caught in the division when the general manager moved on. Somebody new came in and I was associated with the prior regime. I fell out of favor.

I'd only been here for four or five years, but that was a very defining circumstance in terms of growth and realizing how important it is to establish yourself as your own person in your own role—so you don't get caught purely by circumstance. In that situation, I had to make a choice. I could stay where I was and do something there, or I could move to another part of the business that was much more core to the rest of the company. I took the counterintuitive next step because it would give me more experiences that were much broader, and would help me three to five years down the road. It worked out great, and I did learn a lesson: Don't get caught in a situation where you get thrown out because everything from the prior regime gets thrown out. Don't be dependent on the strength of the people above you. It is a powerful lesson.

Be aware if you are aligning yourself with a certain star. You really need to be aligned with multiple stars, particularly in a large organization that is going to continually change. Leaders are going to come and go. The main thing you have is the strength of your reputation, and you build on that day in and day out by the decisions you make.

I do think that perception becomes reality in the absence of anything else. It is important to be active in your own career in understanding how you are being perceived. That means asking your employer or manager how you are doing. Find out what the perception is. Somebody once told me that exposure far outweighs actual performance. If people are not familiar with your work or who you are, they are going to fill in the blanks themselves. They will make assumptions. Sometimes that may be good. Sometimes it may not be good.

Don't wait for somebody else to define your strengths for you. You bring a lot to the table. Step up with your ideas and solutions. Any leader is glad to have somebody willing to take on more so they don't have to hire more people. That means saying, "This is what we need to do; this is how I am going to do it." Does that mean doing everything yourself? No. If you are able to develop other people to take on more, you don't have to be involved with everything. Find others with the same passions whom you can bring on board to help.

Women tend to want to be 100 percent sure before they do something, whether it involves a discussion or a recommendation or turning in the results of a project. There is an overdelivery mind-set. You really only have to be about 80 percent sure. If you can let go of that overdelivery mind-set and see how far your peers are taking things, you will benefit. There are ways to do more without working at 150 percent of your capacity. It's about the boundaries you want to set. Find other people with the same passion and ideas.

We have a unique culture here. People are attracted to Coke because of what the company stands for. It always lands on the side of doing the right thing. You hear that time and time again. So, being here, you feel like you are part of something a little bit better than your average company. We do wear the Coca-Cola red a lot, but that comes from being proud.

I'm really proud to be here. It all worked out just great. ■

Rose Kleyweg Mitchell, who is exuberant in her love of her work and of her company, admits she has learned plenty about women making their marks in male-dominated workplaces. She certainly has made hers, but she is way too humble about it.

She began her interview session by saying, "I don't know why they want me in the book. I'm a small fry."

Rose, Rose, Rose. Would a man ever say that?

"No," she admits. "No man would say that."

She is approachable, yet edgy—a rose of a woman who has learned to believe in herself by working hard and continuing to move.

38 Work Your Tail Off
Rose Kleyweg Mitchell
Senior Vice President, Education & Governmental Affairs
Hy-Vee Inc.

I was a high school English teacher in a small town in Iowa. I didn't like it because it was too small and isolating—it was lonely. So I applied for a job at the largest school in the state, in Des Moines, and I got the job. I was thrilled, but lo and behold, I didn't like that either.

A lot of teachers have second jobs, but back in the late 1970s, part-time jobs weren't that plentiful. A friend recommended me for a job at a grocery store and I remember going to the interview dressed as professionally as I could in a nice orange linen dress—it was button-down, and it was my favorite.

I said, "Excuse me; I'm looking for Mr. Budd." He said, "Are you Cindy's friend?" I said yes. He said, "You're hired!" It happened right there, aisle two, against the green beans. That was how I got into this wonderful company. That's the story.

It was the most fun job I'd ever had in my life. I'd been a teacher, I'd done factory work, office work, restaurant work, fast-food chicken work, and I'd detasseled corn, which was the worst for teenagers in Iowa because they'd bus us to the fields and we'd pull the tassels off the ears so they'd pollinate. What a nasty job.

But I loved working in that grocery store. I loved the people, the action—everything about it. I couldn't wait until my teaching job ended at four o'clock so I could get in the car and go to the grocery store.

I was about twenty-two years old and nine months into this part-time job when an opening came up at corporate. The posting listed a number of skills—training, knowledge of this or that, and knowledge of accounting—and when I saw that I thought, "Gee, I can't do that," so I forgot all about it. A day after the deadline, Mr. Budd said, "Rose, didn't you see that posting about that training job at corporate? Why didn't you put in for it?" I said, "I didn't think I would get it." He said, "Well, Cindy put in for it. I see you doing that job. We need you there."

Well, I went through three rounds of interviews. They even canceled one of the interviews because there was this raging snowstorm, but there I was, still driving there in a blizzard, and since I was the only one who drove in, I stayed in the home of the human-resources director and played bridge with the family into the night. I got the job.

If Steve Budd hadn't nudged me, I would not be here today. I did not have enough confidence in myself, and I was so fortunate that he did.

I quit teaching. The structure of the public school system was very hard for me at twenty-one years of age. I had students in my classes who were seventeen, eighteen and nineteen years old. One asked me to the prom! So walking out of the classroom was relief. Absolute relief. When I told the principal and some of the teachers, they were sneering, "You're going to work for a grocery store?" as if the teaching profession were so noble and glamorous that I was downgrading myself to work for a grocery company. But the rest of the story is really the American dream. I work for this company, and I love the company so much! I have had so much fun!

When I got promoted, that was a scary moment. I closed the door and cried and thought I couldn't do it. After I got over that pity party, I knew I had to do it. I got a book on instructional design and I did it and it was the most successful thing I ever did. It was the biggest accomplishment that pushed our company forward in terms of training and profitability. It had a huge impact and parts of it are still here today.

Everybody has always had more faith in me than I do in myself, but I always pull it off. I've pulled myself up by the bootstraps really quickly and thought, "Well, you can do that. Just figure it out, Rose. Just figure it out."

I am a kid from a blue-collar family, and the first one to go to college. I just worked my butt off in this business. I was sent out into the field and I was dealing with all men. The executive operations guy, who became the CEO and chairman, told them, "Now guys, we're putting a woman on the road. Mind your manners. Mind your language. Behave." He was protecting me as best he could, and you know, the guys were nothing but supportive and helpful. I was like a sponge. I soaked up everything.

My boss gave me some really good advice. He said, "You'll be out there and you'll have extra time. While you are out there, ask the store people and other supervisors about their jobs. Just learn. Learn everything. Get to know people." That was the best advice I ever got, because when I got promoted, I knew so much about all the departments. I wrote training manuals and I'd really built a base of knowledge that carried me through that assignment.

At some point, I complained that I didn't have a job description. My boss looked at me and asked, "Do you really want a job description? Do you want to be defined that narrowly?" And of course I didn't. So I have avoided that. I get to go everywhere. I do government affairs today. I do food safety. I get to dabble in recycling. I'm so fortunate—I got great advice.

I was the first in everything I have ever done at Hy-Vee. The first woman, the first job of its kind—every single job has been a first. I'm still the first senior VP. I didn't realize the impact of what I was doing until I was going to become an assistant vice president. Then I knew it was going to be a big deal. When I was out in the field, I was just trying to do my thing.

Being a woman helped and it hurt, there is no doubt. Back in my day, I might have been recruited to become a store director. In our company, store director is the position. Even today, it is the No. 1 most desired position. They hire, fire; it's a unique system at Hy-Vee. There are just a handful of spots beyond that job that are desirable. We weren't quite there in the '70s. We got there—to have a woman store director—in the '80s, but I was on a different career path. I am one of those rare birds who was promoted up and was never a store director.

If I were a man, I imagine I'd have been the CEO or EVP by now, just because the opportunities would have been there. There was no woman who seriously moved through the ranks until ten years ago. I have thirty years in. I was just tough enough to hang in there. I can work long hours. I wasn't afraid to work really hard, and I like hard work. I got pretty far anyways, and my salary is on a par. I got "there," although I am just one level short.

That's pretty good for a kid from Sioux City, Iowa. ■

Cristina Benitez is a master of personal definition and redefinition. After college, she taught Spanish. That didn't challenge her, so she went into communications and advertising—even though she didn't know anything about it. Her company had a Hispanic advertising division, and she worked her way up to be senior vice president, where she oversaw accounts with Procter & Gamble. Then she went into direct marketing.

"Time passed, and then it was, 'I'm in my late forties, I'm going to start my own business.' I had clear, almost spiritual feelings that chapter was done and I was ready to move on. I had things to do. I knew something else was on the horizon. One of my mottos is, 'Make it up and make it happen,' So I did."

She founded Lazos Latinos, a specialty Hispanic strategic branding and advertising company in Chicago. The company expanded to include Latinization, which consults with Fortune 500 companies on how to understand and develop their Hispanic employees.

"Two years ago, I started feeling unrest. I knew there was something else coming up because I was no longer getting inspired doing brochures or radio or television commercials," she said. So she wrote the book *Latinization: How Latino Culture Is Transforming the U.S.*, which shows the contributions Latinos are making to the United States.

Ever-changing, ever-ready for the next big adventure.

39 Make Cultural Connections
Cristina Benitez
President
Lazos Latinos

I didn't have mentors when I first started. I had a boss, but nobody who helped move me along. I learned from watching other people and seeing what I needed. I learned by hard knocks.

I learned to take time to hear what others are doing. I had to learn office politics—that over here are the people who are leaders of the company, and over there are the people who wield the control. There are the people whose motives you want to understand. Here is how to support their agendas. Here is how to ask for help. I was afraid to do all of those things. Nobody explained it to me. I didn't understand how important it was to support those people and ask for help. I didn't realize how important it is to make the change agents within the company look good.

I worked at a company in Chicago and didn't understand their corporate culture or play their politics. That is probably one of the reasons my job was downsized. I didn't have clear-cut direction from management about what the expectations were. Because they gave me no expectations, I didn't know how to fulfill them.

I should have spent more time with my boss to work on the goals of the organization with her. I did not go out for drinks after work. I had family agendas that were important to me. It hurt me not to play the social game with people who were important. It is important to develop relationships and see people in an atmosphere that is not always work-related. If you are in a big corporation, you have to play the game. You probably have other things you'd rather do, but you have to pay attention to it. Or do what I did and not be in big corporations anymore.

Our lives today provide us with opportunities to change our passions, and for our passions to evolve. I don't have to stay with a company for however many years it takes to get a gold watch. I have learned that you can have many careers, and can excel in all of them and have passion in all of them.

So much of what I have done has to do with understanding Latinos in this country. I am Latina. The interesting thing is, I don't look Latina. I am pretty Anglo-looking. My mother's background is Welsh and my father is from Puerto Rico. So I stand on both sides of the situation. I look very Anglo, but feel very Latina.

I try to help others understand that there is so much diversity among us. Latinos are from twenty-two countries, and within each country, there is tremendous diversity. The largest percentage here is from Mexico. But they have very interesting and very different cultures throughout Mexico. If someone tells me they are from Ecuador, I'll ask, "Where in Ecuador?" That shows that a) I have a little geography knowledge and b) I am interested in them. It shows I have a true interest in the real Latino culture.

We have a lifestyle that celebrates life. Every time I see Latinos working in a restaurant, planting gardens, having a business meeting, there is a sense of humor and lightness.

The biggest element of the Latino culture, which is very important to us, is our family. Family overrides the bottom line. If something is going on with my family and I have to take care of it, I will do it. Latino families are reluctant to let their kids get out of the nest until they actually marry. They have a hard time letting them leave the nest and go to college. We love socializing. We love getting together with our extended families. We love partying with our families. This is not a common experience for many non-Latinos. But this is a part of the Latino culture—all the time.

To understand us understand our values and life experiences. From that, you build a genuine respect of the diversity between the two cultures.

I have been able to use that cultural understanding to build a business and my understanding of marketing to make me successful.

Marketing taught me a lot about how to present yourself in any environment. Your personal brand is evident in the first seven seconds people see you and get an impression of you. It is important to establish that right in the beginning. Your physical image, voice and delivery all impact the way you communicate with people. Your body language and your posture say a lot about you. You can change it. There are things you can look at and change. You can learn to stand up straighter, move your shoulders back and present.

Think about your personal philosophy and develop a tagline or slogan for yourself. To do that, look at your core values. Some of mine are compassion, respect, curiosity, and passion. Then look at some of your personal attributes. This is exactly what you do when you brand a product. You look at the benefits. The packaging. You look at the presentation. The mission. You go through each one of these segments and then you write down your attributes. Well, I am adventurous, I am creative, I am spirited, I have a sense of humor—so how does this play out? Well, in my case, I am a Type-A personality. That is my DNA. So you go through these attributes and give adjectives to all of them. What kind of packaging am I? I like to be a little trendy, stylish. I tend to dress up a little more than the mainstream does. At home, I am more relaxed.

My tagline evolves. I use it for my personal branding for my business, and for branding my book. Empower, respect and embrace. That includes helping people along, respecting, having compassion. The slogan evolves.

Once you have it, you ask yourself, "How do I promote this?" Well, you just start living it. I start thinking of my tagline, of the different elements of the brand that I like. "Lazos Latinos' mission is to build leadership by embracing, understanding and respecting Latino employees and consumers."

When I created my book, I created a little handout card right away and gave it to people and said, "I am writing a book." That got people interested, and it helped me get interviews with people like Henry Cisneros. You have to learn to talk about yourself in a way that is promotional but not boastful.

Just get out there. I always say, every time you go into a lecture, prepare yourself to ask a question. Prepare to say your name and where you are from. "*I am Cristina Benitez, I am president of Lazos Latinos and I have a book that just came out. I have a question…*" It is a mini advertisement. Always be ready with the next question you can ask. That is an exercise that we all can do. It stretches us.

The other thing is, go up to everybody. Introduce yourself. Say who you are. Don't be afraid to introduce yourself to people. We are all people. It is not that I like networking events, but I can do them. I will say, "I'll stand for this for 45 minutes and make four connections. And I will share something I can do to help each of those people." Titles can be so obtuse when you are introduced, so I will ask, "What was on your desk today? What did you do?" Then you find out what they are involved in. It is important to try to really connect with somebody. Otherwise, you are making small, small, small talk that never ends up going anywhere. ■

Three women started at Procter & Gamble at roughly the same time, back in the day when women at the table may as well have been Martians—women were that rare. **Maria Edelson** started around the same time as two other women featured in this book, Barb Hartman and Helayne Angelus. All three of them talk of how they leaned on each other for support as they blazed a trail in an entirely male-dominated environment.

"We were the Three Musketeers," Edelson said. "We are all about the same age with the same experiences, but Helayne is the one who did all the moving and was much more on the fast track. We were always there for each other. We used to keep each other company to keep each other sane. We'd have lunch together. We were in different cities and we used to bring lunch to the office and talk on the phone for an hour while we ate at our desks. Even to this day, twenty years later, we don't have to be physically together to be connected. It was survival. We were all we had."

Like her colleagues, Edelson has approached her fifties with the recognition that she has role-modeled a strong legacy for those women coming up behind her. Edelson's point? Be yourself, deliver results and get in the game.

40 Don't Be Shy
Maria Edelson

Director of Sales Capability Development, North America
Procter & Gamble

I started at P&G so long ago—it'll be thirty-three years. And when I started, it was me. That was it. There weren't any other women. I went to meetings and I can't tell you how men interacted with women because no one would speak to me. Can you imagine going to meetings where no one would speak to you? They figured that if they ignored me, I would go away.

But I didn't. It was all about surviving.

I was the first woman in the history of the company to be promoted to the "band three" level. It was 1980. Three minutes later, they promoted my very best friend, Barb Hartman, right behind me. But I was three minutes ahead.

I always say that you have to speak up for yourself. You can't always accept the immediate response and you really have to continually push the envelope, and do it in a way that you don't alienate people.

In the 1990s, I got a new manager who truly, truly believed in me. He could count on me until the cows came home and he took care of me and promoted me to a band four. Finally, I said to him, "Joe, I'd like to do more for the company and be considered for band five." He said, "Maria, you could do the work. But the experience you would need in order to be prepared for that work would mean moving to Cincinnati." I told him I could commute, but he said, "Sorry, it is out of the question." End of discussion.

I called him and said, "Joe, I can't live with myself or act on behalf of my family without satisfying the question. I would like to meet with Steve (his boss) and ask him about commuting to make sure he feels the way you do." You could have heard a pin drop on the other end of the phone. He'd supported me and had been my mentor and my advocate, and there I was, wanting to go over his head. I said, "I know you know I can do the work, and I believe you want me to have this experience. I know we are both frustrated because I can't have this experience while staying in New York. So let's go to your manager. I can't put all of my eggs in your basket. I need to check this out." He asked if I wanted him to be at the meeting. I said, "Of course."

We all had lunch. At the end of it I said, "Steve, I would like to be considered for more responsibility. Joe and I both agree I am capable of more work. I can get the experience from New York."

Steve looked at me and said, "I think we can do that. I can't tell you we are going to do that tomorrow, but you will be considered for the first job that becomes available."

You could have knocked Joe over. Nine months later, I get a phone call that said,

"We have a job opening in Cincinnati and we're going to let you commute."

It had been a big, big risk. I tell people the story and hear them gasp. But to the day that Joe retired, he remained my strongest supporter.

There is a real lesson in that. Do not lie down, roll over and play dead. It is not a question of being confrontational or adversarial. There is a right and a wrong way to do these things. If you take the high road, enroll people and be a partner in the solution, you can have a positive outcome.

Another lesson is to have principles and stick to them. I have a lot of idiosyncrasies. One is that I do not tolerate any bad language. Not at home, and not at work. Ever. In the '90s, I was in Rhode Island calling on CVS with my manager and his manager. We were in the car and, all of a sudden, the conversation went into the sewer with the f-word. I said, "If you are going to continue to do this, we are going to have trouble getting to the airport." I stopped the car, turned it off, then turned myself around to look at both of them. "You both have young children. If you talk this way, your daughters will talk this way. Do you want your daughters to have gutter mouths?" Well, they were shell-shocked. I started the car again and nobody spoke for miles. Then we went on as if nothing happened.

Not long after that, my immediate manager told me, "I don't want you to think what you said went unnoticed. I have stopped talking like that at work and I don't talk like that at home. I don't want my children talking that way."

The lesson is, you have to stand up for what you believe in. If you have principles and you believe in them, you have to speak up for them.

Along with my principles, I stand for results. It is all about delivering results. But what I tell people today is this: It's jacks or better for openers. If you play poker, you have to have jacks to open. You have to have results to get in the game today. But great results just get you in the game. It is insufficient if you want to move up the success ladder and have a high-powered career. You need to have the right image and the right exposure. Know what you stand for, what your values are and communicate them in an authentic way. Make sure you get out there and get the exposure you need to get a broad array of people behind you, not just your immediate manager. Are you networking? Do you have a mentor? Are you making contact with people who connect with your business? What are you doing to let people know who you are and what you stand for? Great results and values won't do you any good if you keep them a secret. You have to let people know who you are.

Nobody taught me that thirty-three years ago. I keep telling people that they need to get over the idea that they are bragging. Bragging is embellishing things. I am asking people to simply state the facts. To tell what their results and principles are. Just communicate who you are and what you have accomplished. That is not being a braggadocio or self-promoting. It is simply stating the facts. Is it true? That's not bragging. If it is not true, don't say it.

If you make a big sale or accomplish something on your work plan, you might call your boss and say, "I am sending you an e-mail because I am so proud of my results, and I am writing it in a way so that you can easily forward it on." Then send an e-mail that says, "I'm writing to share great news with you. This was my goal. Here is my result." But suggest forwarding it on because, sometimes, bosses aren't so swift and you have to give them a hint. "Hey, Boss, I am sending an e-mail with my results. I'm writing it so it is easy to forward. And, if you want to forward it, please do. It will show what a great job you are doing training me." Say whatever you need to say to get them to move it along.

As you meet people in different situations, ask for cards. Write people back on e-mail, and keep those relationships active. Find a business connection. Send them updates on what you are doing. There are so many ways to promote yourself, but people have to have the facts.

I am very authentic. What you see is what you get. I am who I am. I have raised my children to believe that you are who you are, and if people won't like who you are, that is their problem. Don't change for anything. That's my strategy. ■

Michele Hanson is a survivor of brutal woman versus woman office politics.

"We are our worst enemies," said Hanson, who knows how far we have come as women and has worked hard to clear the path for younger generations. Hanson remembers when, as an executive at Minute Maid, she looked around in meetings and didn't see any women with whom she could team.

She asked her boss where she could get some support, and she was matched up with an older woman who ran the legal department. "She told me that I was too cute. If I could make myself look uglier, I would get more respect. She said that, as she'd aged, she'd gotten more respect. So she joked that I should get some Coke-bottle glasses. I was not about to give up."

Eventually, Hanson went to the CEO of the company for the funding to build a business case for creating the Network of Executive Women. Then she went about finding fifteen senior-level women in the retail industry who were above the director level who could serve on the founding board. "It took me months of digging and networking to get fifteen women."

It's a phenomenal success story. The Network of Executive Women boasts thousands of individual members, including senior executives, emerging leaders and academics and students. They represent more than three hundred organizations, including grocery, chain, drug and mass retailers, wholesalers, consumer-packaged-goods manufacturers, consultants, sales agencies, associations and media.

Hanson is CEO of ExecuInsight, a consulting firm focused on boosting performance through training, assessment and mentoring initiatives.

41 Learn from Your Failures
Michele Hanson
Chief Executive Officer
ExecuInsight

I have had some pretty phenomenal failures that have led me to learning.

Women aren't built or made to be hierarchical, but here we are, moving up the corporate ladder in a hierarchical environment. A lot of us play the game and move up, but it pisses other women off. Some of us have this male style that fits in well, so we can deal with the men really well. It involves being able to be confrontational. We've got it. But the other women totally hate it. It seems like they are jealous of us. So we focus on dealing with men really well, but not with other women.

We are our biggest obstacle in the corporate environment. Pat Heim (one of the nation's most cutting-edge gender consultants) talks about this. We are genetically wired to do what we do. Women learn how to operate in a flat structure where power is shared. Men learn how to operate in a hierarchy. When you put women in a hierarchical structure, all hell breaks loose with the women below. If one woman gets more power than other women, the others will pull her right back down.

I learned this through failure. We should be focusing on pumping up other women, their power bases, their self-esteem, and finding opportunities for them. We have to learn how to support one another. We could do such amazing things if we all came together.

I have had three instances where I have walked away from jobs because of issues with women. In one job I was a vice president of sales, reporting to another woman. The CEO liked what I was doing and asked me to be involved in their senior executive meetings. He asked me to take on some projects for him. That was my demise. After that, this other woman was out to get me any way she could. She excluded me from meetings and discussions, kept information from me, and there was a lot of behind-the-scenes nasty stuff that I found out about because other people would tell me. She was out to make sure that I was not successful.

There was one meeting that the CEO asked me to pull together. I coordinated all of their strategic planning sessions for the next year, brought their sales teams together, had them look at their accounts and come in prepared to talk about their top-tier accounts. I brought everyone in. This company never had done that before. It was like a new day for them. So there we were at the meeting with all the sales executives and the CEO and other executives.

My boss just started firing off at me. She was absolutely rude. When I was speaking with someone, she looked through the things I pulled together and said, "This is totally wrong. I want you to pull this out of the book right now." She went around the room, pulling it out of all the different notebooks at the meeting.

She told me she didn't want me to talk about the resources my team needed, even though each team was supposed to talk about what they needed. Mind you, we'd seen much success and everyone was so excited about what we were doing by bringing together an enterprise approach for the organization.

Before my turn came to take them through what I was planning for the next year, she said, "I will be introducing your group." There she was introducing the people on my team saying, "Here's what we are doing for the next year, here are our plans," and she took the glory away from me. I quickly interrupted and took over. I know that pissed her off even more.

After the meeting, someone came up to me and said, "It was so obvious to everyone what was going on." Even the CEO came up to me and said, "She is jealous of you."

Now that I look back on it, I had broken that power base where we are supposed to be even and equal. I had done good things, and she was feeling at a lesser power base than me. I should have worked to build up her power and self-esteem.

I spoke to her about it many times, but it never got better. I met with her and asked HR to join us. I said, "Listen, I came to work for this organization because I knew you. I don't know what is going on. I am just doing what the CEO told me to do." That is hierarchical. You do what the boss says.

I told her I wanted to figure out how we could move forward. She then proceeded to rip apart everything I had done since I started. She'd come with notes describing how everything was an absolute failure. I stopped that conversation and said, "I'm here to figure out how we can move forward and work together because if we do work together, we can accomplish so much." By the end of the meeting, she agreed to move together with a positive approach.

But we had a new CEO come in and I lost my support base. Finally I said, "Let's negotiate a package to get me out of here." My boss ended up losing her job.

I think the moral to the story is, if we don't learn how to work together, it will be the demise of all of us.

If you are a successful woman in corporate America, you are going to get hit with this. We all need to learn to deal with it.

It happened other times, in other jobs. It is very, very sad. I take responsibility for all of these things. It is no one else's fault but my own. I had choices. I needed to manage things differently. My style is direct, and I get the job done.

But we need to learn how to better support one another. The world really can be ours, and we really can make changes in this world for women—if we could just come together. ■

The Act of Imbalance

Change places with your child and imagine this: Your mother is a world-class, trailblazing executive who has hundreds or thousands of people who work for her. People cling to her words and jockey for her favor, desperate to impress her...

And, there she is, nagging at you to pick up your shoes.

To the world, she is a title. To you, she is mom.

What the child of the senior executive probably doesn't know is, women executives wrestle with their job performance as mothers more than anything else they do.

When I speak at women's leadership events, I am constantly asked about balance issues. The reality is that there is no issue of balance. It's all about imbalance. It's about making it work so you succeed professionally, raising children who are not juvenile delinquents, and not losing your mind in the process.

So many of the young mothers I meet describe a frenetic cadence they have to sustain as parents and professionals. They always are running to keep up with the demands. Despite their efforts to do it all, they are tortured by guilt because, let's face it, they can never do enough.

Is it selfish to want a career? Is it selfish to want to be with your children? Is it selfish to want ten minutes to yourself?

The women in The NEW Woman Rules have quite differing perspectives and approaches to achieving balance or making peace with imbalance. One difference was absolutely startling to me:

Nearly half of the women in this book who are mothers have husbands who are stay-at-home dads. Nationally, just one in twenty fathers are stay-at-home dads, reports the Bureau of Labor Statistics.

What does it mean when these senior-level women choose this option? Does it prove that the old model was right? That the senior executive needs someone at home running the household and taking care of the kids in order to make everything work?

I think that it suggests that running a household and raising a family are such demanding challenges that every parent needs all the help she or he can get. And that those who make it to senior leadership are in a better position economically to choose that option.

What would happen to those national statistics if every family could afford financially to choose that option? Senior leadership is a demanding world, but is it any more demanding than a world where a woman works two back-breaking jobs to pay her family's bills? I think there are a lot of women who would just love to have that kind of support at home.

Success gives you money and money gives you options. What money won't buy you is the time you have to expend in order to achieve your success. So it may be great to have a husband staying home with the kids, but it doesn't do much for you when you want to be home with them.

The word "priorities" continually came up in interviews. You have to know yourself enough to know and honor what matters most to you in your heart. Find ways to allot your time accordingly, because you only get to live this life once.

I really liked Brenda Barnes's story of stepping down as CEO of Pepsi-Cola North America. She wanted time with her growing-up-too-fast daughters, said she knew she was fortunate to be able to afford the seven-year time-out she took from the corporate world.

Several women in this book sacrificed relocation or promotion opportunities because of their family demands. There were stories of family-first decisions that stalled or even derailed careers. But you won't see a lot of regrets about the choices that were made. You will see a lot of pride as parents.

I was at a NEW mingler where about eighty executive women had come for dinner. This was personal time, where no one felt compelled to put on the success mask and swap egos. What did they talk about? Their kids. About how joyous they felt watching them grow up and get ready to go to college in the fall. One woman talked about her son struggling with juvenile diabetes and how she wants to devote the next phase of her career to fighting the disease when she retires in a couple of years. Another told of her reaction when her daughter accidentally revealed a tattoo of a four-leaf clover on her side while reaching for something in the kitchen. One mother proudly shows off a spray bottle of a cleaning product that her ten-year-old daughter has developed by mixing pantry staples together. The bottle is labeled and the girl even made a flier. Another mom ended a cell-phone call with her daughter who'd just checked in to report that she'd sold a $675 pair of shoes on her summer job. Pictures start coming out of purses and are passed all over the room.

The atmosphere was light and personal. It was happy. The women were happy. And they were proud.

There is sometimes an assumption that women who climb to the highest reaches of the professional world have hardened into being selfish, not selfless, in their quest for power. The stereotype is that the professional woman thinks she can "have it all"—but can't—and willingly sacrifices mommy time to keep moving up.

But the stereotype is wrong. I am convinced of that because of the way everything stops when I bring up the subject of family in the interviews. If you wonder what matters most to these women, ask about their passion for their work. Then ask if they have children. The tone of voice always changes. It softens. The women open up. Maybe they can't always be with their family in body, but they are always there in heart. They have felt their share of guilt for not being around every minute of the day, but you can just see that they really have been there, just the same.

I hope their children feel that.

These mothers function in a hard-driving, often-unforgiving level of the business world that constantly foists expectations on them. What is so interesting is that those expectations seem so insignificant when you contrast them to what these women expect of themselves—as mothers. They truly want to do right by their children.

Finally, these serious questions of balance don't apply solely to women with family obligations. Kim Feil's story shows how easy it is for those of us who don't have children to become so consumed by work that all other signs of personal identity are lost. The demands that children and family make of mothers are so immediate that balance decisions are always right there in full view. But when you are not being pulled on by outside priorities that so obviously need and deserve your attention, it can be easy to slip into the self-neglect that Feil experienced. The good news is that you can wake up to the fact that there is a full, exciting, colorful world out there, just waiting for you to make the decision to embrace it.

I get perspective on this when I think of one of the newspapers where I worked as a reporter. I worked very hard as a reporter, but I noticed something about my job.

If I took a long lunch hour, the paper still came out. If I went on vacation, the paper still came out. If I switched jobs and moved away, the paper still came out. It came out every day, whether I was there—or not. So many of us delude ourselves into thinking we are so indispensable that we must make great personal sacrifice to save the institution. But there aren't a lot of situations in which the business will sink because we take some time to ourselves.

And, forgive the heresy here, but it is only business. Life—in all of its glory—is far more important than the immediate task at hand.

I think of two veteran journalists who loved my newspaper so much that they had their ashes encased in the walls after they died. Instead of having their ashes spread in the glorious Rocky Mountain around them, they chose the newspaper lobby? It said everything about what the paper meant to them and, probably, what they thought they meant to the paper. But, theirs was a sad choice, because decades after their deaths, people didn't care about who they were, what they'd done or what they meant to the history of the newspaper. It was a bit of a joke that there were ashes in the wall. And, aggravating the insult, management removed the remains and buried them in a cemetery when the paper moved to a new building. Management didn't even extend the courtesy of letting them make the move with everybody else.

You can give and give and give and give, and the business will take and take and take and take. In the end, who you are matters so much more than what you did.

The business won't love you back.
It won't.

The NEW Woman Rules on balance:

- It is not about balance because it's just impossible to achieve that kind of constant equilibrium. It's about priorities. Know what matters most, then honor it.
- Set boundaries. When you are juggling too much between home and work, evaluate your work tasks and let the things go that won't "move the needle" of the business.
- It's not the quantity of hours you work, but the quality of hours you put in.
- Be mindful of the 80/20 rule. You achieve most of your benefit with 80 percent of your energy. Let the rest go.
- Don't try to turn off your heart when you are using your head, or your head when you are using your heart. Come to work with everything that you are. Be the same person at home.
- Always remember: The business will not love you back. Have a life outside the business.

Brenda Barnes graduated from college in 1975 with a double major in economics and business administration, but that didn't matter. The country was in a recession and she couldn't find a job. Barnes—who one day would ascend to be the president and CEO of Pepsi-Cola North America and now is the CEO of the Sara Lee Corporation—wound up working at the post office. She was stuck on the night shift, where she sat on a bench, sorting mail and dropping letters—one by one—into the right boxes for delivery according to ZIP code. It was humbling, boring and tedious work made worse by supervisors and managers who would move around like sergeants, yelling at workers and treating them like dirt.

Barnes said she learned plenty watching that.

"People deserve to be treated with respect," she said. "You have to value every level in the company. Without every level working—from hourly on up—the company won't work."

Over the years, she has developed a powerful mentoring philosophy that hits hard at valuing people over ego.

Demand the Best
Brenda C. Barnes
Chairman and Chief Executive Officer
Sara Lee Corporation

I was at the post office for only about six months, and then I was on track. I got my first "career" job, got married, had kids, changed jobs, moved to different cities, worked for bad bosses, worked for good bosses, worked in sales, worked in general management and kept moving up.

For ten years, I'd been trying to do it all.

There are twenty-four hours in a day and seven days in a week. I had to make a list of what was most important to me, and then allocate my time accordingly. Certainly, my work took the most time, but I did nothing else but family. I gave up sleep, I gave up sports, I didn't do as many things with friends.

I never felt I wasn't there as a parent. My kids were fine, but I wanted to be with them more. I wanted time with them for me. I had three children, I was living in a different city from my husband and I didn't want to live that way. I recognized my kids were growing up, and if I didn't do something to be with them then, I would miss the opportunity totally.

When I made the decision to leave, I knew the outcome probably would mean I would never have a job like that again. Once I was comfortable with that, I was ready to leave. I quit my job. I did. I did it because I wanted to spend time with my family. My children were ten, eight and seven when I left.

It was really big news because I was CEO of Pepsi-Cola North America and I'd been on all those lists—you know, like Fortune's most powerful women list and all of that. So, when I left, I was on every morning show and in every newspaper. I was the poster child for whether women could or couldn't have it all. I didn't want to let womanhood down; I just wanted to spend time with my kids.

I came to be very supportive of the right to make personal choices about what is right for your life. My family roots gave me the courage to do what I did, and I don't regret that decision for a minute.

My identity was in turmoil for a while. It took a little while to learn that I'm just Brenda Barnes. I am not just a business title.

I was able to stay active during the seven years after I left Pepsi. I served on ten corporate boards. I was the interim president for Starwood Hotels. I taught classes. I always stayed busy, but the difference was that I didn't have to work day-to-day, and my schedule was predictable. I could control it.

My kids started going to college and being young adults, and I found I still had a lot of energy. I found myself tapping my fingers on the table and saying, "I think I still have it in me. I like doing these boards, but I really like running something." I wasn't actively pursuing it, but opportunity crossed paths with me as I was thinking about it. I'd gotten a lot of calls about jobs, but the timing came together for me with Sara Lee three years ago when I came in as president and COO.

I became chairman and CEO about six months later and launched a major transformation plan that has been very, very challenging. It has tested everything I have learned up until this point.

I still don't think there is anything special or unique about me. I sometimes wonder why people think there is. I work hard, I do my job and I think I do it effectively. I certainly have been ambitious and have a standard of work that I think is high, but I've never thought of myself as special. I always wanted to be the best. I did have that in me, for some reason.

My father had a maintenance position in a factory; my mother raised seven kids and had part-time jobs. They were really smart people and absolutely the best human beings you could imagine. They dedicated their lives to us and worked very hard so each of us could go to college and be educated. They created such a strong bond; each of us always wanted to go home to see them, which we did until they passed away. All of my sisters talk to each other once a week, at least.

We grew up in a Polish neighborhood that was very traditional. My father's peers would ask why he was sending his girls to college. But my parents were very progressive and we all were successful.

I don't remember any sense of competition growing up in a home surrounded by women. I don't feel it to this day, and my sisters would say the same thing. I was brought up thinking it wasn't a zero-sum game. Why would women think we should compete against each other?

But, when I started being a manager, women didn't want to work with women. Why wouldn't you support your own gender? That was crazy to me. It is so counterproductive when that happens. Women should get off each other's backs and get on with it. Who are we competing against in the business world? It's men. They are the ones who have the jobs. You have to win in a pool that is more male-dominated than female-dominated.

In the end, it is not about other people. It is about the job you do. Whether you are male or female, you have to keep focused on the business issue at hand and stay the course to make sure you solve the problem, meet the opportunity and grow the business. The other things don't matter. The politics don't matter. People who can find the way to get the best out of a team and out of subordinates are more effective at progressing; it doesn't matter if they are male or female. It takes an internal trait that says you don't have to be the center of attention.

You don't need to be in the limelight. The real skill is being clear about what you have to get done, getting the facts and data, and then finding the way to make sure everyone is clear on the role they need to play in order to get it done. Always focus on the task at hand—not each other, not on who has the power.

The reason I think I have been able to move up is that I know that. I always know I don't always have to have all the answers. I respect the people on the team and find ways to get them to work together. Over time, if you keep having wins in the marketplace and wins in your business, you end up looking good.

Set high standards. Expect a lot, and help people to stay focused on the objective at hand. It is always about getting the best out of everyone, and that is why diversity is so important. You have to allow your people to bring forth their best thinking and contribute. If there is a bias in the way, you don't get the best from your people. And it is always, always about getting the best out of everyone. If there is a built-in bias against women leaders, what a shame! You won't get the best out of them.

Great bosses value your input. They involve you in what needs to be done. They give you freedom to act on what your job is. They value and support you and they don't hover and micromanage you. They develop you. It is such basic stuff.

Over the years, you realize what a title carries with it in terms of perception. There is a fear factor that comes as you move up. You have to work hard to break it down. You really have to do that. I remember thinking, what am I doing that is so scary to other people? Then, I realized, it is the position. The title carries intimidation. The more senior you get, the harder and harder it becomes to find out the truth. You have to break down the intimidation.

This is a big, big deal. Good leaders know it, and bad leaders don't. The bad create a culture that tells them what they want to hear. Good leaders want the truth because they can fix it and capitalize on it. If people are intimidated and afraid and worried about their jobs, they fear speaking up about something that is bad. You have to create an environment that opens this up. How are you going to fix anything if you don't know about it?

You really have to understand what is going on. You can see anything that is presented to you, either in its full glory or in its full ugliness, or see it in the way someone has wanted to show it to you. You have to sort it out. You have to know you are seeing the real truth. I always have a fear of failure, but it doesn't stop me from knowing that I will fail if I don't know the full truth.

This transformation at Sara Lee could be my triumph or my demise. This company has a long history of being a successful company, but it started going flat. I firmly believed that, without change, it would not have a great future. I am moving us out of being a company that acted as a holding company that didn't pull pieces together to get synergy. We have spun off 40 percent of our revenue. Most CEOs judge their importance by how big their company is—they don't shrink their company by 40 percent. But, we needed that here to change from a holding company into an integrated operating company.

There has been an incredible amount of turmoil. If you do a Google search on me, you'll see a lot of rotten articles speculating on whether or not I will make it. But we are being proven out. We are doing it. You have to have a thick skin in this. If you are going to respond to every negative, you will never get anything done.

There are no secrets to my motives. I want to make this place great. It is astounding what this company has pulled off in three years. Are we getting credit with our stock price? Not yet. That will come. But this company has faced a challenge unlike what anybody has done before.

And that is exciting to me. ∎

Kim Nelson had an MBA from Columbia and was a young, fast-track executive who soared through the ranks while working to mentor women and African-Americans at General Mills. She was also a living, breathing human being who wasn't afraid to face a personal setback so devastating that she risked everything and stepped off the track, out of her job and into her own skin.

43 Play Nice in the Sandbox
Kim Nelson
President, Snacks Unlimited Division
General Mills

I found out I wasn't going to be able to have children the same week that my husband's father died. The whole world came crashing down, and work was put in the proper perspective.

I loved my job, I loved the work, but that was not the life I'd planned for myself.

My reproductive engineer was so sure I couldn't conceive that she wouldn't even take my money for in vitro fertilization. She should have said, "My best guess is you won't conceive," but she said it would not happen. She took away my hope.

She shouldn't have done that.

I always wanted to have a family and children. That was my vision of my life. It was a huge part of me. This all happened in 1997 when I was thirty-six years old, and it was the first time something really rough happened that impacted my ability to work well. I needed a very long break.

That's when I learned everything about my company. I needed General Mills to see me as a human being. I was the director of the family snacks unit at the time and I went to my boss and to the CEO and talked to them about taking a leave. They both said, "Kim, are you okay?" They both told me, "Take the time you need. We will be there for you on the other end." The CEO, Steve Sanger, shared with me that both of his children were adopted. For him to comfort me in such a human way, well, it makes me emotional to even remember that meeting. I took an eighteen-month leave of absence, which is unheard of in the corporate world.

My journey really broke with the career path of onward and upward.

Doing something like that, I had to wonder if it would pull me off the track and whether the company would question my commitment. What would it do to my career? But I took the time because I felt I needed to do it. It was a wonderful, cathartic period. I could look at my life and ask myself if I was doing what I really wanted to do.

I always have been interested in nonprofits, so I worked at a shelter and created a book club for the YWCA that linked African-American professional women with African-American middle-schoolers. It was all wonderfully fulfilling. Then I traveled across country with my husband. We called it, "Kim and Stafford's Excellent Adventure." We camped. We went to all the national parks between here and the West Coast. It was a two-month trip, which no one can do if they are working. We had his father's van.

It was so much fun. I got fit. I ran every day. I prayed. Every single day, I prayed about the kid thing, because the Bible says to ask for what you want and not censor your request.

At the end of my leave, I knew what I wanted for my life. I wanted to come back to work here. I wanted a job. I was negotiating my way back into the company into the area of new ventures, in an opportunity they were creating just for me. They created a team for me with three other high-potential, great people. And they tasked me with finding new ways to energize and sell cereal.

Right as I was negotiating my way back in, I found out I was pregnant. I took the pregnancy test and it was positive. I'd had two miscarriages, so being pregnant really wasn't a certain thing for me. I thought I'd probably miscarry again.

I kept going to my meetings about coming back and waiting for the opportunity to say something about the pregnancy. I was sitting with my boss and I knew I had to tell him. I just said, "I have to tell you something that you are not going to believe." He was an old mentor who knew me personally, and I just came out and told him.

You know, if I were going to get pregnant, it would have been convenient in the eighteen months I'd taken off. This was not convenient timing. But my boss told me how happy he was for me and for Stafford. I was three months pregnant, and the company wanted me to come on back to work, even though I would be there for only six months. I did the job, took my maternity leave, then came back part time for another six months. Then they promoted me to vice president to lead the Cheerios unit—the biggest unit in the company at the time.

It is an incredible story because I wasn't penalized for the time I'd taken off. I knew they liked my work, but you never know how changes like this will impact your career —no matter what they are telling you. But they gave me the promotion.

A few years later, I got pregnant again. All of this was with no intervention, no drugs, no nothing. Just natural. I took an eight-month leave that time, and the company supported me again. General Mills has figured out that women have babies. It happens. And we are the same people and they should remember that they trained us, developed us, and having a baby doesn't change our abilities or competencies.

So that was my first big career event. The next big career event was my biggest failure. It happened early on, when I was a manager in popcorn. I had this great idea that we would enter the price segment of the popcorn category with a terrific brand: HBO Popcorn. It was my idea, pinned right on my back. I am a big believer that you have to take risks. If you float through a corporation without having anything pinned to you, that's a mistake. Remember: high risk, high reward.

Well, HBO Popcorn was a massive failure. It was awful. It just didn't go. It didn't meet hurdles for sustainability in the marketplace and we weren't able to compete with it. It didn't lose the company money, which was good news. But this was the first public failure I'd had. When something like that happens, you learn a lot about your own ability to weather failure. You learn who your true supporters are. You watch who is quiet. You see who tells you to hang in there. One of my mentors called me into his office and picked me up and dusted me off. He said, "You know, Kim, here are the things you did that were great in popcorn." He tried to put it in perspective for me. I left his office, went into the bathroom and I cried because I was so appreciative of how he'd made me feel. You can't get that unless you have a failure to precipitate it.

You learn and it stings and you hate not winning, but you get over it. You get through it. You think every time you walk down the halls, everyone knows what you are going through. But half the people don't even care what goes on in popcorn! You have to learn to get up and swing the bat. It is good to do that. Sometimes you strike out. But, you have to swing it, and swing it again when you get another at-bat.

My third big career event was a good one involving Honey Nut Cheerios. The Cheerios business had been energized by marketing its cholesterol reduction. The problem with Honey Nut was that it was going into houses that had children, but it wasn't being consumed by the adults in the house. The thought with this project was to bring a benefit to the adult, to put something there to give adults a reason to eat Honey Nut. This was messing with one of the company's babies, one of the crown bowls. Cereal is our most important business, so it is very challenging to do anything dramatic there. But this was a great idea. We had all the consumer work done, and my boss was very supportive. So we did it.

We gave Honey Nut the ability to reduce cholesterol. It ended up being a huge success. It generated exactly the results we wanted. That was several years ago and they are still using that strategy. It is still running the cholesterol-reduction campaign. I'm really proud of that. I'm proud of the team that worked for me at the time. It was a flat-out, incontrovertible success.

I was afraid in every one of these defining moments. I was terrified of those risks. But, I believed in what I was doing, whether it was right or wrong. Not everything works. As leaders, we don't want to shut down the innovation that doesn't work. We have to swing the bat.

I have said that I could write a book on how everything I need to know about corporate America I learned from my children. For example, one chapter would be, "No—Me, Mommy." They don't want you to do things for them. Your people, like your children, want to do it for themselves. They want to develop their own skills. You can be their coach. Don't do it for them.

Another chapter would be about recognition. They want to know how great their artwork is, so give them that. They are constantly generating artwork and things they are proud of. They bring something to you, and what they don't want is for you to criticize it and show how it could be better. They want you to say, "Look! How beautiful! Look how you have used these colors!" But, in the work world, some leaders criticize, and they should know that you get more when you see that someone's efforts were complicated, that they did a great job. They want to hear that you think you couldn't have done any better.

Finally, I could call a chapter, "Play Nice in the Sandbox." That is all about corporate politics. I have found that there is so much value in building positive relationships across boundaries in the sandbox. There is absolutely no place for mean-spirited behavior. It's inappropriate. Be somebody whom others want to play with.

I've learned so much from my children. Isn't it funny how it all turned out? ■

Betsy Cohen is a master of running in place at extraordinary speeds. Family priorities rooted her in St. Louis, but her leadership acumen and corporate finesse kept her moving up without moving on. She knows she sometimes has sacrificed professional gains for her personal obligations and commitments, but the decisions have honored what matters most to her.

"I really encourage women not to be influenced by what other people think they should and shouldn't do with their lives," she said.

Cohen is Vice President of Nestlé Purina's veterinary business, Purina Veterinary Diets, overseeing the sales and marketing team of one hundred associates. She also is Nestlé's Sustainability Champion, working with key retailers across all Nestlé products.

Pull People In
Betsy Cohen
Vice President and Futurist
Nestlé Purina PetCare Co.

You are running a marathon, not a sprint.

There are bumps in the road.

That's what I have told myself.

I married a doctor in St. Louis and we have kids. I wanted to stay in St. Louis with my company, and since I wasn't able to hop around, it took more time, planning and effort to put together the right pieces of my career and advance myself along. Patience and persistence.

When you try to build your career in one city at one company, things don't always work out in terms of timing and opportunity. It takes so much persistence and patience if you want to stay where you are. That's hard when you are itchy and you think you should have a different title and more responsibility.

I had to learn to be patient. For people who are driven in their careers and have a lot of long-term goals in their heads, patience can be in short supply.

When I came to Purina, which is now Nestlé Purina, I'd had two years of experience working at Black & Decker. But when we moved to St. Louis and I was hired at Purina, they basically made me start over as a marketing assistant because I hadn't worked in a consumer packaged goods company.

I was a Wellesley graduate with a Harvard MBA and two years at Black & Decker. I would have thought I would have at least come in at the third-year level, but I didn't get any credit for that. I had to start over in an entry-level position. I asked if I could be reviewed early and they said yes, but it took me a while to recoup where I could have been.

The lesson is, if you think you are with a good company, you may have to take something that doesn't seem like it is at the right level or for the right money. Don't let that get in the way of the right decision. I thought Purina was the right company and figured, "Okay, I will make it work."

And so I did.

One thing I have learned is that the projects I worked on got better when I involved more people. Some of the things I did early on weren't as strong as they could have been had I gotten more input from others. It is the difference between being efficient versus being effective. You can be efficient and get something done yourself, but are you being effective? You need consensus; you need to get people involved.

And you have to share leadership of projects, ideas, and successes. If you have an abundance mentality, you realize that if you share success, you will get your share. It takes growing into it to realize there is plenty of success and recognition to go around. If you share it, there is more to share.

I am competitive, but the competition is focused outward. I am competitive about our business results. I am competitive about wanting our team to have great ideas and benchmarks against industry leaders. I don't feel competitive internally very often. I am competing against myself and the goals I have set, about how my team is doing, about how I want to lead and proceed, about how we are competing in the marketplace.

Set your yardstick out there pretty audaciously, and that is how you move forward. If your horizon is too short, you can't really see how you are doing. You can't really measure yourself in a one-year window because the horizon is too short. You can have good luck or bad luck in a year, and a year goes by too quickly. But, in a two- or three-year window, things have a chance to be fulfilled. I am usually looking out two or three years, both in business and personally. You can't always bundle everything you want to accomplish in the next twelve months, but if you expand it out to twenty-four, you can incorporate the things you want to do.

It takes a long time in big companies to reach the levels people feel they are shooting for. It is disappointing because it is hard. There are a lot of talented people out there. That is difficult.

Sometimes it is disappointing being married and tied to a city. There are opportunities as a part of Nestlé that require people to move. The career opportunities are phenomenal for the people who can do it, but it is hard for those who can't.

Do I want to be CEO? Well, when you work for a company like Nestlé, the people who will do that will have taken on international roles. I recognize that my desires and ability to successfully run a business give me the skills I would need to do it. Many have the desire to do it. But, you have to recognize the realities in organizations about what is likely to get you there. You have to temper your desire with realism.

Often, for a lot of good reasons, both men and women aren't willing to "do what it takes" to get those top jobs. Those jobs in every company demand many sacrifices and dedication that are very consuming. Not everyone wants those top roles with what comes with them. But I do hope that those who do want them have the opportunities to push forward.

To get those opportunities, it is important to study the culture and know what is important. In our culture at Nestlé Purina, it means making connections, having a big network, building alliances and trust. I've worked hard to help mentees see that. I had to learn that. I used to think that if I did a very good job, it would be apparent and I would get to take on more. I had to learn to ask to take on more things, and I had to have the network in place so I could ask.

One responsibility I asked for has to do with environmental sustainability all across

Nestlé. I asked for the opportunity to work on sustainability because of my personal interest in the topic and the ability to be involved with other operations across Nestlé and in Switzerland. I had been working to find ways to take advantage of some of the global nature of a company like Nestlé.

Again, if you can't move, it is hard. If I want to stay in St. Louis and stay with the company, I have to find a way to advance the work that needs to be done and expand my opportunities within the framework I have.

I may have made some sacrifices because of it, but I try to stay centered on my own North Star. My husband, sons and I did a lot together. We had dinner together many nights of the week. The Midwest allows for a good lifestyle like that. The commute is short; you can be home. My two sons are now nineteen and twenty-two. Both are very motivated, strong and hard-working. They are good men.

That was the big goal. ■

After high school, **Jeri Dunn** didn't get the fast track. She got on no track.

When she was forced to take charge of her life and make a career, she moved herself forward with a momentum that made her unstoppable in the retail industry.

Then she encountered yet another obstacle, and it almost killed her. Hers is a story that gives us great power—and perspective.

"I've thought that, after I retire, I should go in and talk to young women who, for whatever reason, didn't go to school and got derailed like I did," she said. "With me as a case study, it will prove to them that, with the right attitude and the aptitude to learn, you can do absolutely anything."

45 Ask for More to Do
Jeri Dunn

Vice President and Chief Information Officer
Bacardi Limited

I got married a month after I graduated high school—when I was seventeen. My parents were devastated, and I think everybody I went to school with thought, "Oh boy, she's not going to do anything with her life." Everybody thought I was done.

My first husband and I split up when I was twenty-five. I took a job on the assembly line at a toy company that was literally in my backyard. For the people in that town, the toy company was a great place to work because they worked you through Christmas, then laid you off so you could collect three months of unemployment checks, then brought you back to a guaranteed job. I remember women in the breakroom saying, "I've been doing this for thirty years." Nothing against those women, but that couldn't be me.

It wouldn't.

I was divorced with two daughters—the youngest being six months old—and I had no visible means of supporting them. I had no college degree. I went to my parents and said, "I want to go back to school. Will you pay?" They said, "No, you had your opportunity. We aren't giving you a free ride anymore, but if you move out of your house and move in with us, we'll watch the kids." I did that.

I went to the adult education department at Edinboro University in Pennsylvania and said, "Tell me what I can get a degree in over the shortest period of time that ends with me getting a guaranteed job."

They said I could go into nursing or computer science. I knew I didn't want to be a nurse, so that's how I wound up in IT.

I got an outside job, worked thirty hours a week, went to school full-time and still took care of my kids. It just shows that if you have the mind-set that you are going to make it happen, it will happen.

I hated the courses the entire time I went to college. I hated the programming. The professors said, "Jeri, hang in there, you're going to be great." I stuck with it, and when I went to work, I realized it wasn't about computers. It was about dealing with people. What I do for a living is not technical. It is dealing with people and transforming businesses.

It still niggles me that I never got a bachelor's degree. I look around the room and everybody has a master's, and I'm sitting there with a two-year degree. I used to wonder if I even deserved to be in the same room with those people, let alone have them work for me. But I'm getting better about it. I used to be ashamed to say I have only a two-year degree, but now I will stand in front of an MBA class and say it and not be ashamed of it anymore.

In business, I had to learn that there were things that I just couldn't control. It used to be that, if things went wrong, I felt I was a failure. I want to make sure everything is done right, on time, under budget. But some things you can't control. Sometimes things go wrong!

I have always wanted to make sure that everyone who works for me is happy. They could be bothered by an outside issue like a divorce, a sick parent or something else that has nothing to do with the job. I think the caring I have has been a benefit because people have told me how much it meant that I recognized they were having trouble at home and that I cut them a little bit of slack. People respect that I care about the whole person. That is the good thing. The bad thing is that I can't fix everything that is broken in their lives.

Over time I've learned that, in the office, there are very few people who are going to be my confidant. Anything I say, I'd better figure is going to be repeated somehow, sometime, some way. The big thing about office politics is this: Keep your mouth shut. As soon as somebody opens his of her mouth to say something about somebody else, you have to shut it down by saying, "I don't want you to have this conversation around me." If you don't say anything, he will take your silence as agreement and the next thing you know, he is telling somebody else, "Jeri thinks …"

How did I move my career along? I'd say, "I have mastered the things you wanted me to do. Give me something more to do." It's smarter than saying, "I want a promotion. I want to move up the ladder." I've had a lot of people do that and my response is that, 'You'd better be sure you are doing the job you've got very well before you find the next one." But when you ask for more, you make a statement. And if the boss says, "I don't think you can take on any more," it's a key indicator that you need to ask what you are doing wrong. Asking for more is a smart way to get recognition. It's a different way, and it's a smart way.

When I would do that, I was lucky that they'd say, "We'd like you to try this. Are you game?" The companies I worked for gave me the opportunities I wanted. I probably wouldn't have stayed if they hadn't.

Women are not naturals at self-promotion. I've asked myself a thousand times why that is the case and I just don't have an answer for it. Younger women are better at it. Men find it easy. Men who were growing up in the '60s and '70s had every self-promotion tool at their disposal. They had high school athletics, which women didn't have back then. Guys knew that, every Saturday morning, they could look in the paper and see who was the star on Friday night. It made them more competitive. There was no place for women to showcase their competition. That's why younger women are better at it today. They are getting into sports and into the competition and getting their pictures in the Saturday morning paper.

Five years ago, if I'd have described my career, I would have said it's been a steady ride. But five years ago I hit a big valley. I miscalculated the culture in a company I joined. They'd said they wanted diversity and when I walked in, it was just fifty-year-old white males. It was an emotionally trying time for me, especially because I'd never felt I had been anything but successful. But, in that environment, I felt like no matter what I did, I wasn't going to be good enough.

Finally, I left the company. I made that decision because, five months before, something profound happened in my life that changed me forever. I had a brain aneurysm.

It happened on a Tuesday, when I was giving a presentation at a Michael Hammer conference in Boston. He was introducing me and I felt like my head was going to blow up. I stood there for an hour and fifteen minutes giving my presentation. Afterward, my team members clustered around me and asked what was wrong with me.

"I have a headache," I said. I went into the bathroom and I had severe vomiting. Then I came out and said, "Reschedule my limo for three hours. I'm going to my hotel room to rest." Massachusetts General was right across the street, but I said no to that —I was going to just lie there. So I did, then went to my limo, flew to Atlanta, then went to meetings all the next day. They gave me aspirin, which is the worst thing you can do when there is bleeding in your brain.

Then I flew back to Arkansas and went to work. They said, "If you don't go to the doctor, we're calling your husband." The doctor told me I needed an MRI, and I said, "I have a meeting. I'll be done at 2 and then I'll do the MRI." When I came out of the MRI, the doctor called me in and said, "I want to show you something. You have a clustered aneurysm that is bleeding into your brain. You are going to need surgery— soon." I asked if we could wait until the following Monday because I was going to have some people over and he said, "No, that is not okay. You are going to have surgery tonight and you are going to the Mayo Clinic."

My husband was catching a plane for a trip out of the country, but the doctor said, "Get him home."

The aneurysm was directly behind my left eye, and I went into surgery with no clue whether or not I was coming out alive. I had to say goodbye to my husband and daughter and I had no time to prepare for it. I had to say goodbye to the people I loved the most and didn't know if I ever would see them again.

When, all of a sudden, you have what you hold most dear being threatened, you stop sweating the small stuff. I had been so miserable at work, but after that aneurysm, work was small stuff. If I only have so much time that God has given me, I am not going to be anywhere that I am not happy.

The day that my CEO asked if I was committed to remaining their CIO the way they were operating there, I said, "I have to think about that." I took the weekend and, the following Monday, I went into HR and said, "I want to separate from the company."

The most important thing is recognizing the fit before you walk in the door. Do your homework. Ask questions such as, "How many women do you have in key management positions?" And "How are women promoted?"

Once you get into a company, the way you fit in is by being yourself. It's not so much about liking the people you work with as it is having respect for them.

There are a lot of people I work with whom I don't like, but I sure do respect them.

I love my work, which is why I can't get enough of it. Once I get done doing something and then go into maintain mode, I have to move on. I am a creator. I really like what happens to a business, and facilitating the change. A business that stays stagnant is down the drain. I was always looking for ways to facilitate the change. It is such a great feeling when I implement something that has an impact on the business.

I have been lucky to have worked for companies that gave me great opportunities. And I've sure had a lot of fun. ■

Kimberly Betts pushes her limits in ways that most others don't, daring to venture into uncomfortable conditions to test her mettle. That ability started early, and has served her well in her profession and as one of the leaders of the Network of Executive Women.

As NEW's second president, she is credited with solidifying the concept of the Network into a functioning reality. NEW President Helayne Angelus said of her, "The Network was a collection of hard-charging sales and marketing people, and Kimberly provided the business process infrastructure and transformed the energy into a sustainable enterprise. That's what she did. I love her dearly."

Betts is a senior manager in the retail practice at Deloitte, working with retail clients to help them implement change in process and technology. She previously was the director of communications at Ahold USA.

46 Do It Your Way
Kimberly Betts
Senior Manager, Retail Practice
Deloitte

In high school, I was interested in politics. I was crazy, crazy, crazy about politics, and in college, I was going to take Russian. I had an opportunity to study in St. Petersburg, Russia. Surviving that experience has helped me to adapt to difficult environments—regardless of how harsh they are.

This was back in the 1980s, and Russia was still a spooky, cloak-and-dagger kind of place. From an American perspective, it was a very hard place to be. I was living with people who didn't speak English, and I had to communicate in Russian for six months.

There were no direct phone calls back to the United States, so I couldn't pick up the phone and call my parents. If you needed to make a call, you had to take three trains to get downtown to the post office, then wait in line to schedule a phone call for some time the next week. Then you'd take the trains home. The next week, you'd take the trains back to the office and wait four or five hours because you never got the time you actually were scheduled to have. Then you'd take the trains back.

I remember that when I get impatient about technology.

We'd go into the supermarkets, and you know how our grocery stores are stocked to the edge of the shelves? These shelves were a quarter or an eighth full, and most of the stuff there was canned fish products. I couldn't even recognize what anything was. The produce was awful. I remember sifting through it to find items that weren't rotting.

And, at that time, they still didn't manufacture toilet paper. They used newspaper! Newspaper! I think every kid should spend time abroad. It adds so much perspective to your life.

That was one of the most difficult things I have ever done. It helped me to understand the extent of my own personal endurance, stamina and flexibility. Later on, when I would experience difficult things or difficult people, I'd think back to what I went through in Russia.

I grew up in grocery retail, and that is tough. Some of the operations guys were really challenging, and they'd push to see how hard I would actually work and what I would be willing to do. I thought, if I can survive Russia, I can do this. I still tap into that experience—to this day.

It was so hard. Like running the Boston Marathon.

I did that. I was always a chubby kid. I never had a lot of running talent, but I developed it. I couldn't run a mile when I started, but over time, I continued to grow to the distance I was running. Running Boston was one of my "before thirty" goals. I was living there at the time. I wanted to do it because I wanted to see if I could do it.

Running a marathon tests your mental capability as much as your physical capability. You get to a point where you have to shut off the pain so you can keep moving.

I didn't sleep the night before the marathon because I was so nervous. I was running on adrenaline. I'd run some half-marathons as part of my training, so I knew I could run thirteen miles. But it got harder at miles fourteen and fifteen. And, in the Boston Marathon, there are a series of hills at miles sixteen and seventeen called "Heartbreak Hill." If anything is going to break you, it is going to be Heartbreak Hill.

Once I started up the first hill, and then the second, I found myself running near a seventy-year-old guy who was going about the same pace as me. It was his tenth marathon. I looked at him. I was twenty-nine, he was seventy. If he could do it, I could do it. I kept running and running. I knew that if I could get beyond Heartbreak Hill, I could get through the race. At miles twenty-two and twenty-three, there were just a few more miles. There were so many people yelling at the side of the road—it was insane—and people were screaming at me because my name was on my shirt. I was thinking, "I am going to die, my anatomical diaphragm is going to burst from my body," but people were screaming my name. I kept going. I made it through Copley Square and I could see the banner that said, "FINISH." I could see my time, and it was about four-and-a-half hours. My goal was to come in under five. I crossed the line and threw up about twenty times.

That was another time when I learned what I could do physically and emotionally. Remember, I was a fat kid. I redefined myself as someone who was healthier, more athletic. I was the student-body president, not the jock. So, running a marathon was the height of getting past the fat, smart, geeky kid from primary and high school.

I stretched myself. I do that in my work. I continue to push myself to figure out what I can do. I like to use the muscles I don't normally use. I don't want them to atrophy. I don't want to get lazy. When things get tough, I think to myself, "I can do this. It may be really difficult, but I lived in a country that didn't manufacture toilet paper, and I ran a marathon."

I learned the most important things in life the hard way. I have a blue-collar background. The work ethic was always an important value in my family. The minute I turned sixteen, I was working. I grew up thinking that if I worked hard, good things would come. You work hard, work hard, work hard.

But I learned that working hard was not enough.

You have to work hard to manage the perceptions people have of you. And you have to manage your network. Key players within the organization need to understand who you are and what you are doing. Men do this really well. Women don't. Self-promotion is not something that is high on our "Make sure you do this" list. We are so used to getting things done. We take a lot of pride in the quality of our work.

Well, when I was at Stop & Shop, I was working so hard, and I was still getting passed over for promotions. I thought I was doing all the right things, but the people around me were getting promoted and I wasn't. I wondered what I was doing wrong.

Feedback is priceless, and real feedback is something we never get nearly enough of. A very trusted mentor, friend and adviser told me, "Kim, you are working hard, but people don't know your value proposition. They don't know why this organization can't live without you." I'd been working like a crazy person and I was not about to go talking about myself. That wasn't my shtick. I don't enjoy the spotlight that much. So how could I put out that "value proposition" and be authentic about it? That is really challenging. My work *should* speak for itself. I spent the time I needed to spend in denial, and then I took some deliberate, targeted steps to change. It took me a while to figure out how I could do it and not feel I was being fake. I am never going to be one to go into the CEO's office to talk about how fabulous I am.

This adviser helped me figure out how to get the same result in my own style. I got other people to promote or advocate for me. I had them help create visibility around me. They helped some of the key players understand what I was doing and what my strengths were. They drew attention to me, but it wasn't overt and it didn't make me uncomfortable.

I learned something else the hard way and that is, you can't do everything yourself. There is so much more power in numbers. You just need to ask for help. Sometimes, that is hard to do because we are prideful and think, "Oh my God, if I have this job, they will expect me to know what I am doing. I shouldn't ask for help." We all deal with confidence issues. I talk with women who have done amazing things but who still question their own ability and capability. That gets in the way of asking for help. But, when I ask for help, I am constantly awed by what people are willing to do.

I just got promoted and I need my hundred-day plan. I went to the NEW Executive Leaders Forum last week and figured those were the people who could really help me. Everyone I asked said, "Absolutely. What do you need? I'd love to help."

Sometimes we feel like we are supposed to carry the whole load on our own. But we have such incredible resources—especially in a group like the Network, with this powerful, successful, talented and smart source of help and support. I am constantly humbled by it. ■

Vicki Escarra's job at Delta Air Lines was intense, lucrative and had her poised to fly even higher in the corporate stratosphere. A tug-of-war between work-life balance led her to make a decision that involved enormous professional sacrifice and, ultimately, great personal reward.

A grueling run of decisions changed virtually every aspect of her life, and now she has the golden hindsight of knowing that the hard part was just taking action in the first place.

Escarra leads America's Second Harvest, the nation's largest hunger-relief organization, with more than two hundred food banks and food-rescue organizations in its membership.

Understand Who You Are
Vicki Escarra

Chief Executive Officer
America's Second Harvest

I was the executive vice president, chief customer service officer for Delta Air Lines, a job that entailed managing Delta operations at 315 airports around the world, 15 call centers and roughly 52,000 employees. The CEO spoke to me about opportunities to be promoted to chief operating officer, and said the one thing that would assist me was to take thirteen weeks and go to the Harvard Business School class for an accelerated MBA. I had two daughters, the oldest of whom was fourteen at the time, and the Harvard class meant I would have been gone for the summer.

At the time, I had been at Delta about twenty-two years. I was hired as a flight attendant with a degree in psychology and business, and I'd worked my way up. I never expected I would ever be the No. 3 or No. 4 person in the company. I had a lot of confidence that I would be a very good chief operating officer—good for the overall business and direction of the company. But was it more important for me to go to Harvard, or to be with my daughter at a vulnerable time in her life? Those teenage years are very trying, and watching what was going on with my daughter gave me the sense that it was not a good time for me to go. I made a decision, which is what working mothers do every day.

I didn't go.

The CEO promoted a peer of mine.

I am often asked if you can "have it all" if you are a working parent. I think you can, but you can't have it all every day, you can't have it all every week and you can't have it all every year. Some days, you are a great executive. Some days, you are a great mother. Some days, you are a great wife. Some days, you are a great friend or a great daughter. But, to have a happy and fulfilling life, you have to be grounded enough to understand that you have to make choices if you want to have it all.

I really respected the CEO, Leo Mullin. I remember telling him, "I appreciate the opportunity to go to Harvard. It was a dream of mine, but I can't go right now because I have a teenager and I feel she needs me at home. If I am not there for three months, I have the feeling it won't be made up. He said, 'I understand that. You are making the right choice.' "

I did know it meant I would not get the promotion. That is always disappointing. To think I gave up going for a role I felt I was capable of handling, something I was actually more competitive for than the people in the race with me! It was actually better that I wasn't promoted, because my path has taken a different course. Not being promoted was one of the reasons I eventually left Delta and am now working in the nonprofit world. Because of that, I just completed the happiest year of my adult life.

Your work is not your entire life. Having that sense about balance has been very important as I have gone through my life. Be very clear what your priorities are and recognize that you are going to have to make some tough choices, whether it is going to a child's birthday party or declining a promotion or being available for aging parents, or commuting for an out-of-town promotion. If you decide to take on these complex roles of running businesses, having children and being a good spouse, you will have to make these tough decisions. Having it all comes with a lot of choices.

My daughter is now a senior at Stanford. She just came home Friday. She made straight A's; she is very healthy and well-balanced. Granted, straight A's are not a mark of happiness or an indication of being well-balanced, but they do show that she is on a road to success.

I left Delta after a twenty-eight-year career. It was three years after 9/11 and the airline industry was dramatically different. I wanted to position the company so it was in good shape, and then very consciously and knowingly give my resignation. I took a year and a half off and rethought what I wanted to do in the second phase of my professional life. I spent a lot of time with my younger daughter, who was fourteen at the time. I rethought my marriage, which was not a healthy relationship.

I am fifty-two now. Making the decision to divorce in my late forties was tough. Did I want to spend the rest of my life with that person—where six out of seven days were not good—or would I be happier recognizing that I might not be spending the rest of my life with anyone? I really grappled with it. I worried about what was right for my kids. I ultimately decided that it was best for everyone if my husband and I were not together. It was the toughest decision I have ever had to make.

But once I made it, everything else began to fall in place. I recognized I did not want another corporate job. I did not want to live in my hometown of Atlanta anymore. I wanted to broaden my horizons.

I told executive recruiters that I was interested in nonprofit, with issues of poverty, education or issues involving women and children. I was one of the top candidates for CEO of Habitat for Humanity, a position that I would have enjoyed, but they asked me two questions that were difficult for me from a personal-integrity point of view.

They asked me how I would feel about praying before every meeting. I responded that I was not comfortable with that. I pray a lot on my own, but the whole issue of church and state should remain separate, and I am not comfortable praying in front of people at work.

Also, they wanted me to move to a small, small town in Georgia. I was straightforward. I am interested in a larger city. If they were interested in moving their headquarters to Atlanta, I'd have considered it. The position was offered to a really great guy, a minister, and it turned out to be a very good thing for them.

The prayer thing was so personally against my own integrity and not aligned with my character. It wasn't right for me. Having the courage to understand who you are and what is important will allow you to grow and be yourself and fulfill your mission in life.

I interviewed for the CEO job at America's Second Harvest and, before the second interview, I went unannounced to the food bank in Atlanta. I told the receptionist I was learning more about food banking and asked if the director would have a few minutes to talk to me. We talked about the vision and mission of the organization, how America's Second Harvest supports more than 200 food banks that feed 25 million Americans. Nine million of them are children, 3 million are senior citizens and, of the remaining 13 million, half are working. So the notion that the people who don't have enough to eat in this country are the homeless people standing on street corners is not true. Close to 85 percent of the people we serve are either working two jobs at minimum wage, are retired or can't work.

This was the work I was waiting to do. I got the CEO's job and moved to Chicago.

My challenge is taking all of these nonprofit food banks and having them operate as one nonprofit. The pay is a lot less—actually, a third of what I was making before. But, I had a long career at Delta Air Lines that afforded me the opportunity to make a choice like this. One of my best friends laughs that, if I'd taken another corporate job and made another couple of million dollars, I would have just found a charity to give it to. I do get paid very well in this job, but the real pay is visiting the kids who come to our soup kitchens and soup pantries with their families, and knowing that we are providing them with food, and that it likely will make a difference in their ability to learn and be educated and somehow break out of this cycle of poverty.

This is exactly what I was looking for. ■

One of **Julie Washington**'s favorite quotes comes from Benjamin E. Mays, the famed African-American minister, scholar and activist who said, "The tragedy of life doesn't lie in not reaching your goal. The tragedy lies in having no goal to reach. It isn't a calamity to die with dreams unfilled, but it is a calamity not to dream. It isn't a disgrace not to reach the stars, but it is a disgrace to have no stars to reach for. Not failure, but low aim, is a sin."

Washington has aimed high with great heart, defining her purpose in human, more than professional, terms. She has achieved wildly but has found her greatest success by holding close the things she values most.

By title, she is the director of shopper marketing for Procter & Gamble North America. She'll quickly remind you that what other people call you doesn't matter: "What matters is what you answer to."

To her, leadership and purpose have as much to do with her other titles at home, at church and in her volunteer efforts as they do with her place in corporate America. She has proven her commitment to expanding the presence and power of women and minorities in the workplace by active hiring efforts and a consistent effort to create, sponsor and support their leadership councils.

48 Take Off Your Mask
Julie S. Washington

Director, Shopper Marketing
Procter & Gamble

Earlier in my career, I didn't want people to get too close to me. I definitely wore a mask. I saw work as a transaction: You pay me, and I will do great work and deliver great results in exchange for compensation.

I thought promotions had to come through results. If I worked hard and delivered nothing short of excellent results, they had to promote me. But I learned early on that promotions don't come just because of results. They come because of results plus relationships.

That's why I didn't get the first promotion when I'd expected it. I'd delivered great results, I had great ratings. But what I didn't have were the relationships. I was a one-woman show. I knew what I could count on me for; I knew I could deliver the results. But they didn't know. I hadn't tried to get to know people.

I was wearing the mask because I didn't think others needed to know all about me. They just needed to know that I showed up for work with a plan to win. But people in power want to promote those who can deliver the results and those they know. They didn't know me because I was wearing the mask.

I went to our most senior African-American leader in the company and asked him what it was that I was missing. He explained, "Your results are great, but they don't know you. They need to know they can count on you to be sensitive and be a full leader." My promotion came a few months later, but the lesson was important.

You have to have a plan, a consistent message, supporters who can help you with a SWOT (strengths, weaknesses, opportunities and threats) analysis. This self-awareness is important before any self-promoting occurs. Don't be afraid to brag and say what you have done. Practice and prepare so when you publicly share your accomplishments, it sounds polished and genuine.

This strategy is just like brand management. You do consumer research, determine your communication statement, and develop your advertising campaign.

My mentors and coaches taught me to be willing to ask others for help. To never underestimate the power within you or your team, because it isn't until heat is applied that we know there is a whistle in the teakettle. Keep the end goal in mind at all times—that vision will encourage and strengthen you during challenging times. Seek to give your teammates the assist versus needing to be the one who scores. Remember the small things: anniversaries, special occasions, thoughtful gestures, and saying thank you.

And go into the deep water.

I heard Dr. E. K. Bailey deliver a sermon during a revival church service called, "Launch Out into the Deep." It's about the willingness to launch into deep water. Deep water is where you find great fish. But in order to be in deep water, you must be willing to assume great risk. You have left the safety of the shore, where you could just step back. If you cast out from the beach, you will get only minnows and crabs. You have to be willing to go into the deep water.

When storms come, as they will, you may not be able to get back to the safety of the shore quickly. Yet deep water is the only place you will find great fish.

Success is defined differently by all of us. Some would say it is a title, but I say it is all about purpose. If you have pursued your purpose with passion and you can look back in the mirror and say, "I haven't let you down," that is a rather successful journey on this road called life.

I don't chase the ever-elusive work-life balance. Balance implies that you will obtain a state of equilibrium or equality. I don't think that is real. I don't know anything that allows you to stand with a foot on one side and an equal foot on the other. Life is constantly changing. It's not about balance. It's about priorities. That was one of the most important things I had to learn.

I went to a class on the "7 Habits of Highly Effective Leaders," and the woman running it had us list the things most important to us, then prioritize them. When I looked at my list, God was on it, my husband, my kids and work. And that was the order in which I felt they were most important. God, husband, kids and work. Yet when I looked at what was getting the most time in my life, work was getting the majority of the time and God, husband and kids were fighting for what was left over.

It was like someone had shaken me awake. It was very clear. At that time, I had only one child. Now, with three, I am very clear about my priorities and I can easily walk away from something at work to go to ice-skating lessons—with no regrets and no guilt.

I don't try to do too much. I can't do it all. I enjoy my work, I am passionate about what I do, but I am also very clear about my purpose. ∎

The rawest moment in any of the interviews for this book occurred with **Barbara Hartman**, when we dared to go into the territory where few women will publicly venture.

"The one thing I don't spend enough time on is me. The working out and the being over-weight…" she said.

There it was. The topic.

Her weight. Then my weight. And then we talked about self-esteem.

Self-esteem is the one thing that dogs virtually every one of us the minute we wake up as we start flogging ourselves for our personal flaws. It might be your wrinkles, it might be the shape of your nose or the size of your breasts or, well, it is probably your weight. That's the most common thing. But we all seem to have something that makes us be mean to ourselves.

"It is hard to talk about, because in a life of accomplishments, it is a considerable failure," Hartman said. "The way I get through thinking about it day to day is that, someday, it will be time for me. I am so proud of my life as a wife, and equally—if not more proud of—my life as a mother. I am proud of a fantastic career. But this is the one area I continued not to fix. No matter how much people say that all you have to do is put yourself first, get up a half-hour earlier and work out, it doesn't matter. You have to do it, and I haven't done it."

She told me about her three best friends—women she has known since she was twelve—and all three are thin and gorgeous. "I have real self-esteem issues when we take our infrequent girls' weekends because I see how other people relate to them, versus me. My career is, by far, the most accomplished. My family is a great family. Yet I feel less than them because of how I look."

She deals with it by looking at the total picture, which is amazing. But this one nagging issue—weight—continues to hold her back. "Sometimes it makes me feel very low. I know it can be done, but I haven't chosen to do it."

Her time to focus on herself is coming. She's fifty-four, she can consider retirement at fifty-five and she knows she's on the verge of something huge. It goes back to one of her mottoes: You only have one life. Live it now.

49 Live Your Life (You Only Get One)
Barbara S. Hartman

Vice President, Customer Business Development
North America
Procter & Gamble

Something happened to me at work on January 9, 1997, and it completely changed me. I was a human resources associate director with our company and we were doing a panel interview. That was the last interview before the decision was made for someone to join the company. A woman named Arati Sharangpani was the interviewee. I don't know what happened. I fell in love with her. I'd read her file and thought she might be one of those magnificent people you don't come across every day. On her application, she'd written a lot of examples of how she impacted students at the University of Michigan. I felt she would be a person I would want to know. She was captivating. Not only did I offer her a job with P&G, but I promised her she could come to Chicago, which was what she wanted. But, at P&G, we don't promise people locations when we offer jobs. I was breaking rules left and right.

She accepted the job on the spot and proceeded to hug me, which also doesn't happen in interviews. I told her I would watch over her career.

She left the interview and took a cab to the Cincinnati airport.

She got on a plane back to Michigan.

The plane went down.

She died along with everyone else on that plane.

I didn't find out until late that night that she'd been on that flight. My grieving started with guilt. Maybe, if I hadn't had such a long interview with her and asked her so much, maybe she would have gotten an earlier flight. Or maybe if I'd talked longer, she'd have taken a later flight.

Our CEO called me and said Arati's parents wanted to talk to me. I thought they were going to blame me. I was so afraid to call, but when I did, I found out she'd called her parents after the interview. She'd told them that she'd just had the best day of her life.

Her parents wanted to thank me. Her life's goal was to work for Procter & Gamble, and she reached her goal on her last day.

They asked me to give the eulogy at her funeral, which I thought was strange. This was someone I'd known for two hours. But the Hindu religion believes in reincarnation. It was important that I give the eulogy because I'd had the last meaningful conversation with her. They also asked me to speak at the memorial service at the University of Michigan—where six hundred people had shown up. Arati was that spectacular.

It is an important story for me because none of us knows what will happen next.

We just don't.

We take everything so seriously, but we shouldn't. I used to have a boss who said, "Let's remember: We sell toilet paper." He was one of the great people in my life.

I was an education major in college. I was going to work for P&G for one year because they offered me the job. I thought they were crazy. I had no interest in selling—or so I thought. My interest was in teaching, in helping special-education children. But P&G paid twice what they paid special-education teachers, so I was going to do it for one year.

I forgot to quit.

I am now at a point in my career where I have nothing to lose. I have had a fabulous career here and have loved just about every minute of it. I want to spend the rest of my time making sure that other people—particularly women—can say the same thing when they have put in their thirty-two years. So, I say exactly what I think—all the time. There are benefits to being fifty-four. That has to be the safest birthday I have had because I can consider retirement at fifty-five.

I made a major career decision to turn down a job in 1984, and that cost me ten years of vertical growth. It was a job I'd wanted. No woman had ever had it. It was to be associate director for developing businesses. Women hadn't achieved that level yet. I turned it down because it required me to move to Cincinnati. Six weeks before I got that offer, I'd met my husband. During the first eight years of my career, I told the company, "Move me anywhere. I am single. I am very location-flexible." I kept getting promotions in Chicago. And then I met my husband.

One of the sayings that guides me is, "You only have one life." At age thirty-one, I met this man who I knew was going to be my life partner. They were giving me the job I wanted, but I said, "I have met this man who I know I am going to marry." They said, "How long have you known him?" I said, "Six weeks." They said, "Are you crazy?" I said, "Perhaps." But you only have one life. That part of my life was about to be fulfilled. I had to say, "I can't take that job right now. I may be wrong. I doubt it." So I turned it down and someone else got the job, and I was basically taken off the promotion list.

Not as punishment, but because you didn't get two chances back then.

I did marry my husband two years later. So, the way I thought about my career at that time was, get the best result that anyone at that level could ever get, and become so good at what I did that, if something ever changed and I could get a better job at a higher level, they would pick me. I would get the results. I was going to be a role model.

I will tell you that I did look for other jobs, because I realized I had potential at a higher level. But I realized I was a good fit with the values and principles of Procter. And, I loved being a part of this company so much that I was willing to stay at my level, have this fantastic husband and two great kids. But I did look. I was pretty open about it. I had nice opportunities. But it didn't all fit for me. The great thing was that things did change and I once again was given great roles with significant vertical career growth in P&G. The key was to achieve significant results in anticipation of change.

You get one life.

Another one of my sayings is, "Go beyond." No matter what I do, I want to feel I go beyond the norm, whether that is at work, at being a wife, or at being a mom. I don't always succeed. But I am always trying. ■

Marie Quintana knows better than anyone what it is like to be the outsider. She moved to the United States from Cuba in 1961 and, even though she was only five years old, her parents relied on her to learn English quickly and interpret for them. She learned how to adapt, focus and thrive—skills that have served her quite well in the corporate world.

Her career has moved through so many gyrations, from her days at IBM in leadership sales roles to her time at Perot Systems, where she was a strategy consultant working with international clients. In between, she built a hugely successful consulting firm.

"I have always felt I could jump off a high building and land on my feet," she said. "That excites me."

Now, at PepsiCo, she drives the corporate strategy for multicultural markets. It's the latest role in a career that has soared because of the hard, confidence-building lessons of her childhood that ultimately helped her to plunge into change and comfortably take risks.

50 See the Stars, Not the Ceiling
Marie Quintana
Vice President of Ethnic Sales
PepsiCo

We arrived here in November, the year of the Bay of Pigs. It was my mother, brother and me. My father was already in the United States on a short-term job. We had only the clothes on our backs, and we basically moved into a refugee project.

I was told we were going on a short trip to the United States. My father had a two-month job, working in a sugar refinery in Louisiana. It was such a scary time for me.

In Cuba, I could hear the military marching in front of our house. There were bombs going off at night. You couldn't go outside. My grandfather was taken to prison in the middle of the night. It was very scary, and my mother was very afraid. I could see that she was frightened. I remember how sad it was for her to leave her mother and father and everyone she knew.

I don't think anyone thought we were leaving forever. Everybody thought it would just be a period of time before the government could get back to some sort of democracy.

I grew up very early because of that experience. I was the oldest child, and even though I was only five, my parents looked to me to quickly learn the language and help them assimilate in the new culture. When anything difficult happens in my life, I go back to that time.

People would say things in English and I didn't have any idea what they were saying. We moved to Reserve, Louisiana, for my dad's job, but there were no Hispanic families there. I remember being in first grade and not knowing how to raise my hand and ask to be excused to go to the bathroom.

In the second grade, I started to become fluent in English. I had to learn it quickly because my mother and father weren't going to. Mom really thought they were going back, and they didn't see their role as trying to fit in. I felt my family was in crisis and it was my responsibility to step up.

I was a very serious student, and my teachers were trying hard to help me. I stayed late, had extra tutoring and started to make friends. But I didn't fit in. I remember picture-taking day, and we were told not to wear anything white. They wanted us in colors. But I told my mother I needed everything white, and she went to the cloth store and made me a white skirt and white shirt and even white gloves. I remember looking around the schoolyard and there was every color but white.

I had it all backwards. I totally didn't fit in. It was really rough. I learned so much.

Actually, I am still learning about those years. I learned a lot about adversity and having to fit in when no one really wanted to accept me.

As I progressed through school, I began to realize I was embarrassed that my parents could not learn English. I was tired of carrying the burden of having to interpret. My mother never could talk to my teacher. She couldn't communicate about homework. I had no one to help me with it. I didn't want her speaking Spanish in the grocery store because everyone would look at her and know I was different. I got tired of it all.

I was living in a town where we were the only Hispanic family. There was a lot of prejudice in that small town. I remember being called "spic." But I also remember families opening up to us in church. The whole experience helped me to understand racial issues for African-Americans and Hispanics. It gave me courage and it built character.

My parents—I love them to death—but they were not into this country. They didn't want to be here. My mother was still mourning her family and her country. So I had to learn to validate myself when things went wrong. I had to figure out that it was going to be okay. My parents were loving and protective, but they were from a country and culture that was completely different from what I was living in.

Those years taught me that you can do anything if you put your mind to it. My parents were supportive of anything I tried to do. At some point, after so many hard times, they turned into optimistic, wonderful people who recognized how blessed we were to have all these opportunities in front of us here. We had the whole spectrum of possibilities.

I never saw that ceiling that holds people down. I thought, "I can do it. I just have to work very hard. I always have to work harder than the person next to me." I came into a country that was not my country, and if I was going to succeed, I'd always have to work harder than the person next to me.

I have a very different career path from most people in the corporate world. I really wanted to be a psychologist. I was very interested in people's behaviors and motivations. I majored in psychology and wanted to do counseling right away. I wanted to work with people immediately. I got my master's in social work at Tulane University and I wanted to work while I got my Ph.D. in psychology. My first job was at the state outpatient clinic in New Orleans, where there was a team of psychiatrists and psychologists. I ran the Hispanic clinic and did counseling.

I learned a lot about myself.

I learned that I am a Type-A person who needs results. I'd be counseling a family through a crisis for a month and a half, and then a month later, we'd be back. I'd be thinking, "Wait, I thought I fixed you." I knew very quickly that I was going to go into business.

Psychology gave me an incredible background for understanding family dynamics and human behavior, and that helps me to understand the true consumer, the true shopper, from a completely different perspective.

Business suits me better. I've been in leadership sales roles with IBM and Perot Systems. I also started my own consulting firm that had several key projects. The one thing I know from my background is how to adapt and change.

Don't be afraid to take risks. If there was ever a point in time that I said, "No, I don't know enough, I'm not ready, I can't," I would have missed out on the next experience. It is all about the chain of experiences. Each one has enabled the next one. In totality, they have given me such a rich grouping of skills that I draw from every day. You can learn whatever it is you have to learn. You find the experts and the people who are going to support you.

Never give up. In those times I've had where I think, "There is no way that I can do this," I step back and find the people who have lived through valuable experiences and I get the answers.

You can get past whatever barrier you have in your mind. Just step back and get the big picture to find the answers. The answers always come.

I have always had to know how to adapt to change. It starts with you. You can't find the answers on the outside. You have to know yourself, take care of yourself and find ways to validate what you do. When you start looking for validation of who you are or of your accomplishments from people on the outside, you will always be searching for something you will never find.

I have a lot of humility in my life. A lot of things have brought me to my knees. When those things happen, I realize how much I should give back to those who have given me so much. I think how much I owe to the ones who are coming up behind me. There is accountability and responsibility with what I have today. There is a purpose, and that purpose is to give back. ∎

Kim Feil has traveled a road that has swallowed many professional women. Early in her career, she worked too long and too hard. She was all too willing to sacrifice her present to the demands of her job.

It didn't add up to much. Feil described an awakening that redefined her life and her mission. Professionally, she has more than twenty years of experience in marketing, sales and strategic planning. Personally, she's got a passion for everything she does. She has had to learn to create her own equilibrium.

"I am not the smartest person in the world, but I am often the most passionate," she said. "People often fail because they give up when barriers are thrown at them. They don't feel—not just see—that end goal. But, there is a will and unflappable desire to get it done that creates the momentum to make impossible things happen. It is amazing how much other people draw on that energy."

She has made significant changes in her career, both in the industry and in roles as a consultant. I asked her how she adapts so well to change. "Like everyone, I have moments of self-doubt," she said. "I always think of that song from *The King and I*: 'Whenever I feel afraid, I hold my head erect, And whistle a happy tune, So no one will suspect, I'm afraid... Make believe you're brave, And the trick will take you far, You may be as brave, As you make believe you are.' "

51 Set Boundaries for Yourself
Kim L. Feil
Chief Marketing Officer
Sara Lee Food & Beverage

learned a few personal lessons the hard way. The first took me fifteen years to learn, and that was this: Stop overworking. I come from a good, hard-working, German farmer stock—the kind that is all about putting your head low, picking the weeds and knowing good will come your way. I plowed my first fifteen years of soil by what I now realize was not necessarily productive overwork.

I went five years without a vacation. How stupid was that? I could have had two months to travel the world and discover new things, but I worked. I might have taken a day to go to a doctor or dentist, or to have lunch with my mother—but I wouldn't leave the office, shut off the phone and discover something new. One year I flew 250,000 miles for work, so the idea of getting on a plane again didn't appeal to me. I should have taken a week off and taken cooking lessons. I should have tried something different.

After graduate school, I had an incredibly broad array of interests: tennis, cooking, gardening, horseback riding, and a lot of other things. But once I started working, I basically did nothing other than work. My awakening came when I realized I couldn't go to a cocktail party and have anything to talk about other than my work.

I married someone I met at work. We worked at three companies together and the main thing we had in common was work. We would come home and we would start talking about what happened at work that day.

I'd call my mother and listen to her talk and I would have nothing to share. It was so very narrow on my side of the world, and I found myself not being invited to do things. It created a lot of loneliness, and I am not, fundamentally, a "be alone" person. I am not a hole-up-in-the-bedroom-and-be-by-yourself person. I love to entertain.

I was thirty pounds heavier than I am now, and that wasn't who I really was. I lived to work. That is what I did. I felt ugly, I felt unhealthy, and I put myself on a serious diet and started working out. I picked up tennis. I threw myself into my hobby of renovating houses. I got a house with a swimming pool and started swimming a lot. I met different people, tried new things and it was all a real awakening. I look back with regret at those lost vacation weeks and being too old when I was only thirty-one. But I came out of it and focused on the things that I loved. I lost thirty pounds in three months—I just vowed to do it.

I learned to set boundaries. Boundaries are really about making it clear to people that there are things that are really important to you personally—and not being afraid to say it. It is not about the quantity of hours you work, but the quality of hours you put in. It is okay to say, "I can't do this unless we trade this out or move the deadline on this." I used to take it all on. I used to work really late and start really early, but I don't think that was the most effective use of my time. I would have gotten a lot more done by setting boundaries and limits. An example is that I play tennis on Monday and Wednesday nights, and I have to be gone from the office by six-thirty—period. That is a simple example of setting limits that define a capacity for doing quality work. I am open to others doing that because of my own experience with it.

Another thing I learned is, the last 3 percent is not worth it. I used to believe that, unless something was perfect, it was flawed. That is not true. What is important is sifting through the garbage, identifying the most important elements and delivering those. Anyone who operates as if the last 3 percent matters will 100 percent fail today. The speed of decision-making and the quantity of decisions that have to be made are so vast now. There is no room for overdeliberation. Identify the most relevant actions and do them very well. Have the ability to triage a business problem. Forget about the wasteful 20 percent and go after that core 80 percent that matters the most.

As women, we are gatherers. Men are hunters. But we gather it all, we pull it all together. We spot every detail and men go for the kill. Frankly, I think we can all go for the kill instead of doing too much gathering. We can get lost looking for the herbs when we don't have a steak to put them on.

I read somewhere that the happiest people are those who can appreciate things around them. I now appreciate my health and my friends and family and getting up every day. I have a heightened sense of why those things are important in my life. I still work hard. I thrive on working hard. But I am working a whole lot smarter and am really balancing it with a lot of fun.

Careers can either happen to you or you can manage them. The first half of my working life, I let my career happen to me. In the second half, I am managing it. With the ebbs and flows, I have found that sometimes you have to choose an ebb. People talk about it like an ebb is something that happens to them. But you can choose an ebb as well.

So often, women who don't have children throw themselves into their careers. Women with children often choose ebbs to raise and manage their families. Women who don't have children often don't choose the ebb. But they can. It's okay. Sometimes, the flow of a career requires absolute sacrifice, which is okay as long as it is not always. It is about boundaries. Sometimes I choose pure sacrifice. There are times when I have to give that. But then I say, "Okay, I had to do that. Let me balance it out again." ■

Meg Whitman called, interrupting me from bidding on something I didn't need on eBay. In the five years since I first interviewed her, she's been at or near the very top of Fortune's list of the 50 Most Powerful Women in American Business, and eBay has grown from a pop shopping phenomenon to a consumer behemoth.

Whitman used to get media attention for being effective in spite of her technological ignorance. That's all changed. "I can't go toe-to-toe with a schooled technologist, but I've learned a lot about technology over the years. I have a good grasp."

No kidding. Since she got to eBay, she took the company global. "Now, more than half of our revenue comes from outside the United States." She introduced the "Buy It Now" option, which offers consumers a fixed price on items. Then she launched eBay Motors, which is now 25 percent of the company's gross volume on the website and 10 to 15 percent of its revenue worldwide.

Buying PayPal in 2002 changed the trajectory of eBay. "One day, we woke up and realized it was being offered on 10 percent of eBay listings. We dug deeper and saw that it helped fill a significant customer need, and we bought the company. We didn't realize the accelerator we'd bought." Right. People like me can sit at home and click the mouse four times and, next thing you know, the mail carrier is on the porch with the goods.

Studies show the average Fortune 500 CEO lasts less than five years. Whitman has been running eBay since 1998. I asked her what's next, and she said her advice to new CEOs is to never answer that question. She never imagined she'd love doing this so much—for so many years.

52 Constantly Reinvent Yourself
Meg Whitman
CEO
eBay

The company, the product—everything is endlessly interesting. I am energized every day, every week, every month. I'm always saying, "Hmmm, I didn't know that. That's interesting." As long as it is fun and interesting, it is easy to stay around.

I joined eBay in January of 1998. The previous year, there were thirty employees and we had $4.7 million in revenues. Today we have 15,000 people and do roughly $7.5 billion in revenues in thirty-five countries in fifty-five locations with three major business units.

When I think about it, it's like, "Well, this turned out really well. Who knew?" and yet, there are certain times when it seems so overwhelming. It has been a constant reinvention of what I do. Running a $4.7 million company and a $7.5 billion company are not the same thing at all. I used to know everyone who worked in this company. Now I am lucky if I know 400 or 500 people well. The way I manage has to be different.

The first thing I learned is it's all about the right people in the right job with the right behaviors at the right time. My challenge is making sure my top 125 people are exactly matched to the right job and the right time. The trick at eBay is always the right time. At the rate we are growing, the jobs are constantly changing.

I've learned that it is far better to have the right strategy and less -than-perfect execution. What is a disaster is having perfect execution against the wrong strategy. The business is so dynamic; you need strategic agility in our business in order to compete. You have to be willing to change your strategy. You have to have the right strategy. You can't be focused on perfect execution when you have the wrong strategy.

Our merchant services were growing nicely and doing very well with no real competitive threats. Enter Google Checkout. We had to accelerate our plan to get large merchant ubiquity by four to five years. We had to react fast and nimbly. You can say it would take nine months to fill the sales force, but we had nine days. Would it have been better if we'd built it in nine months? Yes. But, we had to get out there and meet the needs of large merchants.

Someone said, "Perfection is the enemy of 'good enough.'" It is. In our business, and in many businesses, you have to get started, get it out there. We are in a business where we can do that because we're Web-based. We can change things overnight.

My husband tells me I'm not very detail oriented, and I'm not. That works in this business. I've always been very agile. That's part of my personality.

I try to leave the executive persona at the office because it doesn't work that well at home. I'm a different person at home. I'm a mom first and foremost at home, and secondarily a wife. Kids and husbands are not your employees. I am married to a professor of neurosurgery at Stanford, and I am very lucky that he completely stepped up to the plate when I got to eBay. Households don't manage themselves and he was a huge partner in that. Everyone has to solve this dilemma on their own. There is no silver bullet here, and no playbook. Figure it out in the context of your kids and significant other and support system. When the kids were younger, we did our jobs and we did the kids. I'd joke that my house did not look like Martha Stewart had just left it. Something had to give along the way, and it turns out it was fine.

There are more women in senior leadership because women are finally getting to critical mass. When I went to Harvard Business School, 11 percent of my class was women. Now it's 50 percent. You have women in their mid-forties to fifties to sixties and you are starting to get to critical mass, or the tipping point, in leadership. Look at (PepsiCo CEO) Indra Nooyi, or (Kraft CEO) Irene Rosenfeld or (Sara Lee CEO) Brenda Barnes. It's because we have been in the pipeline for so long. Most of us graduated college between 1975 and 1982.

My sister was six years older than I and, when she went to college, none of the Ivy League schools were co-ed. She could go to women's schools, or the University of Pennsylvania. But in the intervening six years when I came around, they were all co-ed. I wonder how much of an impact occurred when they opened those institutions of higher education to us. The women who were five or six years older than I had a huge influence on me and my generation. Gloria Steinem was a huge influence. She made a difference and was cutting edge. And Bella Abzug. I bet if you asked girls who Bella was, they'd say, "Who was that?" They might not even know Gloria Steinem. But they were the pioneers of my generation. They made it happen. Somehow, when you don't live through the challenges of a generation, you don't care about it. But it was important for all of us.

I am absolutely a feminist. Absolutely.

I get asked all the time about advice for younger women. I say, the world is your oyster. You can go to whatever school you can get into, whatever job you can get into. Put your head down and do the best job you can do with the tasks assigned to you. If you are constantly in the neighborhood of good things happening, if you are a great team member and easy to manage, you will do great.

Over the years, I have learned that the best development tool we have is the job we put people in. All the classes, coaching and mentoring are only useful if you have them in a job that will structure them and coach them. I have learned more from the jobs I've been in than all the mentoring and coaching I have had. If you get the job right, you really have a chance of growing great executives.

Eight years ago, I said I would stay here for ten years. It seemed like it was eons away. It feels like it was a few minutes ago. I'm still here. I'll stay as long as I am the right person in the right job at the right time for the company. ■

Conclusion

I
am
typing
very,
very
slowly
because
I
don't
want
this
moment
to
end.

I'll miss talking to these women. I'll miss this book. I'll miss you.

If you ever wonder if you are doing the job you were meant to do, remind your-self that you deserve to love your work as much as I love mine. I got paid to do this. Seriously—they gave me money! *And yet, this is the most fun I have ever had as an author.*

Oh, wait. I said that when I finished my novel. And Mustang Sallies. *And …*

And, if you aren't this crazy about your work, you need to make some changes. It is in your own bliss that you will find your power.

I've shared with you the rules from all of the great women I've interviewed here, and now I will share mine:

Don't settle.

Do what calls you.

Make up your mind to achieve at the highest level because you deserve it as much as anyone.

Lean on your sisters, and they will get you there.

Make it happen.

There is so much possibility out there for you, and all you have to do is embrace it. Others will help you—if you let them. Don't stand timidly at the sidelines waiting for your big chance. Go get your mentors. Network at the highest level. Know you belong anywhere.

Be your true self. You are your greatest asset, so work it. And don't be afraid of your role models. I am so lucky that I grew up as a journalist with a healthy irreverence for positions of power. People who intimidate others don't intimidate me—they become my mentors and friends. Don't let fear or awe keep you from those who can help and inspire you. Let them teach you so you can teach others.

Most of the women in power today began their careers in male-dominated environments where they were the only women at the table. They endured insults, discrimination and, I'm certain, a great deal of anxiety. They made it, and they are absolutely set on bringing the next generation of women leaders up behind them.

They want to help you. Let them. Don't be afraid to ask for help and make connections with anyone, regardless of where they fit on an organizational chart.

See yourself as belonging at the top, and you will belong at the top. See yourself achieving at that level, and you will achieve at that level. See yourself winning, and you will win. Don't roll your eyes. It's very simple and very true.

I hope your life is filled with the kind of challenge and fun that I have experienced and that your work gives you great joy and possibility. You may think it is cliché for me to say that you can do anything if you believe you can, but it is a truth I have learned. You deserve everything, so open yourself to achieving it.

I am so happy right now. And sad. I don't want this moment to end, but I feel so lucky to have had it. What a ride. ■

About the Author

Fawn Germer once had a boss sit her down and tell her that she'd never be more than she was at the time: a newspaper reporter. In the decade since, Fawn has written two best-selling books and has become one of the nation's most sought-after women's leadership speakers, keynoting for the nation's largest corporations.

This marks the release of her greatest effort yet, The NEW Woman Rules, which was published by the Network of Executive Women and includes interviews with more than fifty of America's most powerful women in the retail industry.

When Fawn left daily journalism to write her first book, it was rejected fifteen times—by every major publisher in the country. She persevered, and then had her choice of publishers. She received her first copy of Hard Won Wisdom one day before the Sept. 11 tragedies, and had to promote her book—and herself—at the most difficult moment in our history.

She worked tirelessly to market the book, even sending Oprah's producers twenty-nine letters. Once Oprah told the world, "If you want to read a very inspiring book, read Hard Won Wisdom," Fawn's speaking career took off.

Her second book, Mustang Sallies, hit best-seller lists within two weeks of its release. The book looks at how strong women can find success by being themselves in a world in which there is so much pressure to be like everybody else. If features personal interviews with everyone from Hillary Clinton to Martina Navratilova to Erin Brockovich.

This acclaimed investigative reporter has worked as a Florida correspondent for both The Washington Post and U.S. News & World Report. Her distinguished reporting career earned her numerous state and national awards, including four Pulitzer Prize